Ramification of Human Rights in India

Ramification of Human Rights in India

Anoop Kumar Singh
Assistant Professor (S.G.)
P.G. & Research Deptt. of Sociology
D.A.V.College, Kanpur, U.P.

SERIALS PUBLICATIONS
NEW DELHI (INDIA)

First Published - 2011

ISBN: 978-81-8387-421-2

Published by

SERIALS PUBLICATIONS
4830/24, Prahlad Street, Ansari Road
Darya Ganj, New Delhi-110002 (India)
Phone : 23245225 Fax : 91-11-23272135
E-mail: serials@sify.com

Contents

Foreword vii

Preface ix

List of Contributors xvii

1. Violence Against Dalits: A Human Rights Perspective — 1
   ARVIND TIWARI

2. Human Rights Concerns: Perspectives and Context in Developing Societies — 50
   P. N. PANDEY

3. Human Rights and Development in a Tea Garden Setting of Assam — 58
   VIRENDRA PAL SINGH

4. Paradigms of Human Rights Awareness — 80
   DIWAKAR SINGH RAJPUT

5. Violation of Human Rights Among Indian Tribal Communities — 85
   UDAI PRATAP SINGH & VIJAY KUMAR

6. Ground Reality of Human Rights Declaration — 142
   RAVI PRAKASH YADAV, RAGINI DEEP & PUJA ROY

7. Gender Equality in India: Constitutional Provisions and Human Rights — 158
   D. K. SINGH

8. Development, Forced Displacement and Resettlement: A Human Rights Perspective — 176
   A. K. SINGH

9. Human Rights, Women and Panchayati Raj Institutions in India — 197
BIRPAL SINGH

10. Terrorism and Human Rights — 210
V. P. SINGH

11. UNO's Human Rights Declaration: Historical Context and Sociological Perspective in a Developing Country Like India — 220
D. P. SAXENA

12. Global Ageing: A Triumph and a Challenge to Protect Rights — 231
YOGENDRA KUMAR SRIVASTAVA

13. Human Rights Violation and Women Empowerment: With Special Reference to North East India — 243
SANJOY ROY

14. Social Work Practice and Human Rights — 267
KIRTI VIKRAM SINGH

15. Struggle for Human Rights Towards Equitable Society *(A Study With Regard to a Group of District Bahraich U.P.)* — 284
ALOK CHANTIA, PREETI MISRA & ROHIT MISRA

16. Human Rights and Women: An Ignorance — 307
NIRMALA KAUSHIK & MANJU

Index — 315

Foreword

Contemporary human rights discourse is based on a rich legacy of ideas and expressing the simple idea that human beings have rights that require notion gives human rights a formalistic character that translates the abstract ideas of human rights theory in to concrete programs of action. It strengthen notion of entitlement in human rights discourse and provides a legal basis for ensuring compliance.

The roots of the contemporary conception of human rights can be traced to the period of 'renainance and enlightment'. The first half of the twentieth century was marked not only by the prevalence of colonial rule in the large part of the world, but also for the rise of authoritarian Government and the establishment of the facist and aggressive regimes in many countries of the world. No doubt the respect for human rights has increased and its observance too, however, gross violation of recognized norms continues unabated in all parts of the world though there is difference of degree only. There are large-scale breaches of civil and political rights, as well as economic, social and cultural rights such as rights to life, rights to adequate standard of living, right to freedom of speech and expression, right to protection from torture and inhuman treatment, police atrocities etc. The obligation set-out in the course of international conventions and treaties for the protection and promotion of human rights accepted by the different countries are flouted flagrantly by them without impunity. The most formidable challenge to the human rights is their abuse by governmental agencies themselves.

Education on human rights is of great importance and it is viewed as an essential contribution to the development of human rights culture violation of human rights is widely rampant, violation of human rights is in the homes, the streets, the public officer and educational institution.

Here arises a question - how can such a paradox be resolved? Virtually, spread of awareness about and protection and promotion of human rights, respect for each other's rights and fulfillment of our obligation towards the fellow beings and the society only possible solutions.

The contents of this book are fascinating as it discuses the various dimensions including emerging issues of human rights viz: rights to environment, rights to women, rights to leisure etc.

The book would be of immense value to the researchers, academicians, law makers, social scientist, N.G.O.'s and social activist, along with all concerned who are committed to strengthening policy, objects and understanding of human rights jurisprudence and its philosophy taking in to account its relevance and potent challenges in the 21st Century.

This work deserves a praise from all those who champion the cause of human rights.

Professor, I. S. Chauhan
Former High Commissioner of India in Fiji
Vice chancellor, Barkatulla University
Vice chancellor, M.P. Bhoj (Open) University

Akshay Tratiya
16 May 2010

Preface

Through myriad struggles and movements throughout the word 'Human rights' has become an arena of transformative political practice that disorient, destablizes and at times, even helps destroy deeply unjust concentrations of political, social, economic and technological power. The transformation from the modern to the contemporary 'Human rights' paradigm remains inconceivable outside movement for decolonization and self-determination. Like wise, the movement of contemporary human rights must take account of the struggles for the elimination of apartheid, and movement directed to realization of women's right and human rights, the human rights to difference, and the integrity of environment.

Human rights as insurrectionary praxis provides diverse map of the illegality of the dominant and also of the mass illegalities of the subaltern peoples. The violence of the oppressed provides as much as the violence of the dominant, a matrix for the emergence of human rights, norms and standards.

The concept of Human Rights is an ancient universal and inherent phenomenon and is as old as humanity in the Indian Society. 'Human Rights' have not been defined in any document dealing with subject. The expression human rights was adopted only in the present Century with the expression of previously known as 'natural rights'.

With the spread of democratic values, revolution in information technology and consequent rise of popular awareness aspirations, the concept of human rights has assumed national and international significance. It is often argued that this concept originated in the west and got embodied in the UN Declaration in 1948. They stress that the British Magna Carta (1215AD) which for first time formulated human rights and liberty of the individual against the authority of the state and which was followed by the petition of Rights (1627) laid the foundation of this concept. In reality however, it was a struggle in England between the barons and landed aristocracy on one side and the king on other during all these years in which people were nowhere in picture. In fact, western ideas of rights and liberties were conceived in a particular socio-political framework in situation of oligarchy, feudalism and highly restricted franchise.

In India on other hand references occur as early as in the Rigved to several civil liberties such as tana (body), Skridhi (dwelling house) and Jibasi (life). Long before Hobbes, the Indian epic, Mahabharata, described the civil liberty of the individual in a political state. Ancient Indian society was a highly structured, and well-organized affair with the fundamental rights and duties not only of individual, but also of classes, communities and castes were clearly laid down. The concept of Human Rights in thus not entirely western in origin nor, it is very modern. India emphasis on perceiving human rights through the prism of duty or by giving first priority to duties and then talking about rights for bringing harmony, love and generosity in the society Reason for this difference from the west is routed in cultural moorings.

Generally there are three distinct sets or generations of human rights. The first set or generation lists civil and political rights. The rights to a fair trial, freedom of speech and religion, freedom of movement and assembly, and guarantees against discrimination fall within these political and civil human rights.

The second set or generation are economic, social and cultural rights. This set of rights attempts to ensure each resident of a country an adequate standard of living on the resources of that country. Under this second set of human rights, everyone' has the rights to a standard of living adequate for the health and well-being of himself and of his family, including food, clothing, housing and necessary social services.

These rights are termed as positive rights, in that govt. and individuals must take action to preserve them.

A third and final set of human rights involves collective rights among nations. This set of rights is the least developed among the there types of human rights. The promotion of collective human rights reusing inter-governmental cooperation on world issues (eg. environmental protection and economic development) The third set of human rights indicates the solidarity among nations and individual form a core value of Universal Declaration of Human Rights.

With this backdrop, it is intended to look into the structural and functional aspects of the human rights. Moreover, inquiry of rights pertains with aged people, vulnerable groups, women, displaced has been focused in this book.

Prof. Arwind Tiwari's paper titled *"Violence against Dalits: A Human Rights Perspective"* explores the genesis of violence against dalits and analyse how violence is embedded in the caste structure of Indian society.

Three-pronged strategy of Indian Constitution provides legal safeguard to dalits in form of protection, compensatory discrimination and development. Ten case studies by author manifested the current scenario presented about dalit aristocracies in India.

Prof. P. N. Pandey in his paper *"Human Rights concern: perspectives and context in developing societies"* examines the concept of human rights through the prism of Asian Societies and find that concept has been coined in the Western Cultural framework, so the European Societies are interpreting the concept, concern events in his framework and therefore this is not accepted by the Asian Society. Western countries should considered it as a dynamic procedure of international norm setting giving priority to the significance of national and regional peculiarities including historical, religious, cultural and social backgrounds.

Dr. Virendra Pal Singh in his paper titled *"Human Rights and Development in a Tea garden setting of Assam"* explain human rights situation in the tea gardens of Assam. It was stated and revealed by author that tea garden workers were not only exploiting by contractor in various ways as well as they are being treated as slaves by planters.

Dr D. S. Rajput in his paper *"Paradigms of Human Rights Awareness"* stated that social awareness is important tool nowadays to protect and uplift human rights. To promote the environment of rights protection knowledge, Awareness, Networking, Participation, upliftment, reformation is appropriate model and region specific to inhance and control violation activities.

The paper titled *"Violation of Human rights among Indian tribal communities"* by Dr. U. P. Singh and Vijay Kumar examines violation of human rights among Indian tribal communities. The rights concern with land, forest and water of tribals are being violated by the Bureaucracy, Government and middlemen. The social evils like bonded labour, prostitution, child marriage and child labour were also emphasize in this paper as a hurdle in the development of tribal and as well as these evil creates background for the violation of fundamental rights of tribal. Several tribes across the India and cases of aristocracies against them presented in details by authors.

The paper titled *"Ground reality of human rights declaration" by* Dr. R. P. Yadav, Dr. Ragini Deep and Dr. Puja Roy explain three generations of human rights. In the light of three generation of Human rights paper explores that in India despite of U.N. Declaration, large section of women, child and Dalits are deprived from the even rights to live, food and shelter. Women are being raped, children are being exploited. These are the blackspots in the civil society.

Dr. D. K. Singh's paper titled *"Gender equality in India: constitutional provisions and human rights"* describe the provisions about gender rights, equality and safeguards inherent in constitution. The author emphasize on the human rights, education teaches both about human rights and for the human rights and take responsibility for teaching, defending human rights.

The paper on *"Development, forced displacement and resettlement: A human rights perspective"* by Dr. A. K. Singh inquires the dark side of development. Mega industrial projects, dams etc. focused themselves on the economic outcome only instead of tangible transformation in the quality of life of the habitats development-induced displacement always creates ruckus for the people because resettlement polices are not appropriate to cope with expectations of people.

The author has developed two categories to describe the process of land acquisition and displacement. One is the developers and another is developees. Developer has seen their interest in making money with the help of corrupt bureaucrat, middlemen and influential people of villages. That's why developers easily made possible the land acquisition process by violating govt. norms, while developees asked to bear the disproportionate cost of economic development. The author has also mentioned two types of non-economic cost. two set of cost. The Rule of Law cost (ROLC) and The Human rights Cost (HRC). In nutshell Dr. Singh suggested that before initiation of any project EIA (Environmental Impact Assessment) and Social Impact Assessment (SIA) is inevitable so that social and ecological cost of project could cut down.

Dr. Birpal Singh is his paper titled *"Human Rights, women and Panchayati Raj Institutions in India"* explore Women's rights as political rights in panchayati raj system in his study of PRI's of M.P. Theoretically 1/3 reservation has been given to women in three tier system of PRI's to some extent they have became politically empowered and now in the process of decision making they are playing key role in the family and society.

Despite of all these, embedded discrimination in the structure of Indian Society on the gender basis became hurdle. Several instances of violation of human rights of women was seen in the study. The study focusses that due to lack of awareness about plans and policies, illiteracy lack of confidence, prevalent customs and traditions at village level make difficult their political panticipation.

Dr. V. P. Sings in the paper titled *"Terrorism and human right"* describe that human rights protection is an inseparable part to fight against terrorism. This suggests that respecting human rights may indeed help us to incur security.

The paper titled *"UNO's Human Rights Declaration: Historical context and sociological perspective in a developing country like India"* by Prof. D. P. Saxena explores the historical background and as well as social frontiers of UNO's declaration. The author strongly contended that commission and committing could not protect the human rights of people. There is need to create social environment for the protection of rights and for the education of human rights, so that established social fabric can change.

The paper titled *"Global Ageing: A triumph and challenge to protect Rights"* by Dr. Yogendra Srivastava raise very relevant issue of Ageing in paper. Due to betterment in the field of medicine the number of aged people in Indian Society has been increased. The rights of older persons safeguarded by commission of human rights through economic and social council. The aged should be enabled to enjoy a life of fulfillment health security and contentment and that they should be treated as integral part of the society.

Dr. Sanjay Roy's paper *"Human Rights violation and women empowerment: With special reference to North East India"* access that how protection of human rights leads to women empowerment and vice-versa how violation of human rights became hurdle to women empowerment.

According to author human rights violation of women has been a worldwide phenomena and almost all the countries of the world irrespective of forwardness or backwardness of that particular country. In case of North-East whenever govt. proclaim the 'Disturbed Area' to several states of North East then the instances of harrowing accounts of violation of human rights of women traces. It is really shocking that Army personal, were the main culprit of violation of rights of women, social workers need to take some directions to develop strategies and to address intersectional discrimination and subustantive equality through building collective consciousness collective mobilisation, caacity building, providing legal aids and secure rehabilitation because author is self a social work scholar.

In a paper titled *"Social work practice and human rights"* by Dr. Kirti Vikram Singh explores relevance of human rights to social work. An important starting point in the integration of human rights into practice involves adherence to social work ethics Dr. Singh has analyse the pragmatic aspect of human rights, in this process the tactics used for the realization of human rights of target group were discussed, the tactics viz. ICC, BCC, CCD are the key components of the analysis.

The paper titiled *"Struggle for human rights towards equitable sociaty"*, by Dr. Alok Chantia, Dr. Preeti Mishra and Dr. Rohit Mishra analyse in his paper struggle of Dhankut Community of Bahraich district, U.P. towards equitable society Dhankut is an isolated group; it has no caste identify of its own. They are not recognized by the adjacent communities of the district. Due to living at single place, poor economy and non-recognition by other communities, they are practicing cross-cousin and parallel cousin marriage in order to save their lineage.

The paper titled *"Human Rights and Women: An Ignorance"*, by Dr. Nirmala Kaushik and Dr. Manju attempts to make aware Womens about their rights and if find violated then protest must be there. The author says that Women's are facing psychological and physical problems.

This book 'Ramification of Human Rights In India' discusses ground reality of Human Rights declaration, violence against Dalits gender equality in India and Human Rights Global Ageing: Challenge to protect rights, social work practice and human rights, Human rights, women and Panchayati Raj Institution in India. Terrorism and Human Rights, Human rights violation and women empowerment with special reference to North-East India, Human Rights concern in developing society, Historical and sociological context of human rights declaration, struggle for human rights towards equitable society, human rights and development in Tea garden setting of Assam, Violation of human rights among tribal communities, human rights awareness model and human rights of displaced.

This volume would be of immense value to the researchers, social activists, social scientists and legislators along with all concerned who are committed to strengthening policy, objects and understanding of human rights philosophy from different perspectives and corners.

Of course, it is meaningful addition to the existing literature of sociology of human rights.

Many persons have helped and encouraged me in bringing out this volume. I would like to record our sincere thanks to Professor I. S. Chauhan former Vice-Chancellor of Barkatulla University, Bhopal and as well former High Commissioner of India in Fiji, for writing the foreword. My thanks is also due to Dr. D.S. Rajput, of Sagar University to motivate me time to time to complete this task. I would also like to thank our family for their continued support and encouragement. Finally, I thank to Sri S.K. Jha owner of Serial publication, New Delhi for bringing out this volume.

Dr. A. K. Singh
Asstt. Professor
Deptt. of Sociology
D.A.V. P.G. College, Kanpur

List of Contributors

Arvind Tiwari, Professor and Chair Person, Centre for Socio-legal studies and Human Rights, School of Social Sciences, Tata Institute of Social Sciences (TISS) Deonar Mumbai.

P. N. Pandey, Professor of Sociology & former Dean Faculty of Arts, Banaras Hindu University, (B.H.U.) Varanasi.

Virendra Pal Singh, Professor & Head, Centre for Globalization and Development Studies, Allahabad University, Allahabad.

D. S. Rajput, Associate Professor, Deptt. of Sociology and Social Work, Dr. H.S.Gour, Central University, Sagar, M.P.

U. P. Singh, Associate Professor, Deptt. of Anthroplogy Lucknow University, Lucknow.

R.P. Yadav, Faculty member in Deptt. of Industrial Relation & Personnel Management, T. M. Bhagalpur University, Bhagalpur (Bihar).

Vijay Kumar, Subject Expert, Deptt. of Anthropology. Lucknow University, Lucknow.

D. K. Singh, Associate Professor, Deptt. of Social Work, Lucknow University, Lucknow.

A. K. Singh, Assistant Professor (S.G.), Deptt. of Sociology,D.A.V. (P.G.) College, Kanpur (U.P.)

Birpal Singh, Assistant Professor (Panchayat Admin. & Nyay Panchayat, National Law University, Bhopal, M.P.

V. P. Singh, Assistant Professor (Law) University of Petroleum and Energy Studies, Dehradun, Uttranchal.

D. P. Saxena, Retd. Professor & Head Deptt. of Sociology, D.D.U. Gorakhpur University, Gorakhpur.

Yogendra Srivastava, Assistant Professor (Law), National Law University, Bhopal, M.P.

Sanjay Roy, Assistant Professor, Deptt. of Social Work Assam University, Silchar, Assam.

Kirti Vikram Singh, PR (ELM) & Visiting Faculty ASODL, Amity University, Lucknow.

Alok Chantia, Lecturer, Deptt. of Arthnopology, J.N.P.G. College, Lucknow.

Preeti Mishra, Assistant Professor (S.G.) Deptt. of Human Rights, School for legal studies. B.R.Ambedker Central University, Lucknow.

Rohit Mishra, Director, Finding Research & Development Foundation Lucknow.

Nirmala Kaushik, Assistant Professor, Deptt. of Applied Psychology, G.J.U.S.T., Hisar, Haryana.

Manju Assistant Professor, Deptt. of Applied Psychology,G.J.U.& S.T., Hisar, Haryana.

1

Violence Against Dalits: A Human Rights Perspective

Arvind Tiwari

Introduction

Liberty, equality, justice and human dignity are the basic principles of contemporary society. Although injustice, discrimination and inequality are social phenomenon, their nature and extent differ from society to society. At the same time, there have been constant efforts to fight these problems in human history. Indian society is no exception to this. However, injustice inequality, violence and discrimination in India exist in the worst form by way the social stratification and hierarchy that are directly linked to religion and caste. Caste plays its role in both ways i.e. as a system and as an institution (NCTE, 2003).

Organised violence directed against members of identified groups/communities has been a distinct feature of the Indian society for quite sometime. Though violence does take place in the process of change in many societies, and particularly so when radical alterations take place in the existing social and power relations, it usually does not choose its victims on the basis of birth in a given social entity. In India, however, this is precisely what has defined the character of violence in relation to certain groups. The country has witnessed increase in both caste and communal violence since independence which the processes of modernization have not abated. Rather, in some respects, it has been intensified by them. While communal violence is a relatively recent phenomenon rooted in the events leading to partition, caste violence has a much longer history and a firmer anchorage. It also has the distinctiveness of being embedded in the social structure of the dominant community itself which lays down the norms of conduct between its more privileged groups and the subdued and subordinated segment. It is this age old caste relationship in Hindu Society which is getting disturbed by pressure of forces both from above and below. The frequency and intensity of violence is an offshoot of desperate attempts by the upper caste and Other Backward Castes (OBCs) groups to protect their entrenched status against the process of disengagement and upward mobility among lower castes resulting from affirmative action of State Policy. The violence takes brutal forms and turns into acts of atrocities against a whole group of people, such as massacre, rape, burning of houses and through more subtle methods like social boycott, which are intended to block their access to basic necessities and services. This phenomenon has to be positioned in the largest perspective of State-Society dynamics in order to understand why it happens and how it can be checked.

Caste Structure

The target of caste violence is largely the people belonging to the lowest rung in the hierarchy of Hindu social order, who are known as the 'untouchables', or Scheduled Castes bound to the rest of the caste society in immutable relationship of rights and obligations. The practice of 'untouchability' characterizes this relationship. The emergence of untouchability in the caste based social order has a complex history with little consensus or clarity on its origin. (Naval, 2000) While some have attributed it to the growth of agricultural civilization in the country and the emergence of agricultural castes, who needed assured access to manual labour for agricultural operations, others have traced its genesis to expansionist phase of Indian civilization which led to the consequent of indigenous inhabitants and their consequent enslavement by the Aryans (Krishnan, 2000). The 'shudras' in the social hierarchy towards the end of the Rig Vedic period represent these enslaved persons who were assigned inferior status, which was related to their birth in that community. (Naval, 2000) Whatever be the explanation of its origin, the institutional structures which governed social conduct in the society are subsumed under the nomenclature of 'Caste System', which broadly represents a vertical arrangement of social division of the Hindu population into four major groups, known as 'Varnas'. At the top of this arrangement are the Brahmin (priestly class), followed by Kshatriya' (the warrior class), and 'Vaishya' (trading and artisan class). 'Shudra' (labouring and service class) stood at the bottom of hierarchy. The 'untouchables' were not a part of this Scheme. However, over a period of time, the exigencies of situation led to the addition of a Fifth group to this classification which was not given any 'caste status' as such, but nonetheless integrally linked to the social order and is referred to as 'untouchables' or 'outcasts'. The membership of this group was determined by birth and could not be changed by individual effort or social acceptance. These four 'Varnas' subsequently transformed/got divided into hundreds of sub-castes, known as 'jati', each 'jati' having its own norms of social conduct. The caste structure is characterized by six important features:

- Segmented division of Society;
- Hierarchy;
- Restrictions of feeding and social intercourse,
- Lack of unrestricted choice of occupation,
- Civil and religious disabilities and privileges of different sections, and
- Restrictions on marriage.

The segmentation of society into four groups represents a tightly divided arrangement, of both status and occupation which is linked to each other in a hierarchical relationship. Brahmins occupy the top slot in the hierarchical ladder and 'untouchables' the bottom. As the caste hierarchy operates around the concepts of 'purity' and 'pollution', 'untouchables' are considered as the most degraded because they perform polluting tasks. The restrictions on feeding and social intercourse incorporates code of conduct for each caste on what one can see and cannot see, what one can and cannot touch and what can or cannot be accepted by a person of one caste from a person of another caste. Restrictions on occupation are intended to prevent any destabilization of hierarchy (Bhopal Document, 2002). Civil and religious disabilities mandate 'untouchables' to live at a distance from the main village, not to draw water from village well, enter the village temple, wear the sacred thread, acquire education or recite the religious texts. Untouchables are required to undertake the most polluting and degrading occupations, such as cleaning filth, including human excreta, flaying dead animals, digging graves, etc. The absolute restriction on marriages outside the caste and, in fact, even sub-castes ensures that there is no mobility from one group to another. Thus, the untouchables face total segregation in all matters, subjected to acute discrimination, do the most menial and degrading jobs and have no right to change their status.

Caste Atrocities: A Historical Perspective

The transition from caste disabilities to commission of atrocities has been traced to 3rd and 4th Century A.D., when varna system faced crisis of deviations from the prescribed social conduct and the need was felt for coercive measures to enforce caste discipline and boundaries. The King emerged as the Upholder of the system. Those who violated the system were subject to severe punishment as well as performance of various rituals. This is how physical violence by higher castes on the lower castes was sanctified. This situation continued for centuries. The persons of suppressed communities acquiesced in this arrangement, as there was no option for them to escape from it. Perhaps they may have been made to believe that life in the next birth may be better if discipline imposed by existing status is adhered to.

During the medieval period some saints, Kabir, Nanak, Ravidas were critical of existing social order and preached a religion of love, compassion and consideration and a more tolerant social arrangement. But there was no protest against the caste system and its social ramifications as such. The prevailing laws continued to support the caste system and the rulers upheld them. During the Muslim Rule in India, some people from the suppressed communities might have converted to Islam as a way out of their degraded status, but there is no evidence that the Muslim rulers ever tried to interfere with the Hindu caste system or reform it. Their strategy of governance may have prevented them from doing so. The British established the rule of law which was based on a concept of equality. The law applied to all persons irrespective of their position. This was a major departure from the pre-British judicial system where caste distinctions were not only recognized but also enforced and differential punishment was awarded, for the same offence, depending on the caste status of the offender. In any case, the suppressed castes neither had the courage nor resources to seek any relief under the new system. But even in the British period caste distinctions remained relevant in matters relating to Hindu Law. The general features of the legal system did not change the status of lower castes, as the overall British policy remained one of non-interference. In matters such as entry to temples, ritual pollution and rights to exclusiveness, the Courts supported the customary laws of Hindus and their view was upheld even at the level of privy Council. There was, however, some difference in the attitude of Courts towards secular public facilities such as streets and roads where such disabilities were not enforced. However, the Courts did not provide any support for removing caste disability in matters which came up before their consideration.

On a social plane, the period witnessed many reform movements in Hindu Society, such as Brahmo Samaj, Prarthana Samaj, Arya Samaj, Ramakrishna Mission. Theosophical

Society, the Social Conference which attacked the caste system and some other features of Hindu social order. These movements, while supporting the four varnas, condemned the inhuman practice of untouchability. Later, during the freedom movement, Gandhiji contributed a great deal towards abolition of untouchability and later founded the All India Haijan Sangh for this purpose. In south, self-respect movement was launched against Brahminical tyranny. It was Dr.Ambedkar, who took up the fight against caste oppression more vigorously through the All India Depressed Classes Federation. Around 1909, the issue of untouchability acquired political significance when proposals were made for special legislative representation for untouchables. In 1917, the Congress passed anti-disabilities resolution. In the 1930s anti-disabilities bills were introduced in Central Legislative Assembly, Madras and Bombay Legislatures. In 1938, Madras Legislature passed the first comprehensive law to remove social disabilities making it an offence to discriminate against the untouchables. In fact, in the publicly supported facilities, such as roads, wells, transport vehicles, etc. as also in other secular institutions, such as restaurants, hotels, shops, the law also prohibited judicial enforcement of any customary right or disability. This was followed by similar legislations in other provinces. Later, initiative was also taken by Madras to facilitate temple entry for Scheduled Castes by making it a criminal offence for any person to prevent any Hindu from entering or worshipping at any temple. Similar Acts were passed in other provinces later (Naval, 2000).

However, the British Government never took positive action to improve the condition of shudras and untouchables and to remove their disabilities. Apparently, the larger consideration of consolidating their rule prevented them from interfering with the customary practice associated with indigenous religions. Thus, at the time of independence, the traditional status of untouchables and caste disabilities, which prevented them from leading a life of dignity and self-respect continued to prevail. It was, therefore, left to the Constitution of India after independence to make the first comprehensive break with the past and to pronounce the policy of abolition of untouchability and declare total equality for the dalits in Indian Society. The Constitution also laid down means to achieve these objectives.

Before enumeration of constitutional and legal measures to curb violence and discrimination against dalits, it would be imperative to clarify the concepts - *Dalit and Violence.*

Who is Dalit?

There has been an intense debate on this question, resulting in two important viewpoints:

(a) that all the socially, politically and economically oppressed sections of the society are Dalits;

(b) that Dalits consist of only those sections of Indian society that suffered as "untouchables". Both the viewpoints are correct in their own ways. But, the untouchables suffer the worst form of discrimination at all levels. While the first viewpoint has the strength of focusing on the wider process of exploitation, it may not adequately represent and reflect the social discrimination to which the untouchables have been subjected. For this reason, the Indian Constitution provides a schedule for these castes and mandates that all the organs of the government treat the Dalits as a special social category and enforce their rights with greater care and commitment.

Dalits have been called by various names: Untouchables, Harijans, exterior Castes, Depressed Classes, Outcastes, Pariahs. In more ancient times, terms such as Mlecha, Chandals, Panchama, Nishada, Avarna, Antraja, Atishuda, Paulkasa, etc., were used. These usages of terms through the times and in different parts of India indicate the spatial and temporal dimensions of the Dalit question (Hargopal, 2002).

Defining Violence

Violence may be defined as application of physical force to inflict injury or damage. It is an intentional act to harm or injure.

It is considered as a persisting feature of social relationships and societies. Violence may not only be understood in physical sense as being the exercise of physical force; it may be mental or psychological; it may also be institutional, i.e. inherent in the institutions of the society itself and operating in a very subtle and imperceptible way. Much of violence found in contemporary society may be classed into three categories. *First,* violence which is used in the commission of crimes may be termed as criminal violence. The violent crimes or 'crimes of violence' fall in this category. *Secondly,* social violence which occurs at the societal level as an integral feature of interpersonal or inter-group relationships. It takes place among the various social groups of society such as caste, communal, political, economic, ethnic, majority-minority etc. *Third,* State violence in which the state uses is force and coercion against its own citizens in a legitimate manner to 'civilize'. These distinctions among three kinds of violence may only be tentative for the purposes of discussion, often; there may be considerable overlap among them. All kinds of violence may be 'criminal' from the strictly legal point of view. But the distinguishing feature of social violence (caste violence) is that it occurs at the societal level during, or as a consequence of some features of social relationships among members of different social groupings. The violence against Dalits can be seen in this perspective. It includes all categories of violence.

Legal Safeguards

The Indian Constitution has provided various statutory and legal safeguards for dalits. The Scheme of the Constitution reflects a *three-pronged strategy* for changing the status of dalits (Scheduled Castes and the Scheduled Tribes) based on the traditional social order. This consists of:

(a) *Protection:* Legal/Regulatory measures for enforcing equality and removing disabilities: Providing strong punitive action against physical violence inflicted on them; Eliminating customary arrangements which deeply hurt their dignity and person; Preventing control over fruits of their labour and striking at concentration of economic assets and resources and setting up autonomous watch-dog institutions to safeguard interests, rights and benefits guaranteed to them.

(b) *Compensatory discrimination:* Enforcement of reservation provisions in public services, representative bodies and educational institutions.

(c) *Development:* Measures to bridge the wide gap between dalits (the Scheduled Castes) and other communities in their economic conditions and social status, covering allocation of resources and distribution of benefits.

In this regard, it is interesting to note how the Indian Constitutional scheme aimed to tackle caste-based and gender-based discrimination and with what result in the last fifty years. The Constitution did not promise absolute equality which is probably beyond human attainment. The Preamble declared the goal as "equality of status and of opportunity". The guaranteed right of equality is framed in a negative language which said, that "the State shall not deny to any person equality before the law or the equal protection of the laws" (Article 14). The issue which immediately challenged the constitution makers was the social reality of widespread inequality and caste and gender-based discrimination. For the people who were treated for long as "untouchable" and discriminated on account of their caste-status, Article 14 offered little in terms of the preambular promise of equality of status and of opportunity. A package of protective discrimination and affirmative action programmes has been conceived and mandated by the Constitution to deal with the situation of entrenched inequalities and discriminatory practices. Untouchaility was abolished and its practice in any form declared an offence punishable under law. This was followed up by the enactment of the Untouchability Offences Act which later became the Protection of Civil Rights Act. Yet another apparently draconian law, the Scheduled Castes and Scheduled Tribes (Prevention of Atrocities) Act, 1989 was also adopted to deal with continuing practices related to untouchability.

The Constitution did not stop with mere elimination of discrimination. It had to fight the consequence of historical discrimination and promote equality of status and of opportunity. Assuming that mere granting of adult franchise would not automatically empower the disadvantaged castes, the Constitution provided for reservation of seats in Parliament and in the Legislative Assemblies of States (Articles 330, 332, 334) for the Scheduled Castes and Scheduled Tribes. Article 335 directed the State that the claims of the members of Scheduled Castes shall be considered in making of appointments to civil services consistent with the maintenance of efficiency of administration. A National Commission for Scheduled Castes is to be established (Article 338) to report to the President of India on the working of safeguards and measures that should be taken by the State for more effective implementation of those safeguards.

Acknowledging the need for positive action against discrimination, the Constitution not only prohibited discrimination by the State on grounds of religion, race, caste, sex or place of birth, but empowered the State to make special provisions, apparently discriminatory in favour of Scheduled Castes to overcome existing disabilities and to advance social justice [Article 15(4)]. All disabilities and restrictions based on caste and race in the matter of access to public places and resources have been removed by appropriate legislative policies.

The picture that emerges from the Constitutional scheme of equality against caste based discrimination in Indian society is positively re-assuring as far as law and State action can go. One may even concede that substantial progress has been achieved in the elimination of caste-based discrimination in society particularly in places where education and economic development helped to improve the quality of life of people generally and the disadvantaged sections in particular. At the same time, it many other places in the country the change, if at all, continues to be distressingly slow and painful. Some attribute this situation to caste-based politics perpetrated by political parties with the connivance of vested interest, others blame the sad state of governance including neglect of education, land reform and local self-Government for the continued denial of equal opportunities to dalits; yet others find the State apparatus not showing sufficient interest in implementing the anti-discrimination laws and in promoting affirmative action programmes officially proclaimed. Whatever be the reason for the malaise, it is a matter of regret that despite progressive laws and an egalitarian Constitutional scheme, the plight of dalit groups in Indian society is as bad as ever for which the State has to own accountability and explain before appropriate forums (Menon, 2003).

To give a clear expression to Constitutional provisions, an impressive range of legislative measures have been enacted to end discrimination against dalits. These inter-alia include:

- The Protection of Civil Rights (Anti-untouchability) Act, 1955.
- The Bonded labour (Abolition) Act, 1976
- The Scheduled Castes and Scheduled Tribes (Prevention of Atrocities) Act, 1989.
- The Employment of Manuel Scavengers and Construction of Dry Latrines (Prohibition) Act, 1993.
- Various Land Reforms Laws.

It was foreseen by the framers of the Constitution itself that an effective mechanism would have to be created to watch whether the intended benefits of various laws and programmes are reaching to dalits since they would not have the strength to avail them given their weak an vulnerable position. The Constitution itself, therefore, created the first watchdog institutions for safeguarding the rights of dalits (SCs and STs) in the institution of Special Officer. This was later converted into a National Commission. Subsequently, other watchdog institutions were created, each looking into specific area of vulnerability, starting from National Human Rights Commission (NHRC) followed up by National Commission for Women (NCW) and National Commission for Safai Kamacharis (NCSK). These Commissions are addressing various issues related to dalit rights, however, violence and atrocities against dalits have not shown any credible reduction.

International Standards Applicable to India

Various International Human Rights covenants and conventions applicable to India, include:

(a) Universal Declaration of Human Rights 1948,

(b) International Covenant on Civil and Political Rights, 1966,

(c) International Covenant on Economic, Social and Cultural Rights, 1966,

(d) International Convention on Elimination of all forms of Racial Discrimination, 1965,

(e) Convention on Elimination of all forms of Discrimination against Women, 1979;

(f) Convention on Rights of Child, 1989,

(g) ILO Convention No .29 - Forced Labour Convention, 1930,

(h) ILO Convention No. 111 - Discrimination (Employment and Occupation) Convention 1958,

(i) ILO convention No. 107 - Indigenous Peoples Convention 1957.

All the above have been signed and ratified by the Government of India. In addition, the Convention against Torture and Other Cruel, Inhuman or Degrading Treatment or Punishment (1984) has also been signed but not yet ratified. There is pressure on Government of India to ratify it since mechanisms have been provided against the practice and torture and Courts and National Human Rights Commission have also issued directions in this matter. These international instruments lay down norms and standards for treatment of individuals and groups and protection of their rights. As a result of these conventions, Government of India is required to submit periodical reports to the concerned international organizations monitoring their enforcement. The concerned Committees of these organizations make observations or furnish comments on the reports submitted.

Despite the affirmative action and compensatory discrimination permitted under the constitution and the range and scope of measures envisaged under these provisions, the regrettable fact remains that social injustice and violence against dalits - (SCs & STs), have not as yet been eliminated. The challenge therefore lies in translating these legal provisions into reality and in strict enforcement of the existing laws. The key lies in the vigorous implementation of the full range of existing legal provisions.

Violence & Crime Against Dalits: The current scene

The crimes against Scheduled Castes/Scheduled Tribes reported to the police are broadly categorized under two categories:

(1) *Under the Indian Penal Code (IPC)*

- (a) Murder
- (b) Hurt
- (c) Rape
- (d) Kidnapping and Abduction
- (e) Dacoity
- (f) Robbery
- (g) Arsan
- (h) Others (other unclassified IPC crimes)

(2) *Under Special Laws*

- (a) Protection of Civil Rights Act, 1955
- (b) The Scheduled Castes and Scheduled Tribes (Prevention of Atrocities) Act, 1989.

In fact, violence against dalits occurs while serious gaps between policy directions and reality persist. There are many reasons for their historical and cultural, economic and social, political and administrative, to name a few. According to National Crime Records Bureau Report *"Crime in India, 2007"* (NCRB, 2007), the year 2007 has witnessed an increase of 10.9 per cent in crime against SCs as 27070 cases reported in 2006 have increased to 30,031 cases in 2007. This increase was observed in all heads under which data of crime against SCs were collected except Dacoity, Robbery and Cares under Protection of Civil Rights (PCR) Act. Cases registered under PCR Act showed a considerable decline of 49.1 per cent in 2007 over 2006. Kidnapping and Abduction cases reported an increase of 18.6 per cent in 2007 over 2006. Uttar Pradesh and Rajasthan accounted for 20.5% and 13.9 per cent of total cases (30,031) reported in the country followed by Madhya Pradesh (13.7 per cent) It is interesting to note that cases related to untouchability have declined (49.1%) in 2007. This could happen through growing awareness among all sections of society that untouchability is a social evil and the soon we realize this, the better. However, the other side of the story could be that many cases are still not being reported to the police due to various reasons - police as participants in violence against dalits, the Act (PCR) attracts lenient punishment as compared to SCs and STs (Prevention of Atrocities) Act, 1989 and does not provide for compensation or relief to the victim. Offences under Protection of Civil Rights Act, 1955 relating to the untouchability attract a maximum of 6 months of imprisonment and maximum fine of Rs. 500/-. In offences not covered by Protection of Civil Rights Act, 1955, the FIR is registered under IPC whose provisions attract lesser punishment than those of SCs and STs (Prevention of Atrocities) Act, 1989 for the same offence.

The recent report entitled *'Crime in India – 2007'* states 27,070 cases of atrocities against SC communities were reported in 2007. The report states that there were 1,349 cases of rape of dalit women, 674 cases of murder, 332 cases of kidnapping and abduction and 3,814 cases of causing hurt. There were 206 cases under Protection of Civil Rights Act and 9819 cases under the Schedules Castes and Scheduled Tribes (Prevention of Atrocities) Act.

More significantly, the NCRB Report points out that the conviction rate was abysmal, while charge-sheets were filed in 90.6. per cent of the cases, the conviction rate was only 30.9 per cent. A total of 51,705 persons were arrested in 2007 in cases of atrocities against dalits; 65,544 of them were charge-sheeted, but trials were completed only in the cases relating to 13,817 persons. In fact, the conviction rate in Uttar Pradesh is the highest in India (49.4 per cent). Thus only 13,871 could be convicted out of 47,136 persons against whom trials were completed representing a conviction rate of 29.4 per cent.

This 'improvement' in the conviction rate in Uttar Pradesh has been rationalized by many north Indian dalit observers as a reflection of the superior public-political presence and organization network of the Bahujan Samaj Party (BSP). The BSP has developed over the past decade into one of the biggest parties of Uttar Pradesh and interventions of the BSP are much more effective in forums of administration and law enforcement. In fact, these interventions have created a relatively better social environment for dalits in U.P. Until the mid-1980s, dalits in U.P. suffered extreme forms of social discrimination. In hundreds of villages and towns in the State, dalits were not even allowed through the main streets or use public utilities, including transport. Many dalit communities were even treated like slaves by the upper & OBC castes. So much so, women of many dalit communities were, as a rule, sexually oppressed by upper and OBC castes men.

But all this changed to a large extent on account of the sustained political interventions of the BSP at the grassroots and in the arena of real politics since its emergence in the mid-1980s. The present situation, where at least some dalit communities such as Jatav are able to stand up to social oppression, is essentially the result of the BSPs initiatives. This is evident from the registration of a higher number of cases relating to atrocities against dalit communities. Further, a large number of these cases are related to grabbing of land owned by dalits by members of other communities, including upper castes and Other Backward Classes (OBCs). The flipside is that this social awareness and militancy are not shared uniformly among all dalit communities.

Forms of Human Rights Violations against Dalits

Broadly, human rights violations against dalits are reported in the following forms:

- Denial of access to common water sources.
- Denial of access to common temples.
- Right to walk into the caste Hindu areas with footwear or ride a by Bicycle or a scooter.
- Supplying tea to dalits in separate tumblers.
- Insult to dalit women (mass rape, paraded naked etc.).
- Threats against contesting in an election.
- Objection to taking a marriage procession in a caste Hindu locality.
- Refusal of demand for higher labour.
- Protest against occupation change.
- Marriage with non-dalit
- Barbar service
- Priest service
- Discrimination at school
- Public transport.
- Manual scavenging
- Bonded labour
- Devdasi system

It is evident from the above that dalits are still discriminated at socio-economic and political levels by the caste Hindu. The discrimination does not end here. To it worse forms discrimination also happening among various constituents of dalits. For example, the scavengers are segregated and required to do odd jobs such as removing human excreta and cleaning dry latrines, cleaning of roads etc. The other sections of dalits do not share food, water etc. with them. This section silently suffers untouchability in its myriad forms – for instance, denial of access to common water sources, public road and temples, shops and schools. Seldom they protest their humiliation. Thus, numerous are the ways in which dalits are tormented. They are murdered and maimed; women are raped; their children are abused and deprived of schooling; they are dispossessed of their property; their houses are torched, they are denied their legitimate rights and their sources of livelihood are destroyed. Adding to the long list of violence on dalits, the following are some illustrative cases relating to violence and crime committed against dalits in recent years:

Case I

On September 5, at Kaundampatti in Dindigul district of Tamil Nadu State, Sankan, a Dalit agricultural worker, was forced to drink urine – for having lodged with the police a complaint of trespass against a caste Hindu, following a dispute between them over a piece of land. Sankan had to suffer many atrocities during his five-year long struggle against his caste-Hindu landlord to get possession of the land. In his complaint, Sankan stated that the landlord had collected nearly Rs.1 lakh over a period of 15 years through deductions from his wages, as the price of the land. An equally horrifying incident occurred at Thinniyam village in Triuchi district on May 22. Two Dalits, Murugesan and Ramasami, were forced "to feed each other" human excreta. The "crime" they committed was that they stood by another Dalit, Karuppiah, who was engaged in a prolonged struggle against a former panchayat president and her husband to recover an amount of money he said he had given them as a bribe to get a house allotted for his sister.

Both incidents are related to the growing aspiration of Dalits to own land, either for cultivation or to build a house, and the continued opposition or indifference of caste Hindus and the government in this regard. Ironically, the principal accused in the Thinniyam incident, the panchayat president's husband, is a retired teacher, while in the Kaundampatti incident one of the alleged perpetrators of the act is a Chennai-based police constable, who belonged to the village.

While a first information report (FIR) has been registered with regard to the latest complaint, a case has been registered in connection with the earlier matter. In connection with the Thinniyam incident, 10 persons, including the former Panchayat president and her husband, are liable to face charges under the Scheduled Castes and Scheduled Tribes (Prevention of Atrocities) Act and the Indian Penal Code. People's Watch-

Tamil Nadu, a Madurai – based non-governmental organization, has taken up both the cases with the National Human Rights Commission and the National Commission for Scheduled Castes and Scheduled Tribes (Frontline, October, 2002).

Case-II

On October 15, five Dalits were burnt to death at Dulina village in Jhajjar district in Haryana. The official explanation was that the five men, who were skinning a cow on the Farookhnagar-Jhajjat road on Dasara day, were brought to the police post by some people accusing them of cow slaughter. Matters got worse, or were allowed to get worse, from there on as the crowd swelled into a murderous mob. Within hours, the grisly deed was accomplished, because of what is being touted officially as a case of "mistaken identity". This implied that the mob thought that the five persons were members of a specific minority community and lynched them. It is difficult to ignore the subtle meaning behind the "mistaken identity' theory as it presupposes that had the five not been Dalits, the lynching would have been a natural outcome of the general attitude towards a specific community.

The State government and The National Commission for Scheduled Castes and Scheduled Tribes conducted inquiries. The question that rankles one is whether the reports have been able to do justice to the five lives that were want only, taken. First, neither of the two reports has even gone into the factors that triggered the mob frenzy. The SCs and STs Commission goes a step farther to state that the incident "does not appear to be a case of atrocity on (the) SC&ST community which presupposes prior knowledge that the victims belonged to (the) SC&ST community. Strange indeed, for if it is not a case of an atrocity against Dalits, and not a communal attack either as the five persons were not members of a minority community, then was it just a spontaneous reaction from a largely peace-loving crowd returning happily from the festivities of Dasara?

The role of the police, which was highly suspect, has hardly come under proper scrutiny. Both reports have mildly castigated the police but have hardly recommended any strong action against them for failing to protect the lives of the five innocent persons. But most important, while failing to look into the deeper reasons, the two reports have consciously given a clean chit to the role played by communal organizations.

The Commission also legitimizes the aspect of "public sentiment" in the entire episode. The system of awarding contracts for skinning dead animals was rot prevalent in Jhajjar and "perhaps the victims were not aware of this fact and they had started skinning the animal by the roadside, which was mistaken as an incident of cow slaughter for the purpose of skin arid meat." This "perhaps had hurt the religious sentiment on the day' of Dasara festival." The "public sentiment's were aroused through rumour on the basis of a mistaken identity that all these people belonged to another religion and their very act was against the basic tenet $_0$f the religion of the dominant Hindu community," the report observes - Who were the turnout-mongers? And who mobilized the crowd These are some uncomfortable questions the report has left unanswered. According to one of the members who authored the report, the job of the commission was not to be "investigative". It was meant to ensure that adequate relief and compensation were provided to the families of the deceased (Frontline, January, 2003).

Case-III

This incident involves the mysterious disappearance of Karan Singh, an elected Dalit Sarpanch of Pehrawar village of Rohtak District of Haryana State. Pehrawar is dominated by Brahmins. Around 800 Brahmin families and 100-odd Dalit families live in the village. Needless to say, it is the Brahmins who wield more social and political clout in their village.

According to Bharpai Devi, at 10 p.m. on October 12, 2004 her husband was taken away by some members of the Brahmin community for a meeting at a dairy. He never returned. Karan Singh, village residents said, was under pressure for a long time from a Brahmin organisation called the Gaur Brahmin Shikshan Sanstha, to 'gift" away 20 acres (eight hectares) of prime shamlat land. Another influential group had been pressuring Karan Singh not to oblige. The sarpanch was caught in the dispute. The sarpanch was not obliged to give away any such land without a two-thirds majority of the panchayat. And it was quite likely that the sarpanch had become a victims of State-level political tussles. While the president of the Sanstha owes allegiance to the Haryana Vikas Party (HVP), the other faction is allied with the INLD.

What was most shocking was the reluctance of the administration even to take cognizance of the fact that the sarpanch was missing. On October 16, 2004 after making several enquiries regarding the whereabouts of her husband, Bharpai Devi went to the police to file a First Information Report. The Station House Officer (SHO) allegedly refused to register it. She named the persons who had taken away her husband but the SHO appeared uninterested. He reportedly told her that the villagers had assured him that the sarpanch would return. Bharpai Devi, who is a Class IV employee in the State government approached political parties and Dalit groups. On October 17, she met the District Commissioner (DC) along with members of the Ravidas Samaj Mahasabha, where the officer gave strict instructions to the Superintendent of Police and the SHO to take immediate action. But no action followed. (Incidentally, SHO Vijender Sharma had reportedly suggested that she use "Tantrik Vidya to locate her husband".)

An FIR was registered on November 25 after a massive protest demonstration - was held and a memorandum was submitted to the Governor. Fearing that the sarpanch may have been murdered, various organisations came together to form the Pehrawar Sangharsh Samjti,

This is not the first time a member of the lower caste has gone missing in Pehrawar. In 1998, a Young Kumhar woman, Mohini. was kidnapped, gang-raped and murdered by upper-caste youth. For a long time, no FIR was lodged and the police maintained that she had run away" with somebody or that her family, being poor, must have sold her off. An agitation was launched and it was later revealed that some village youth had allegedly murdered her and thrown her body into a canal.

Finally residents of the village searched for the body and found the remains. Forensic tests revealed the corpse to be that of Mohini. The family of the woman, isolated and humiliated, left the village. Thus, harassment of Dalits appears to be a regular phenomenon in the village.

Pehrawar is not an exception. A few months ago, a woman Dalit sarpanch was dragged by the hair and beaten in public at Gandhra village in Rohtak district. The victim of a conflict between dominant caste groups in the village, she was being pressured to take decisions in favour of one particular family. Similarly, in Kharkhara village, en route to Meham, a Dalit woman was dragged through the village at pistol-point and raped. The family had to agree to compromise and no case was made out against the culprits. In Harsola, Kaithal district, some 200 families that were attacked fled their homes. They were later pressured into withdrawing the cases registered under the Scheduled Castes and Scheduled Tribes (Prevention of Atrocities) Act.

Karan Singh may not be found at all. But the fundamental problem in the latest episode as well as otter previous incidents involving Dalits is the partisan role played by the administration. There is also a growing feeling that major political parties are reluctant to view such incidents with the seriousness required (*Frontline*, January, 2004).

Case IV

Jagir Singh, a dalit agricultural worker in Punjab, refused to work on Jat-owned fields without wages. Punishment was promptly delivered. Jagir Singh was beaten and his face blackened with dung before he was paraded through the village with shoes strung around his neck. This ritual humiliation illustrates, if nothing else, the fact that local elites think that they can punish Dalits with impunity. Gurcharan Singh, the husband of the village's woman sarpanch. and another landowner, Jagtar Singh, were later arrested for the offence, A third suspect, Chinder Singh, the son of the sarpanch, is evading arrest. Dalit activists in Punjab say dozens of such cases go unreported.

In general, the State apparatus pitches in on the side of village upper-caste elites. At about the same time as the Jagir Singh outrage, the police evicted a Dalit family from homes allotted to them under a landless-labour protection scheme at Lehri village, near Talwandi Sabo. Buta Singh's family was allotted two tenements in 1974, but since these were already occupied, it took over two other vacant properties. Without serving legal notice - or, indeed, following any other procedural formalities - the police threw out the Buta Singh family's belongings and helped another family usurp the plot. Buta Singh's wife, Sarabjit Kaur, claims the land-grab had the backing of a local Shiromani Akali Dal (SAD) leader.

Often, violent reprisal follows Dalits efforts to secure the protection of the State apparatus. On June 11, Binder Kaur and her son were attacked and beaten up by a group of assailants outside her home at Bhisiana near Bhatinda. The attack came shortly after her husband Bikkar Singh insisted on pressing charges after the attempted rape of his daughter-in-law by members of the upper castes in the area. Binder Kaur's efforts to file a complaint were rejected by the local police, who, she says, made her place her fingerprints on a blank sheet of paper. Nor was she medically examined for injuries sustained in the course of the assault. The family received threats in the wake of its decision to pursue the case, but received no protection from the local authorities (Frontline, July, 2004).

Case V

A dalit women Sarpanch of Mohai Kala village in Chhatarpur District of M.P. was beaten up, stripped and then paraded naked by upper caste men as she did not pay them Rs. 50,000 from the village development fund. The women ordeal did not end here. Even after her repeated requests, the Police did not file an FIR. After local political intervention the police lodged the complaint on fourth day of the incident.

According to Sarpanch Indira Kushwah (45), local goons - Lakhan Shukla and Santosh Shukla - had been harassing her for the last six months for money. She said, "Lakhan used to threaten me. He wanted the money which I had received under the village development fund. He said the money should be given to him because I, being a Dalit would not know how to spend it."

"On June 17, 2006 evening when I turned down their demand, the two, armed with rifles, came to my hutmet, dragged me and my children out and started beating me. He and his men then stripped me and paraded me naked in the village," She alleged, "No one came to my rescue. Even my children were not spared. They too, were beaten up," She said.

"When I went to the local police station, I was told to go back to the village. No one will beat me again," she lamented. On Wednesday SP legislator Vijay Bahadur Singh Bundela took her to district collector, who gave instruction to the police to take action but said he could not comment till an inquiry was conducted (*The Times of India*, Mumbai, June 23, 2006).

Case VI

A gutsy Dalit teenager fought off a gang rape attempt but lost her right arm when the frustrated men chopped it off in revenge in an Uttar Pradesh village. Interestingly, the local police station, which refused to register an FIR initially, did so only after the intervention of a top police official.

It all happened when 15 year old Anju of Chinta K Purwa village in Auraiya districts, went to her family owned agricultural land. Local goon Viresh Yadav, who has been stalking her for quite some time, followed her along with two accomplices. They dragged the girl to one corner of the land. As Anju resisted and tried to flee, Viresh and his friends chopped off her right arm with a sharp edged weapon. In an even more daring act, they carried away the severed arm. As she lay in pool of blood, villagers rushed to the spot after hearing Anju's scream. They took her to the LLR hospital in Kanpur. Local police refused to register a complaint by Anju's father Lal Singh Kanjar. It was only after the labourer approached DIG (Kanpur zone), the local police lodge an FIR. By the time police reached his home, Viresh had fled along with his family.

"Contrary to the claim of Anju's family investigations so far show that the victim had a relationship with the accused, "Auraiya SP said. He also said that some villagers told police that since Anju's father asked her to break up with Viresh, she tried to commit suicide by jumping before a train. Though she did not die, the attempt cost her right arm (*The Hindustan Times*, 2006).

Case VII

Two lower caste youth of Angri Lohar were killed, in Amla police station area of Betul district MP, for deposing in court against upper cast people in a murder case. On 13th June, 2006 around 5pm while returning from market to their village Khapa Katheda they were lynched to death. They had deposed before the court in a murder case in which people from same upper cast group had burnt three lower cast women of Angri lohar community to death. This is third such incident in last three years where people belonging to lower cast community have fallen victim to violence of upper cast mob. In mid of 2003 two men and women of Pardhi community of village Amrawati Ghat of Multai block in Betul district (SP's MLA Sunilam Hails from Multai) were stoned to death. Since all the political party right from Congress, BJP to Samajwadi parties supported them, they were acquitted. Taking lead from it, immediately after the acquittal, in the month of August 2004 in village Khapa Khateda lohar were burnt to death.

Killing of lower cast people was not common in Betul since one A. K. Singh became SP of Betul law and order situation in Betul district had gone out of hand. During his tenure first incident occurred where all the accused were acquitted it prompted upper cast community to inflict violence on lower cast people. During his tenure tribal were gang raped and tribal youth was killed to death by Liquior contractor. The SP has changed the pratice led down by him are continuing (e-mail from Shramik Songhu to TISS faculty on June 14, 2006).

Case VIII

In a shocking incident a fight over a game of cricket between school boys escalated into a full-fledged caste war that led to three Dalit boys were being forced to drink urine by upper-caste landlords in Ferozepur District. The incident took place at Patrewal village near Abohar. All the victims belong to the Rai-Sikh community. Jagir Singh said it was during a cricket match that his son Nanak Singh, a Standard VIII student, picked up a fight with his upper-caste classmate, Amardip Singh. Following this, Nanak's relatives Amardip's resident, but they were abused and forced to leave. "Amardip's father, Gurdip Singh Jakhar, even threatened to teach us a lesson," Jagir said.

"A few days later, a group of Jakhar landlords accosted our relatives who had come from the neighbouring Bulla village." Jagir said, adding while his younger brother, Balwinder, managed to flee, three other boys - Gurbas, Bittu and Piara - were dragged to the residence of the Sarpanch, Gurdas Singh, where the landlords urinated in their juttis (shoes) and forced them to drink it at gunpoint.Gurbax, the oldest of the trio said, "Apni Jutti vich peshab kar ke saanu pin nu kiha" (They urinated in their shoes and made us to drink it). 'Later, the boys were handed over to the police where they were kept in custody for eight days. When a former panchayat member, Malkiat Singh, went to meet the Sarpanch to seek the release of the three boys, he was asked to produce two relatives of Nanak Singh Later, two uncles of Nanak, Balwinder Singh and Kulwant Singh, were kept in police custody for 11 and eight days, respectively (*The Indian Express*, 2005).

Case IX

Honour killings, which are widespread in some of the economically advanced states such as Punjab, Haryana, U.P. (western region) are perpetrated under the grab of saving the 'honour of the community, caste or family. The acts of violence include public lynching of couples, murder of either the man or the women concerned or both, murder made to appear as suicide, public beatings, humiliation, blackening of the face, forcing couples to eat excreta or drink urine, revenge, rape and public killing forced incarceration, social boycotts. The largest number of cases were found to have occurred in Punjab, Haryana and U.P. One reason for the increased visibility of such crimes is the trend of more and more girls joining education institutions, meeting other from different backgrounds and castes in establishing relationships beyond the confines of caste and community. Such individuals are targeted so that none dares to breach the barriers of caste and communities. Significantly, in the majority of cases it is the economically and socially dominant castes that organize, instigate and abet such act of retribution. These honour killing occur within forward and backward castes and backward castes and dalits. In Muzaffarnagar district in Western UP, atleast 13 honour killings occured in 2003. In 2002, while 10 such killings were reported, 35 couples were declared missing. It is not surprising that no such category of crime exists in government records. In fact, there is refusal even to recognize this phenomena. Data for such incidents are seldom available and they would mostly be classified under the category of general crimes. Moreover, most of such cases go unreported and even when reported, often FIRs are not filed and post mortems are not conducted. Caste panchayats have come to play an increasingly important role especially in situations when political patronage is also exists (*Frontline* Feb, 2004).

Central theme of honor and violence is the subordinate position of girls and women in all castes and communities. A women chastity is the "honour"of the community and she has no sovereign right over her body at any point of her life. The retribution is particularly swift and brutal if the she crossed caste and class barriers to choose a lower caste man as her partner. In many of such cases men were from dalit community and the women were either from OBCs or upper caste. Hindu.

More recently, giving a clarion call for a war against honour killings and panchayat directed violence against inter-caste marriages, the Supreme Court in July 2006 gave an omnibus direction to the police across the country to take stern action against any one harassing any couples, who are major and have tied the knot after defying caste or religion. The court observed that "intercaste marriages were, in fact in the national interest as they could be a potent weapon to destroy the caste system, which is a curse on the nation". Referring to "honour killings" the bench said: "There is nothing honourable in such killings ..... In fact they are nothing but barbaric and shameful act of murders committed by brutal, fudal-minded persons who deserve harsh punishment. Only in the way we can stamp out such act of barbarism.

The court gave two fold directions: First, it asked the administration and police authorities throughout the county "to see it that if any boy or girl is a major and undergoes inter-caste or inter-religious marriage with a women or man who is a major, the couple are not harassed by anyone nor subjected to threat or acts of violence". *Second,* it said "Any one who gives such threats or commits acts of violence either himself or instigates them is taken to task by constituting criminal proceedings by the police and further action is taken against such persons as provided by law".

Case X

The recent massacres of a dalit family in the village of Khairlanji in Bhandara district of Maharashtra on September 29, 2007, and violent protests against the massacres in different parts of Maharashtra after desecration of a statue of Dr. B. R. Ambedkar in Kanpur have once again brought centre stage issues relating to a long neglected section of socially neglected, economically and politically deprived people across the country. The bone of contention of this gruesome incident was a piece of land, which was owned by a dalit - named Bhaiyyalal Bhotmonge and the dispute was with some upper caste villagers. Axe bearing attackers, allegedly from backward Kumbi caste, flushed the four bodies in a canal. The investigation was handled in a slipshod manner and it was only the pressure exerted by Dalit organizations and others that brought the Khairlanji murders to the notice of general public. A report prepared by a government agency, Yashwantrao Chavan Academy of Development and Administration (YASHADA, based in Pune) has seriously indicted Senior Police Officials and doctors for their attempt to cover up the rape of Surekha and Priyanka Bhotmonge, two of the four victims, and recommend stringent action against them, including making their co-accused under the POA and treating them on par with terrorists. The Report established that "there was dereliction of duty on the part of all the officials in the District and there was a deep rooted conspiracy towards suppressing the crime and the evidence". The Report has made the following recommendations:

- Negligent officers, instead of being merely transferred/ suspended, should be made co-accused. Inquiry under Prevention of Atrocities Act, 1989 should be initiated against them. They should also be denied service benefits like pension and gratuity.
- Atrocities on Dalits be viewed on par with terrorism and the accused be dealt sternly under provisions of a stringent act to control organized crime.
- The government should conduct a survey of all villages to find out if untouchability is prevalent anywhere. The government grant of the village be stopped if any instance of untouchability is found.
- In case of reports of discrimination or atrocities in a village, local-level functionaries such as talathi, anganwadi worker, gramsevak, police patil, etc. be suspended immediately.
- A section on atrocities be included in the school curriculum and teachers be given special training on equity and social justice.

The Lessons Learnt from Khairlanji Massacre

The Khairlanji incident would not have taken place had the police and the administration acted on the complaint made four years ago by Mrs.Surekha Bhotmonge, who was among the four dalits murdered in the village in Bhandara district on September 29, 2006. On July 20, 2002, Surekha had sent a letter to the then Divisional Commissioner of Nagpur , an IAS officer, pointing out the threat issued to her family by some villagers and the indifferent attitude of the police in acting of her complaint. She had sent copies of the letter to the Inspector General of Police, Nagpur Range and Superintendent of Police,

Bhandara district and local MLA. But no one of them acted on the complaint. Only after massacre, the State has taken action against all senior police officials and the Civil Surgeon of the District and a Dy. Superintendent of Police and has given a compensation of Rs. 2.5 lakh along with a job to Bhaiyyalal, the only survivor.

The evidence on record shows how the State, that is the political establishment, has failed to curb these human rights violations against Dalits. For example, after coming to power in Maharashtra in 1995, the Shiv Sena - BJP government began withdrawing over 1,100 cases registered under the Scheduled Caste and Scheduled Tribe (Prevention of Atrocities) Act, alleging that these cases were false and were registered out of personal bias. The State Government also declared that it would ask the Central Government to amend the Act to limit its 'abuse'. The withdrawal of cases effectively sent the message to be police not to register the cases and ensured that it would not be taken seriously. Similar incidences have also been reported from Uttar Pradesh and Rajasthan states as well. This shows that the political establishment is not serious to implement the law effectively. If the Scheduled Caste and Scheduled Tribe (Prevention of Atrocities) Act get implemented effectively, it would not be surprising to see more hostile statements coming out from the political establishment against the use of the Act.

Given in this context of State apathy. Dalits have no one to turn to except themselves when their human rights are violated. With untouchability persisting unashamedly in state institutions like schools and police stations, in public spaces like temples and shops, in farms and markets, and in homes and hearts, Dalits still live in India waiting hopelessly and sometimes in anger, for the long-betrayed dawn of equality. (Tiwari, 2007).

Caste Violence and Untouchability in India: The Current Scenario

The "Report on Prevention of Atrocities Against Scheduled Castes" released by National Human Rights Commission

(NHRC) in November 2004 has taken a hard look at the status of dalits and recommended measures to ensure that the laws meant to protect them from atrocities and violence are implemented by the State with sincerity.

The study begins with looking at caste-related violence from a historical perspective to help understand the background of "organised violence directed against members of identified groups/communities", which has been "a distinct feature of Indian society for quite sometime". What characterises the violence against Dalits is that unlike other incidents of organised violence, the victims are "chosen on the basis of birth in a given social entity". Violence against Dalits, therefore, "has the distinctiveness of being embedded in the social structure of the dominant community itself'. It is this caste-based, hierarchical structure that "lays down the norms of conduct [for relationships] between its more privileged groups and the subdued and subordinate segment" - Dalits are kept at the bottom of the social ladder, as "outcastes" and "untouchables" outside the four-net Structure.

The report says: "It is this caste relationship in Hindu society which is getting disturbed by forces of pressure both from above and below." "The frequency and intensity of violence," the report observes, "is an offshoot of desperate attempts by the upper caste groups to protect their entrenched status against the process of disengagement and upward mobility among lower castes resulting from affirmative action of State Policy [enshrined in the Constitution of India]."

This lopsided development and half hearted moves to ameliorate the conditions of the poor have generated only desperation and frustration all around. Growing unemployment and loss of jobs in the wake of deteriorating economic conditions over the past 10 years or more under the reforms regime have also added to the misery of the poor.

Whenever atrocities against Dalits involving loss of life and property are reported, human rights and Dalit activists complain that the police are generally reluctant to file cases under the stringent provisions of the Atrocities Act. They generally book cases either under the Indian Penal Code (IPC) or, at best, under the Protection of Civil Rights (PCR) Act, 1955, much milder than the Atrocities Act. This often results in the culprits going scot-free. The Atrocities Act was enacted mainly with the intention of giving more teeth to the earlier Untouchabilitv (Offences) Act, 1955 (amended and renamed the PCR Act), and not creating a deterrent against physical violence. The Act brought new types of offences under 'atrocities" against Dalits by non-Dalit persons and provided for more stringent punishment for the guilty.

The report states: "Under-reporting of the Atrocities Act is a very common phenomenon and therefore the decline in the number of registered cases does not provide a true picture of the incidence of atrocities." It quotes several studies to show that all reported atrocities are not registered under the Atrocities Act. "The non-registration of cases, apart from reflecting caste bias and corruption, has also been attributed to the pressure on the police to keep reported crime rates low in their jurisdiction," says the report.

The geographical distribution of atrocities from 1995 to 1999 indicates that the largest number of cases have been reported from Uttar Pradesh every year. This is primarily because Uttar Pradesh has the largest population of Dalits compared with other States. Further, the report recommended 150 measures to the State to implement the Atrocities Act with all sincerity and with all the force at its command.

This aside, Mandar (2006) stated that children in rural India learn early the rules of caste, even as their country races into the 21st century. A survey of practices of untouchability in 565 villages in 11 states reveals that in many as 38 per cent government schools, Dalit children are made to sit separately while eating. In 20 per cent schools, Dalit children are not permitted to drink water from the same source. The recently released report of perhaps the first nationwide survey of the continued prevalence of untouchability, jointly authored by Ghanshayam Shah, Sukhadeo Thorat, Satish Deshpande, Amita Baviskar and Harsh Mandar, finds such untouchability in all local state institutions. A shocking 27.6 per cent Dalits are prevented from entering police stations and 25.7 from ration shops. Thirty-three per cent public health workers refuse to visit Dalit homes and 23.5 per cent Dalits still do not get letters delivered to their homes. Segregated seating for Dalits was found in 30.8 self help groups and cooperatives and 29.6 per cent panchayat offices. In 14.4 per cent villages, Dalit weren't permitted to enter the panchayat building. They were denied access to polling booths, or forced to form separate lines in 12 per cent of the villages surveyed. Despite being charged with a constitutional mandate to promote social justice, various local institutions of the Indian State clearly tolerate and even facilitate the practice of untouchability.

Dalit settlements are most often segregated from the main village. Such traditions are reproduced by government, when building Indira Awaas housing colonies for Dalit or by NGOs such as in the post-2001 earthquake reconstruction programmes in Gujarat. In nearly half the surveyed villages (48.4 per cent), Dalits were denied access to water sources. In over a third Dalits were denied from the shop, the shopkeepers kept the goods they bought on the ground and accepted their money similarly without direct contact. In teashops, Dalits were denied seating and had to use separate cups.

There was found to be great, and at times violent, intolerance of displays of well-being, or public celebrations by Dalits. In many villages, bans operated on wedding processions on public (arrogated as upper-caste) roads. In 10 to 20 per cent villages, Dalits weren't allowed even to wear fashionable clothes or sunglasses. They could not ride their bicycles, unfurl their umbrellas, wear chappals on public roads, smoke or stand without head bowed. Restrictions on their entry into Hindu temples averaged 64 per cent in 11 states, ranging from 47 per cent in UP to 94 per cent in Karnataka.

The research established that such restrictions endured even after conversion of Dalits to egalitarian faiths. In Punjab, 41 of the 51 villages surveyed reported separate gurdwaras for Dalit Sikhs, Dalits who worshipped in gurdwaras frequented by upper-caste Jats were served in separate lines at the langar and were not permitted to prepare or serve the sacred food. In Maharashtra, despite mass conversions of the Mahars to

Buddhism, Dalits were denied temple entry in 51 per cent villages. In Kerala and Andhra, there are divisions in the church between Dalit converts and others, and discrimination even against ordained Dalit priests.

Untouchability persists even into death. In nearly half the villages, Dalits were debarred from access to cremation grounds. In Maharashtra, Dalits have their own cremation grounds but these are permitted only on the eastern side of the village, so that the upper-castes aren't polluted by the winds that pass from west to east.

The study reports discrimination against Dalits in the labour market. Although normally Dalits are coerced into agricultural labour in unfavourably condition, sometimes even of bondage, they are excluded in the lean agricultural season, when work is scarce for all and therefore upper-caste workers are preferred. In 25 per cent of the villages, Dalits were paid lower wages than other workers. They were also subjected to much longer working hours, delayed wages, verbal and physical abuse, not just in 'feudal' states like Bihar but also notably in Punjab. In 37 per cent of the villages, Dalit workers were paid wages from a distance, to avoid physical contact. The study also found evidence of discrimination between non-Dalit and Dalit workers, evidence of caste surmounting proletarian solidarity.

The large majority of Dalits is landless. In the few cases where they were landowners, they were denied access to water for irrigation in more than one third of the villages. In more than one third of the villages. In 21 per cent villages, they were denied access to grazing lands and fishing ponds, and violent upper-caste opposition was reported when Dalits encroached onto or were allotted government lands for cultivation or housing.

Untouchability was found to extend to consumer markets. Dalits producers in 35 per cent villages were barred from selling their produce in local markets. Instead, they were forced to sell in the anonymity of distant urban markets where caste identities blur. This imposes additional burdens of cost and time and reduces their competitiveness. Caste-taboos apply particularly to products like milk – in as many as 47 per cent of the villages with cooperatives, Dalits were not allowed to sell milk to the cooperatives or private buyers. In a quarter of the villages, they were prevented from buying milk from cooperatives.

Dalits are therefore not only disproportionately burdened with poverty to start with; caste discrimination in labour and consumer markets condemns them to lower wages with harder work in uncertain employment and restrictions on their access to natural resources as well as the markets for their products.

Even more than in secular and religious public spaces, the practice of untouchability endures most in upper-caste rural homes. In what people regard to be their private sphere. Our survey confirmed that in as many as 73 per cent of the villages Dalits were not permitted to enter non-Dalit homes, and 70 per cent would not eat together. Even Dalit researchers in this study were denied entry into upper-caste homes. With untouchability thus persisting unashamedly in state institutions like schools and police stations, in public spaces like temples and shops, in farms and markets, and in homes and hearts, the Dalit still lives in India waiting hopelessly and sometimes in anger, for the long betrayed dawn of equality.

The Challenges on the Way

The illustrative cases and findings of research studies presented above are only example in nature of the innumerable dalit human rights violations that go on unabated even today. This aside, major findings of two research reports mentioned above are a sad commentary on the state of affairs of our republic. It is noteworthy to mention that the illustrative cases show the growing aspiration of dalits to own land, either for cultivation or to build a house, and the strong opposition of indifference of upper and OBC communities and the Government.

Failure of Legal Safeguards

It is not physical violence along that the legal safeguards fail to end. Legislative measures such as the one seeking to end manual scavenging have for years existed only on paper.

Reservation in education and government jobs has not brought about the desired level of upliftment, even after decades of implementation. Even the small gains effected through legislative measures are now under threat in the face of the government's policy of liberalization, privatization and globalization.

One principal source of continued caste violence is the lack of implementation of existing laws designed to protect the rights of dalits. The SCs & STs (Prevention of Atrocities) Act, 1989 (hereafter POA) is a powerful weapon that provides legal redress for victims of caste violence. However, a misguided monitoring system coupled with the governments indifference to enforce the Act has led to its utter ineffectiveness. The government in general and the Criminal Justice Administration in particular must be held accountable for non-implementation of Constitutional and legal safeguards for protection of dalit rights.

Dalits in India suffer a wide range of Human Rights violations, despite legal safeguards that are suppose to protect them. Dalits are also often the victim of violence by those high on caste system, and by those in caste which are just above the Dalits in the system, (OBCs) who consider any improvement of the position of Dalits a threat to their own position.

Violence against Dalits is currently punishable under the Scheduled Caste and Scheduled Tribes (Prevention of Atrocities) Act 1989. This Act and the 1995 Rules made there under are very impressive legislative and administrative framework for the protection of Dalits. Many State governments have also set up special units to deal with what is commonly called "civil right protection". However, it is widely accepted that the above said Act and the special units have failed to provide relief to Dalit victims of atrocities. Large part of the Act have been ignored by State Governments-usually because of a lack of political will, the disinclination of officials to acknowledge social injustice, caste bias in the criminal justice system, and the absence of any concrete mechanism to monitor systematically the implementation of the legislations. Abuses against Dalit communities frequently go uninvestigated and unpunished, and those who take action to seek redress, there is a wide spread feeling of impunity among those committing atrocities against Dalits.

About the reasons for the atrocities on the SCs/STs, the Report of the Commission of the SCs/STs 1998 observed, "Some of the major causes of atrocities and other offences against Scheduled Castes and Scheduled Tribes are related to issues of land and property, access to water, wage payments, indebtedness and bonded or forced labour. Issues of human dignity, including compulsion to perform distasteful tasks traditionally forced on Scheduled Castes, and molestation and exploitation of dalit women are also involved. Caste related tensions are exacerbated by economic factors, which contribute to violence. It is the assertion of their rights, be they economic, social or political, by the Scheduled Castes and Scheduled Tribes and their development, which often invite the wrath of the vested interest. Disputes during elections, animosity due to reservation, jealousy due to increasing economic prosperity, violence related to the process of taking possession and retaining Government allotted land, tension due to refusal of SCs to perform tasks such as disposal of dead cattle or cutting umbilical cord, are manifestations of the resentment of the high caste against increasing awareness among Scheduled Caste, assertion and prosperity among the SCs. Like land, water is another sensitive issue. Accessibility of drinking water and water for irrigation and disposal of water removed from water logged areas become issues that can trigger off atrocities on SCs. Castiest favour during religious and social ceremonies, disputes arising during sowing and harvesting operations, and removal of crops from the granary after harvesting, have also been known to cause tension. Increasing awareness and empowerment of SCs, manifested in resistance to suppressions, also result in clashes".

The Scheduled Caste and Scheduled Tribes (Prevention of Atrocities) rules 1995 provided for transport and other expenses for victims to enable them to attend hearing and in the case of women for an attendant to accompany them and covering of wages lost during days attending hearings. However many studies found that many sections of the Rules had not been implemented in majority of the cases including provisions for travelling and maintenance expenses. Often women simply do not have the money to pursue a case and having no economic independence, if their family do not support them in pursuing the case, they drop it.

Police frequently refuse to file First information Reports (FIRs) when Dalits approach them to report crimes. Most often police register the case under very light sections of the IPC and also dilute the gravity of the atrocity cases. This is often because the police act at the behest of powerful local interests who may be behind the crimes. Officials often act under the influence of political parties or dominant social groups who want to keep Dalit communities suppressed. In numerous clashes between caste groups, police have regularly sided with members of other caste groups against Dalits. While Dalits can complain about non-registration of FIR's to higher authorities, action taken on the basis of such complaints is often too late and fails to provide the direct protection against threat and harassment necessary to ensure that complaints are pursued. It is also reported that social activists who are fighting against caste discrimination are subjected to attack and harassments both by state and other powerful interest. Other methods of harassment included the filing of apparently false criminal cases Under Sec 151 of the Cr. P.C. which allows police to preventively detain people they suspect may commit a crime is being used regularly to detain dalit rights defenders.

Although the POA is a powerful and precise weapon on paper, in practice the Act has suffered from a near-complete failure in implementation. Ironically, the primary obstacles to implementation are intended to be the primary enforcers of the Act—the lowest rungs of the police and bureaucracy that form the primary mode of interaction between state and society in the rural areas. Policemen have displayed a consistent unwillingness to register offenses under the Act. This reluctance stems partially from ignorance. According to a 1999 study, nearly a quarter of those government officials charged with enforcing the Act are unaware of its existence. (Human Rights Features, August, 2003).

A bigger obstacle is faced by victims who actually manage to lodge a complaint. Failure to follow through with cases is alarmingly apparent at the lowest echelons of the judicial system. The statistics speak for themselves: out of 147,000 POA cases pending in the courts in 1998, only 31, 011 were brought to trial. Such delay is endemic to the Indian judicial system. Although the POA mandated the creation of Special Courts precisely to circumvent this problem, only two states have created separate Special Courts in accordance with the law. In other states, existing Sessions Courts have been designated Special Courts, while still being asked to process their usual caseloads. Since many different Acts require the creation of Special Courts, such Sessions Courts are often overloaded with a number of different kinds of "priority" cases, virtually guaranteeing that none of these cases receive the attention they are mandated to receive.

Even if cases make it to trial, the POA also suffers from abysmal rates of conviction. Out of the 31,011 cases tried under the POA in 1998, only a paltry 1,677 instances or 5.4% resulted in a conviction and 29,334 ended in acquittal. Compare this to the conviction rate in cases tried under the Indian Penal Code: in 1999, 39.4% of cases ended in a conviction and in 2000, 41.8%. Judicial delay is just one cause of this low conviction rate; the lapse between the case being registered and the trial means that witnesses who are often poor and face intimidation in the interim, turn hostile and the case becomes too weak for a conviction. The long wait also results in many plaintiffs losing interest. Judicial bias against Dalits is rampant and unchecked, and court decisions frequently bear the mark of such bias. (Human Rights Features, August, 2003).

So why has there not been more public outcry about the dismal failings of the POA? Within the government, shoddy monitoring systems have prevented effective action from being taken. Although not statutorily mandated to do so, the National Commissions for Scheduled Castes and Scheduled Tribes (NCSCST) monitor the implementation of the Act. The National Commission for Scheduled Castes and Scheduled Tribes only reports to the Central Government, although it primarily monitors compliance to the POA in the States. The NCSCST has state offices that report to it, but those are vastly understaffed and only have an advisory relationship to the state legislatures. Such a monitoring system depends on the central government's commitment to Dalit rights for enforcement of the NCSCST's recommendations. The sorry record of the POA is ample evidence that this commitment is lacking.

The structural flaws of the monitoring system have instead led to a lot of futile finger pointing about the failures of the POA. For example, in 1998, the NCSCST recommended that States conduct awareness programs through NGOs about the Act for citizens and government officials. In its reply to this recommendation, the Central Government placed the responsibility for organizing awareness programs with the States. However, there was no indication that the recommendation would be referred to the States, nor was there any provision for follow-up between the central government and the States. Such instances of passing the buck are not exceptional; most of the recommendations, particularly those relating to land reform laws and special court creation, are referred to the States without any provision for follow-up.

According to SAHRDC outside of the government, the steadily growing movement of NGOs also seems to be misguided. Rather than holding India to its existing legislative commitments to Dalits in the POA, the leading Dalit voices push pie-in-the-sky agendas. The recommendations at the end of the bleak "Black Paper" released by the National Campaign for Dalit Human Rights include such absurdities as taxing corporations in order to fund Dalit programs and allocating 20% of the GDP of the country in order to fund programs meant specifically for Dalit welfare. Astute recommendations that underscore what is already in the laws – mandating the creation of special courts and the recruitment of a minimum percentage of Dalits in all local police forces – lose their weight in the midst of such impractical recommendations.

More recently, alarmed by the public outrage over the Khairlanji massacre, a Union Ministers panel on Dalit affairs has recommended amending the PoA to make all guilty officials, irrespective of the caste they belong to, liable for punishment. It is noteworthy to mention that Section 4 of the PoA Act, which prescribes a jail term of a minimum of six months upto one year for dereliction of duty by public servants, bars penal action against scheduled caste and schedules tribe officials. In fact, Khairlanji may spark off a debate on the popular view that placing SC and ST officials in field (Khairlanji in Bhandara District where a dalit family was brutally murdered on September 29, 12006, had an array of dalit officials including the IG, SP, DM, ADM and the local inspector) helps ensure justice and weed out caste bias in cases against dalits.

Gender Perspective

Dalit (Scheduled Castes) women constitute 16.3% of India's total female population and 47.96% of the total SCs population. 81.45% of them live in rural areas while they constitute about 12% of the urban population. The plight of Scheduled Castes women is evident from the fact that even the sex ratio of Scheduled Castes women per 1000 male is only 922 as compared to 944 for the general population (Black, Paper, 2002). This only shows that gender inequity operates even among those Scheduled Castes, where women are earning members at par with men. Further, the dalit women are doubly vulnerable. Firstly, they have to share the economic burden of the family on equal terms with those of men and, in addition, the entire household burden as well. They get married early and have to experience frequent pregnancies. Economic independence of dalit women has also not improved their social position, because women bear the brunt of lack of access of their entire community to basic services. They have to shoulder the responsibility of collecting fuel wood and water, and, at times, even edible articles from long distances which drains their energy.

Their hardship is even more pronounced because a large number of dalit households are women-headed due to either husband's desertion or his drunkenness. This places the entire burden of household running on their shoulders. The manifestations of inequity against women of all categories also apply in case of scheduled caste women. They are typically the last in the family to take food where men of the family and thereafter the children receive higher priority. Most of them have nutrient deficient food. They experience larger number of child births than upper caste women do. Their access to education and health facilities is poorer than the male members of their communities dalit women also constitute a major workforce of the national economy. As per one study, nearly 89.5% of all adult Dalit women participate in some productive labour (National Campaign on Dalit Rights, 2002). In urban areas, they also function as hawkers, scrap collectors, petty traders, etc. besides earning livelihood as wage labourers in domestic work, construction industry, earthwork, beedi/agarbathi manufacture, candle making, garment and embroidery work. All these employments are characterized by low wage, irregular work, absence of social security, vulnerability to sexual exploitation and dependency on middlemen and employer. Women labour, in general, irrespective of caste, is relatively underpaid and unrecognized and labelled as unskilled. These disabilities may be operating even more adversely against dalit women. As per one study, nearly 31.6% of all children from Scheduled Castes communities are child workers, dalit girls constitute perhaps the largest segment of that child labour. While there is a general literacy gap between Scheduled Castes and members of general category, the gap is even wider between SCs women and SCs men. The position is much worse in BIMARU States [Bihar, Madhya Pradesh, Rajasthan, UP].

SCs (dalits) women bear the brunt of violence against their community. The number of rapes committed against SC women has shown an increasing trend (NCRB, 2004). The mass rape is used by upper caste militias as a weapon to break the morale of the entire community. Rape is used as a political instrument and these women become the target of anger and wrath of the dominant castes. The women are singled out for other indignities like being paraded naked by upper caste people even for petty disputes. Women are also subjected to most obnoxious practice of prostitution in the name of religion such as the Devdasi system where children between 6 to 8 years belonging mostly to families of dalits are dedicated to God, cannot marry and are raped by temple priests and upper caste men and eventually auctioned off into urban brothels. In times of extreme hardship, such as natural calamities women are forced to sell their bodies for the family to survive. In certain communities under customary practices, women are sent for prostitution as integral part of social survival or auctioned like a commodity as a punishment for violating customary injunctions (A. N. Sinha, Institute of Social Sciences, 2002). Under superstitious beliefs, certain mishaps in the family are attributed to witchcraft and women (usually SC/ST) are branded as witches engaged in this practice and publicly humiliated, grievously assaulted and at times brutally murdered. Traditional healers/customary religious chiefs also lend support to such a belief.

Women constitute a larger number of persons engaged in manual scavenging. In fact, when the entire family is engaged as scavengers, it is its women members who share the larger load of work. It has also been experienced that where benefits have been extended for elimination of manual scavenging to certain families of manual scavengers through development programmes specifically targeted at them, it is usually the men of the family who take advantage of it, give up manual scavenging work and take to alternative occupations. But they continue to permit their women to do manual scavenging for enhancing income of the entire household. This is the worst example of gender inequity at the family level within the community (NHRC, 2002).

Though separate data is not available, there is no dearth of impressions that the benefits of various development programmes, such as distribution of land and other productive assets have, by and large, gone to SCs males and, therefore, have not helped in improving the status of the scheduled caste women within the family as well as outside it. Where women have been targeted for poverty alleviation in the family, the level of investment in projects selected for them is far lower as compared to those for men. Of late, Government instructions have promoted coverage of women in land allotment both as exclusive and joint ownership with their spouses. But separate data on land and assets allotted to SC women is not readily available. In this background, SC women should emerge as a distinct focus of attention and targeting in any future strategy of development for this group.

The Way Forward

It is evident from the above that social injustice and violence against dalits have not as yet been eliminated from our society. It is a matter of serious concern that even after more than five decades of India's freedom and elaborate provisions in the Constitution and legal framework, practices like untouchability, manual scavenging, bonded labour, caste religion/based prostitution (Devdasi system) etc. still exist and more than 160 million Dalits in the 'World's largest democracy' remain at the risk of systematic human rights violations on the basis of the caste into which they are born.

Further, the State has failed to act against its own agencies facilitated in the commission of violence. These agencies are largely - Police and other law enforcement agencies whose personnel are involved in violence against dalits - such as custodial violence, encounter killings etc. It is noteworthy to mention that police are duty bound to register cases, investigate thoroughly free from any caste bias and bring perpetrators to justice failing which dalit victims will continue to suffer.

So far as role of watchdog institutes such as National Human Rights Commission, National Commission for Scheduled Castes, National Commission for Scheduled Tribes, National Commission for Safai Karmacharis and National Commission for Women in combating violence against dalits is concerned state is unwilling to confer sufficient powers on these bodies, to make them effective instruments of delivery of equitable justice.

The entire discourse on violence against dalits revolves around three stakeholders - State, Civil Society and the Dalits. The State has failed to effectively implement laws relating to violence against Dalits. This failure is reflected both in respect of preventing violence against Dalits through various pre-emptive measures as well as in the ability to punish perpetrators of violence after the Crime is committed. The studies have shown that the overall conviction rate in cases of atrocities against Dalits is less than 2 per cent. Very low rate of conviction, deliberate lapses in investigation and delay in disposal of cases in the courts resulting in a large number of acquittals and erode the impact of law and negate the deterrence aspect of it.

At the same time, other forms of human rights violations should not go unaddressed. The false arrests and detentions of social activists are insidious, as they punish those members of the population who attempt to peacefully and democratically claim their rights and protect the rights of others. The exploitation of agricultural laborers and the rigid assignment of demeaning occupations on the basis of caste keeps Dalits in a position of economic and physical vulnerability. The triple burden of caste, class, and gender effectively ensures that Dalit women are the furthest removed from legal protections. Only with the honest implementation of laws designed to protect agricultural laborers and abolish manual scavenging and forced prostitution, and the systematic prosecution of those responsible for attacks on Dalit men and women, can the process of attaining economic and physical security begin.

The Prevention of Atrocities Act (POA) passed in 1989 remains largely an Act on paper. Of the 1,50,000 cases registered under the Act, less than one-third are brought to trial. The conviction rates under the Act are about five per cent compared to conviction rates of about one-third for cases decided under Indian Penal Code. (The Indian Express, 2005). The POA has enjoined the Governments to set up Special Courts to deal with cases of atrocities. But it also empowered governments to declare areas with high caste violence to be "atrocity prone" and appoint qualified officers to maintain law and order. Neither of these provisions has been used with any degree of effectiveness.

The National Commission of Scheduled Castes which is responsible for monitoring the implementation of Anti-Atrocities Law has not been very effective in discharging its functions. Violence against dalits may have its roots in particular social conflicts and political tensions, but by creating a justice system that is unable to discharge its basic obligations we have all became complicit in the kinds of violence and massacres that government have done nothing to prevent.

This aside, caste violence against dalits has little effect on the conscience of the country. They are routinely dismissed away as an empowering sign of India's eternal backwardness. But though caste violence has its roots in the Indian social structure, violence and brutal exertions of power against dalits are routine to politics in many states. The policies of the state are centrally responsible for producing the violence, the state decides whom to arm and whom to protect, politicians encourage violence to teach opponents political presence and the violence continues even when upper caste domination of politics has ceased to be a reality. Indeed a close perusal of new forms of violence against dalits will highlight the fact that the perpetrators are as likely to be aligned to OBCs and other non-twice borne castes as they are likely to align to traditional upper castes.

In crux, it is urgently required that dalits should gain awareness about their rights and entitlements, use the available channel and mechanisms to obtain justice when found with violation, increase their presence in all levels - political, business, bureaucracy, in police and judiciary, promote organizations and build alliances that support their struggle and acquire the new skills to negotiate a respectable deal for themselves. The civil society organisations, academia, dalit organisations, media and concerned citizens can take up issues relating to violence against dalits to the State, bureaucracy and judiciary through various means. In this regard, proper execution of regulatory and development programmes would be helpful to curb human rights violations against dalits. They should also conduct social audit of the implementation of major recommendations made by NHRC, National Commission for Scheduled Castes and the National Commission for Scheduled Tribes in their reports concerning prevention of atrocities against dalits.

The NHRC (Report on Prevention of Atrocities Against Scheduled Castes, 2002) has made the very useful recommendations to curb violence against dalits. These include identification of atrocity, violence prone areas as well as regions where untouchability is practiced, preparation of action plan to control it, and conduct of three-tier training programme for police and revenue officials and annual workshop for District Magistrate and Superintendent of Police on the implementation of the laws in this regard. It has also emphasized that Panchayati Raj Institutions could play a pivotal role in curbing violence against dalits.

The Scheduled Castes and Scheduled Tribes (Prevention of Atrocities Act) has potential to bring about change by sending the message that Human Rights violations against dalits will not go unpunished. The implementation of Atrocities Act and other legislations, however, depends largely on the ability and willingness of the police to follow proper procedure, overcome caste biases and use of forensic tools to ensure equitable justice for dalits. In fact, police reforms shall be integral part of the Agenda for dalit organizations to prevent violence against dalits. This aside, quality education to dalit children can be a great lever to start making a difference. Imagine if all our young children (dalit and non dalits) were educated, how much easier it would have been to us to address the practice of untouchability and educated population would have better governance and far better accountability from our political and bureaucratic establishments.

More recently, the Central Govt. has launched a very promising project – "Bharat Nirman". In the Prime Minister's words, "It is four year action plan. By 2009, we hope to ensure that every village is electrified, has a telephone connection, is connected by a pucca road, every habitation covered with drinking water supply, add a crore of additional hectares of (land that has) irrigation as well as 60 lakh more houses for the houseless". To achieve these formidable goals a massive sum of Rs.1,74,000 crore will be spent, towards which World Bank has already agreed to release one billion every year. This is part of its annual commitment of providing totally $3 billion every year (*The Hindustan Times*, Mumbai, 2005). This is an admirable scheme and, if fully implemented, it will certainly change rural life significantly. This will also help to curb human rights violations including violence against dalits arising mainly due to socio-economic deprivations. The key to success is "How is the Project going to be implemented and what are the structures of the governance that will be used to ensure these goals are achieved? Perhaps NGOs, civil society organisations, academia, media and dalit activists may keep track on effective implementation of the scheme in its latter and spirit.

While the rhetoric of all round development talks go on, hundreds of dalit and their families across India are being butchered. And we let that occur. It happened like this almost every other minutes fault or no fault.. 'Dalits' are stripped, paraded, disgraced, and even then if some amount of dignity is left, it is nullified with a gang-rape and finally hacked to death. So, for the 160 million vulnerable 'Dalits' and Scheduled Castes, development is just fiction and injustice a norm. And that goes on to indicate how much we have developed and on what growth trajectory we actually stand, as a nation. The bleeding dead corpse of 'Dalits' scream aloud the appalling developmental divide. To then blow the trumpet of development is nothing but a complete shame on the part of the polity and the civil society. No matter at what pace India grows, how much it has in forex and to what extent it's political class champions the cause of the underprivileged through commissioning committees and provisioning reservations, till the time India makes sure that being 'Dalit' itself is not a sin enough to be punished through brutal rape and murder, every achievement if futile. And all development elusive, because at the end, we have failed to create a humane society.

References

A. N. Sinha Institute of Social Studies (2002), Musahar: A Socio-Economic Study, p. 38, See also Compulsion of Women to Sell their babies for Customary Practice in an Article 'Auctioned Girl Commits Suicide, *The Hindu*, August 20, 2002.

Bhopal Document (2002), Chartering a New Course for Dalits for the 21st Century Government of Madhya Pradesh, pp. 16-17

Crime in India (2004), National Crime Records Bureau, Ministry of Home Affairs, Government of India, New Delhi, p. 292.

Frontline (2002), Preying on Dalits, October 25, p. 39.

Frontline (2003), A Carnage and a Clean Chit, January 17, p. 4.

Frontline (2004), Dalit Anger in Haryana, January 16, pp. 37-38.

Frontline (2004), Resisting Oppression, July 16, p. 41.

Frontline (2004), The Dalit Carnage: A New Perspective, November 19, pp. 30-32.

Haragopal G. (2002), : Rights and Dalits: Law and Reality, *Journal of National Human Rights Commission,* Vol. 1, p. 1.

Human Rights Watch (1999), Broken People, Caste Violence Against India's Untouchables, p. 25.

Krishnan, P. S., Keynote address delivered at the National Seminar on 2000 Implementation and Impact of SCs/STs (Prevention of Atrocities) Act, 1989 on the Scheduled Castes organized by Centre for Social System, School of Social Sciences, New Delhi, JNU.

Mandar, Harsh (2006), Freedom's Just Another World, *The Hindustan Times,* August 15, 2006.

Menon, Madhav (2003), Keynote Address. Protection of Human Rights Against Racial Discrimination and Related tolerance: An Indian Perspective. Quoted in the Report on National Seminar and Public Consultation on Racism, Racial Discrimination, Xenophobia and related tolerance, published by National Human Rights Commission & National Law School of India University, p. 5.

National Campaign on Dalit Rights (2002), Black Paper, also letters from Divakar, N., National Convenor and other both dated May 9, 2002 addressed to Prime Minister and Chairman, NHRC. Quoted from NHRC's Report, 2002, *op.cit,* p. 160.

Naval, T. R. (2000) Law of Prevention of Atrocities on Scheduled Castes and Scheduled Tribes, pp. 4-7. Quoted in the Report on Prevention of Atrocities Against Scheduled Castes, 2002, published by NHRC, p. 1.

National Council of Teacher Education (2003), Discrimination Based on Sex, Caste, Religion and Disability, p. 14.

National Human Rights Commission, Statement of the Chairman, NHRC while Inaugurating a SAARC Conference on Practice of Torture. Quoted from NHRC's Report, *Ibid.*

National Human Rights Commission (2002), Report on Prevention of Atrocities Against Scheduled Castes.

Sakshi (2000), Dalit Human Rights Monitor, Andhra Pradesh, p. 152.

Shramik Adivasi Sanghatana (2006), Lower Youths Lynched to Death Email for TISS faculty on June 14.

South Asian Human Rights Documentation Center (2003), Human Rights Features - 83, Prevention of Atrocities Act: Unused Ammunition, August 31

The Hindustan Times (2006), U.P. Dalit Girl Resists Rape, Loses Arm as a Result, p. 7., February 14, p. 3.

The Hindustan Times, (Mumbai, 2005), Civil Disobedience by Bhaskar Ghose, October 24, p. 8.

The Indian Express (2005), Dalit Made to Drink Urine Over Cricket Row, January 5, 2005.

The Indian Express (2004), Forgotten Murders, November 30, p. 8.

The Times of India (2006), Dalit Women Sarpanch Paraded Naked, June 23, p. 17.

The Times of India (2006), No Honour in Honour Killing, July 7, 2006.

Tiwari, Arvind (2007), Human Rights Violations Against Dalits: A Case of failed State, *The Indian Journal of Social Work,* 68(1), 73-87.

2

Human Rights Concerns: Perspectives and Context in Developing Societies

P. N. Pandey

> *"Justice without force is impotent and force without justice is a tyranny"*
> **Pascal**

I would like to begin with aforesaid statement of Pascal that justice must have vigorus strength in it to benefit the needy and application of force devoid of justice is certainly torture or tyranny. The universal declaration of Human Rights on 10th Dec. 1948 by the General Assembly of the United Nations was a benchmark event. The second World War (1939-1945) witnessed the untold miseries and violation of Human Rights as result of the negative uses of modernity, which turned as holocaust or genocide as described by German social scientist Zygmunt Bauman. The Nari Germany with the help of official machinery and bureaucracy set up the gas chambers in which thousands of jews were thrown and they were thrown and they were reduced to ashes. The event has certainly shaken the world. The untold miseries of the millions of the people pave the way for the world body. United Nations Organizations and Article 1 of the UN Charter lists the protection of Human Rights as one of the objectives of the United Nations. The very concern of Human Rights can be seen from two view points- The historicity of the Human Rights concern enables us to furnish an argument that is can be seen as informal concerns where all great religious revolutions of Buddhism, Hindusim, Islam and Christianity in one way or the other show a sense of human concerns of justice, righteousness and liberty. A number of hindu treatises and classical literature deal with social and economic justice and discard oppression, exploitation, atrocities and torture. Be that the Vedas and the Upanishads, the preaching the shermons of Buddhist philosophy, of Bible of the chritian world, Kuran Sharif of Islam and Gurugranth Sahib of Sikhism are replete with the cautions against atrocities and exploitations and motivations for promoting the cause of justice and dignity of human being. The holy Bhagwat Geeta consisting of 70 verses divides into 18 chapters depicts about the human concerns of rights and duties and that rights are consequent upon duties.

On the other hand there is formal or legal sources of Human Rights, which have emerged through the universal declaration by the U.N.O. According to western political and philosophical thinking, Human Rights are innate in individual and hence a state that violates them in its laws and interpretation breaches one of the very prerequisites of civil coexistence. the charter of the UN does not define the content of Human Rights. It is perhaps, left to the organizations themselves. The International Bill of Human Rights comprises–

1. Universal declaration of Human Rights (1948).
2. International covenant of evil and political rights (1968).
3. International covenant of civil and political rights (1968).
4. Optional protocol that provides the right for individual petition.

After the World War II, during the last five decades many of the European countries and the United States laid emphasis on Human Rights in their foreign policies. This has affected the texture of international relations.

Human Rights Perspectives in the Developing Societies

Many of the countries particularly of Asia, which are parties and signatory to the universal declaration, feel that using Human Rights as instruments for their political and ideological hegemony there is also a sense of dissatisfaction about the purely western interpretation of Human Rights which focus on delicate matters of culture and identities. In this context, the western slogan of Human Rights is not taken favourably by the Asian countries. Such focus came into sharp contradictions and controversies in the UN conference on Human Rights held in Vienna in June 1993. The perception of Asian continent was presented emphatically by China, Singapore and Malaysia. Stressing that Human Rights are universal and therefore they should be considered as a dynamic procedure of international norm setting giving priority to the significance of national and regional pecularities including historical religious, cultural and social backgrounds. The contradiction of Asian criticism of the western concept of Human Rights is that since there is no single human nature there can not be universal moral law is thee which appeals across the cultural boundaries. Universality of Human Rights is a western imposition on cultures which have different moral conditions and social traditions and hence it amounts to moral and cultural imperialism. There is also an inherent criticism that developed countries of the west, say for instance, the USA, Germany, France, Italy and the UK seek to impose western values on non western societies under the guise of Human Rights. The countries like Singapore and Malaysia had the argument that the cultural matrix within which relations between individual and the state are embedded, are fundamentally different in Asia from the west. The consensus building approach of Asia is collectivist, while there is an overtone of individualistic ethos in the west. Further, the numerous pilling up of the list of Human Rights under universal declaration through international convenants on civil and political rights, social, cultural and economic rights and other international conventions created a major chaos that if everything comes under the purview of human rights then nothing is left for human duties. The western societies with expansionist and establishmentarian ambitions are hankering after the rights and rights only sideling the major concerns for human duties. The Indian philosophical, ideological and classical literature pleads for the prior devotion to duty and duty consciousness. The rights are, according to Indian philosophic tradition and classical jurisprudence, the outcome of the human duties.

I would like to mention here that the social and economic circumstances of Asian countries are not similar for ex., Japan, South Korea, Singapore, Hong Kong are some of the most prosperous countries, while there are poverty stricken countries like Bangladesh, Philippines, Sri Lanka, Bhutan, Nepal, Pakistan and to some extent India. As a sociologist, I perceive poverty, illiteracy, ignorance and lack of scientific outlook as a great cause of the denial of the spirit of human duties and the human rights. It attenuates human dignity and without awareness about human sense of duty there can be no human rights or the capability and persisting attitude to challenge the violation of human rights. Proper social order and political stability are the necessary prerequisite for economic growth there can not be a social justice and human dignity.

The stable political and social order in asia is threatened by the west. The recent earthquakes that occurred in the regions of Indo-Pak borders in the night of Oct. 8-9 have shattered he nerves of the continent. Thousands of people lost their lives, the smiling cities bedecked with parks and towers were reduced to powder. The death destruction and devastation of the area caused by the quake are *Beggar's description*. In such a state of affair, when aida and relief measures are being sent to the victims on borders as well as the neighbouring nations, no human being born and brought up in the milk of humanity can be even imagine of blast and bombardment by the militant mercenaries and hard core terrorist. The two countries viz. India and Pakistan have opened at half a dozen places on line of control under the bilateral reciprocation. In such a delicate moment, the blasts by the terrorists give not only an alarming signal to the violation of human rights but a challenge to the advocates and exponents of human rights. Call it patriotism if you like, call it national honour if you please, call it safety and security if you so choose. But to my mind, it is a nude dance of death in actuality of the human concerns of dignity, honour and social justice.

The concept of human rights is vide and much inclusive of the concerns about oppression, exploitation, atrocity and torture. Freedom from torture and inhuman and cruel treatment or punishment is held as fundamental rights of human beings in the universal declaration of human rights, which consists of 30 Articles.

Art. (5) of the declaration abandons the torture or cruel physical infliction. Art. (7) of the international convenant on civil and political right also provides that no one can be subjected to torture and no one shall be subjected without his consent to medical or scientific experiment. All the member states i.e. 191 of the world community are expected to abide by the declaration.

Human Rights and the Role of the UNO

A human rights concern has become a political idiom of normative expression today. The basic philosophy is to restore a life of dignity, respect and social justice. The British Magnacharta and Bill of Rights, the French declaration of the rights of the man (1789) and the American declaration of independence (1776) and the Indian constitution (1949) show their concern for equality justice, liberty and fraternity. After the 1st world war treaty of Versailles (1919) created permanent mechanisms for international violation of human rights, but the second World War (1939-45) witnessed not only the tremendous loss of private property but considerable degradation of human rights. The suppression of racial and ethnic groups and minorities hammered the conscience of the world. The harrowing groups and minorities hammered the conscience of the world. The harrowing experience of the II World War led to create a belief that international protection of human rights is a pre condition for global peace and progress. The UNO emerged out of the ashes of the IInd World War and attempted to put stress on promotion and fostering of human rights and basic freedom. The very purpose of the United Nations as listed in Art. 1 of the charter includes that, "To achieve international co-operation, in solving international problems of economic, social, cultural and humanitarian character and in promoting and encouraging respect for human rights and for fundamental freedom, for all without distinction as to race, sex, language or religion".

The universal declaration of human rights indicates two sorts of rights- the traditional civil and political rights (Article 2 to 21) and the new economic and social rights (Article 22 to 28). The constitution of India incorporates the first set of rights (Art. 12 to 25 of the constitution) and the second set of rights under the directive principles (Art. 36 to 51).

The ever emerging global consciousness and pioneering role of the Supreme Court and High Courts in India show that the Human Rights Jurisprudence is becoming an important component of any civilized legal system. Violations of Human Rights have become the legitimate concern of the 191 member nations of the world. The human rights movements require to be more strengthened by the academia, judges, lawyers and the social activists in Asia and Africa because the countries of these continents have in built social, economic, cultural and historical diversities. The conditions in the third world countries, especially in Asia, Africa and Latin America are prima facie different from those in Europe and America. The U.S. Germany, France, Italy and the U.K. are moving in affluence and have shifted from industrial to post industrial and post modern state holding control over 80 per cent of the material resources of the world. On the other hand, the countries of Asia. Africa and Latin America are predominantly agration and combating with the challenges of poverty, illiteracy, ignorance, malnutrition, health hazards, sub human conditi9on and indigenous communal and ethnic feuds. Poverty all illiteracy undermine human dignity and without human dignity the question of human rights in futile. Therefore, I would like to argue that the effective judicial system in these countries can play significant role in promoting consciousness conductive to solve these problems and promote a social milieu which will strengthen Human Rights concern. Article 45 of the Indian constitution providing for free and compulsory education for all children uplo age of 14 years, unfortunately, still remains unrealized. The Supreme court of India in case of Unikrishanan, others and state of Andhra Pradesh upheld the view other a article 45 confers enforced and fundamental rights to education of all children with the age of 14 years. The India constitution provides that even during emergency while suspending the Fundamental rights under part III, Articles 20 and 21 shall not be suspended. The rights of life and liberty (Art. 21) and forced testimony against self (Art. 20) have been protected even during emergency.

The universal declaration of Human Rights has a much wide spectrum and includes a number of area concerning violation of liberty dignity and justice ranging frame welfare measures to women, children, forced labour, slavery, labour relation, public and their protection, eradication of hunger, malnutrition, racial and ethnic issues, torture, atrocities and sexual harassment, Dowry death, custodial deaths, terrists and disruptive activities prevention, prison reforms, foreign victims and numerous such other cases which encroach upon liberty, equality, dignity and social justice.

The present state of affairs in the developing countries in general and in India particular are horrendous. India is facing a bifocal problem: one of cross border terrorism and another of Indigenous extremism in terms of Naxalism. The consequences of both are death destruction, devastation and chaos. These event threaten the very foundation of democratic governance. No doubt, among the third world countries India has reason vigorously as a self sufficient and powerful country with its economy, polity, social structure, *vis-à-vis* science, technology electronics and nuclear potential, but a lot of development in diverse areas is still required. The problems of tribal communities the issues concerning their proper rehabilitation caused by establishment of mega projects and industries is a serious concern. Education health are food and shelter and the protection of their cultural identifities, freedom from bonded slavery and forced labour in the regions of

Madhya Pradesh, Orrisa and Jharkhand require special attention to promote among them education and social awareness regarding their rights and responsibilities. The human rights education programme in such areas will be a commendable service to humanity. Further the regional, ethnic, communal, problems and problems of caste conflict and the insult movement emerging from time to time in the Gangetic Belt of India as also in the hill regions especially in North East require serious political and administrative attention. The encroachment upon life and liberty of people, the innocent masses, peasantry agrarian laborers, women and children has to be a eliminated. The criminalization of polities and the entry of politicians into parliament and state legislatures with history of criminal records must be stopped. Thanks to Indian judiciary especially the High Court and the Supreme Courts of India that have taken steady and serious note of the corrupt and dilatory bureaucracy and the criminal politicians and the prevailing, practice of nepotism. It would be unfair to observe and judicial system in India puts constraints in the process of development. As a matter of fact, it is Indian judiciary and judicial activism that have worked as custodian of not only constitution also of democracy. The National Human Rights commission in India has rendered marvelous services to promote the cause of justice, liberty and dignity of the citizens in the country. The emerging social consciousness among the citizens and the public interest writs and petitions in the High Courts and the Supreme Court are, prima facie, evidence that people have sound faith in the India Judiciary.

To conclude, I would like to mention here that the commissions and committees alone cannot fulfill the cherished goals unless a congenial and conductive social Eli mate is created. This presupposes and outlook of persistence of attitude, perseverance of will and forbearances of mind among the people to restore and protect the sense of human dignity, social reciprocation co-operation coexistence and righteousness in the conduct. So, the miseries and catastrophe of the history whether of the previous world wars or the struggle against previous regimes may not be repeated.

3

Human Rights and Development in a Tea Garden Setting of Assam

VIRENDRA PAL SINGH

Human rights are, in varying degrees, included in the national political constitutions of a large number of countries. The United Nations has so far adopted around fifty Human rights instruments, conventions, declarations and proclamations. As many as 180 countries, who have approved several of these instruments, have UN and international obligations to honour, enforce, monitor and implement those Human rights, which they have agreed upon to honour in both letter and spirit. A UN study in April 1993 reports that at least half of the world's population has been suffering from violation or deprivation of their human rights of one kind or another. It states that nearly 1.4 billion people are absolutely poor and another one billion people are marginally poor; besides colossal refugee problems, under-nutrition, millions of victims of racism and 200 million child labourers, the complaints for human rights violations have crossed 125,000 mark as on April 1992 (Sanjaoba 1994: 3).

There are three generations of human rights. The first generation of human rights was largely of negative character, as it had discouraged the state or the government from denying the political rights and freedom to the individuals. But the second generation of human rights is essentially positive in character, as the state has been placed under one form of obligation or another including the international obligation to provide for economic, social and cultural rights to individuals. The third generation of human rights, however, constitutes the collective or group rights like the right to environment, right to development, right of nations to self-determination, right to common heritage of mankind, among others. The contemporary human rights concern mainly covers all the above-mentioned items.

The perception of the government of India towards a complete endorsement of the universal standard of human rights has not been blameless. There are two major contending impressions about India's devotion to the standard setting, monitoring and implementation of the human rights. The governmental case in point is that human rights abuses in India are very much insignificant or have been blown out of proportion by the NGOs and the international agencies. On the other hand, the viewpoint shared, by and large, by the national and international NGOs, the national media and also by the Human Rights Committee of the UN is that there has been large scale, underwritten violation of human rights by the law enforcement agencies and the security forces.

The Indian social system as such had been for millenniums hierarchical, exploitative, oppressive and irrevocably compartmentalized. The *Dalits,* the backward classes, the women, the non-dominant races and subject peoples had been socially deprived from human rights and their torture and oppression had been de-criminalised. Although, after independence the Constitution of India provides certain safeguards to its citizens in general and to this section of society in particular but long standing customs and traditions still support the practice of such inhuman behaviour in contemporary Indian society. In recent years, there has been a trend to highlight and report the incidents of the violation of human rights by the mass media and NGOs but there have been many areas, which have neither attracted the attention of mass media nor of NGOs and Government organization.

The north-eastern region of India is one of those areas where a number of incidences of violation of human rights have been occurred in recent past and have been highlighted and reported by the national and international media and NGOs. But their major thrust has been to highlight and report the cases of state sponsored violence while combating the insurgent activities in the region. In Assam, the major discussion on human rights situation has been centered on tortures by Armed Forces during search of militants and insurgents in civilian areas of the state. But one of the areas where the history of violation of human rights goes back to the time of East India Company is the Tea Garden society of Assam.

The present paper is aimed to understand the status of human rights and development in the tea gardens of Assam. The paper is based on the review of existing literature on socio-cultural life in the tea gardens of Assam as well as on empirical evidence collected from a tea garden village of South Assam.

Human Rights and Under-development in the Tea Gardens during the Colonial Period

India is world's largest producer as well as consumer of tea. India's tea industry produces about 865,000 tonnes of tea every year. India exports about 205,000 tonnes of tea every year. North-eastern region of India has highest number of tea gardens in the country, which are spread over in Assam (1012), Tripura (57), Arunachal Pradesh (20), Manipur (20), and Nagaland (8). In Assam, the tea gardens are located both in the Brahmaputra Valley and the Barak Valley. The districts of Sibsagar and Dibrugarh have more than half of the tea gardens of the state with 355 and 319 tea gardens respectively. The districts having more than one hundred tea gardens are Cachar (115) and Darrang (112). Remaining six districts – Nowgong (34), Karbi Anglong (20), Lakhimpur (20), Goalpara (13), Kamrup (13) and North Cachar (11) have less than fifty tea gardens (Mazumdar, A. 1998: 50; Dey, N. B. 1998: 9).

The origin of tea plantation in India can be traced as back as to 1774 when Warren Hastings was the Governor General in India. It was, however, not before 1840s that the industry could make its room in the world chart (Kar 1980; 1981). The Bengal Tea Association was formed in Calcutta in1839. A few weeks later, preliminary steps were taken by a separate group of individuals for the formation of the Assam Company in London. The two concerns, however, amalgamated soon (Kar 1981:135). In 1840 practically all the plantations of East India Company, except a few, were handed over to the Assam Company rent-free for 10 years. By 1842, there were some 2,500 acres of tea bed under the Company. Till 1853, tea plantation was confined to Sibsagar and Dibrugarh districts only. But gradually private tea gardens also started to emerge on the scene. By 1859, there were in Assam 51 gardens owned by private individuals or private firms spread over the districts of Sibsagar, Dibrugarh, Darrang, Kamrup and Nowgong. Tea cultivation in Cachar district was started in 1855 or 1856 (Kar 1981: 135). The first tea garden in Cachar was established at Barsangan, now known as Kathal, a village in the Chatla Paragna. Towards the seventies Silcoori, Dargakona, Goongoor, Loharbond came in the purview of tea plantation. The plantation in these gardens was undertaken mainly by The Assam Tea Company, Varakhai Tea Company Limited, The North Western Cachar Tea Company Limited and The Cachar & Dooars Tea Company Limited (Dey, R. 1998).

In the first half of the 19th century, the land now occupied by the Assam tea plantation was mainly dense and uninhabitable jungle. For the clearance of these jungles manual labourers were required. But the North-eastern region had been a labour deficit region from the very beginning and the available local peoples were reluctant to take wage employment (Maithani and Singh 1986). Therefore, the labourers were recruited from various cultural, linguistic and ethnic heritages from many other provinces, mainly from Bengal (Midnapur, Purulia, Bankura, and Burdwan), Bihar (Chhotanagpur Tribal region), Orrisa (Ganjam, Kalahandi area), Madhya Pradesh (Bastar, Jabalpur, Bilaspur), Andhra Pradesh (Guntur and Vishakhapattanam), Madras and Eastern Uttar Pradesh (Deoria, Balia, Basti, Ghazipur, Azamgarh, Gorakhpur). These areas were severely affected by famines in the first half of the 19th century and were badly suffering from economic constraints. Most of them belonged to lower rung of the caste society of their region or to tribal communities existing at substantive level of economy and passed through hardship during the period of famines. Therefore, they were recruited as plantation labourers without any trouble (Singh, S. N. 1998). These emigrants as a rule were recruited from the lowest and the most ignorant class of the people. The recruiters did not deal fairly with these emigrants. The planters have adopted a typical system for the recruitment of labourers. According to Bose (1954: 69), "The general plan was that certain persons were appointed by the planters as recruiting agents in certain localities. These persons were known as *arkatis* literally means pilot. The localities chosen were those places where labour would be easy to procure. These places were known as labour recruiting districts. Chotanagpur, the Santhal Paragnas, etc., were noted for famines and acute food scarcity, which were partly due to natural calamities, but mainly to the oppressive system of land revenue adopted by the government to enhance its own revenues. This compelled a major section of the people to live in a floating condition. They could neither maintain themselves on their land nor get any alternative source of livelihood. Most of them, before finally being compelled to give up their lands, had to incur heavy debts which always hung on their necks, even after they had become complete paupers." These people were the targets of the *arkatis*. The labourers were too often entrapped into snares of the recruiters either by fraud or misrepresentation and once they were put in the camp, they were not allowed to escape. In 1859, the Government enacted the Workmen's Breach of Contract Act (Act XIII of 1859), which made certain provisions in order to regularize working conditions and the process of recruitment of all categories of labourers incluuing plantation labourers. But instead of providing facilities to the plantation workers, the planters took advantage of it and compelled their labourers to work even against their will in the name of contract as the Act made the provision of prosecution of the labourers in case of breach of the contract (Kar 1981: 4).Thus, the Act did not protect the labourers against the employer and laid down no conditions in connection with the arrangements for the transit of the labourers to the tea gardens. The contractors did the recruitment of labourers in initial years. At that time there was no restrictions upon the contractors. Therefore, the contractors or *arkatis,* who were ex-convicts burglars, thieves, dacoits etc., adopted typical methods of recruitment. These included loans advanced to the potential victims, tempting young men with liquor, kidnapping of young girls and women and marrying them off in the depots-a-system known as 'depot marriage.' They were brought to transit camps located in Calcutta from where they were sent to tea districts by boats or ships. In 1861, The Indian General Steamer Company introduced its regular services for the carriage of labourers to Assam via Brahmaputra River (Singh 1998). They were subjected to some gross abuses such as deception in recruitment, in sanitary conditions at the depot and on steamers and country boats and heavy mortality on the way to labour districts. The report of Assam Labour Enquiry Committee 1906 gives a description of the situation prevailing at that time, "contractors collected coolies by the hundred of false promises of high pay and light work and dispatched them to the tea districts without taking any sanitary precautions for their welfare on the journey; the result was shocking mortality on the voyage up, while many of immigrants were of caste or constitution which precluded all hope of their surviving many months in the jungles of Assam" (Singh 1998).

There had been reports of violation and abuse of human rights of these poor labourer not only by so called contractors on their way to the tea districts but also by the planters and their staffs who were responsible for the supervision of plantation work. There is enough evidence which indicate that human rights situation was worst in the tea gardens of Assam.

In 1883, some cases of violation of human rights by the planters in tea gardens of Assam were published in a Bengali news paper *'the Sanjibani'*. The reports published in this newspaper were based on the empirical work of a Brahmo Samaj missionary who had visited the tea gardens of Assam. He published two cases which had been tried in the courts and on which judgements had been pronounced in favour of the planters. The English judges always took the side of the planters. Of these cases two became very notorious and created a upheaval in India and England (for details see Singh 2005).

Planters used to pay their contractors and agents a sum of Rs. 120 to Rs. 150 for every recruit under a penal contract. The agents frequently used criminal means such as inducing the victims by misrepresentation or by threats. The observations of Cotton (1911:265), the Chief Commissioner of Assam are relevant in this connection. He pointed out that "the records of the criminal courts teemed with instances of abduction of married women and children, fraud, wrongful confinement, intimidation and actual violence. Due to congestion, lack of food and the hygienic conditions, many died like cattle while still on their way to plantations. The rest were to be sold to the planters. At the expiry of the contracts period, the coolie was legally free but was repeatedly induced under duress to re-engage himself. Thus, having once come to a tea garden, he had practically no hope to return to his native place"(Cotton 1911:265). It is clear from the observations of Cotton that the conditions in the tea gardens of Assam were very exploitative and inhuman. The contractors treated the recruited coolies like animals. The human rights situation in the tea gardens of Assam was worst. There were some other forms of exploitation. "There were a number of cases when the coolies were not paid the higher rate of salary to which they were entitled as per contract. In many cases the rice was not provided at the statutory rate and the subsistence allowance prescribed by laws was not paid to sick coolie or pregnant women. Advances were often illegally debited against coolies on account of subsistence allowance or sick diet, as well as on account of rewards paid for the arrest of deserters and labourers were, thus, bound hand and foot to the garden service. In some instances only a few *annas* found their way into the hands of a coolie as wages in course of the whole year..." (Cotton 1911:265).

Such miserable conditions could be imposed upon the coolies, not because of their illiteracy and ignorance, which was very much prevailing there, but because of their inability to strike work under the binding of the penal contract which they were supposed to sign before they were brought to tea district. If they struck work, they were liable to imprisonment. If they fled, the planters had the right of arresting them without warrant. Flogging and other kinds of torture, with the connivance of even courts of justice, were the common practice (Chattopadhyay 1998:4). It will be more clear from an incident happened in Cachar in May 1921. According to Chakraborty (1992), "the accumulated grievances of the labourers had been crying for redress for a long time. Radhakrishna Pandey, a congress leader of Silchar, Gangadayal Dixit, a cloth dealer of Lakhipur and Deosharan Tripathi, a priest worked among labourers persuaded them not to work in European tea gardens. The situation gradually turned tense and that became explosive. Thousands of labourers of thirteen European tea gardens went on strike on May 2, 1921. Shouting slogans like "Mahatama Gandhi Ki Jay" the labourers numbering about 1300 left their gardens and flocked to Karimganj on their way home. The sudden influx of the labourers made a chaotic situation at Karimganj and stood a threat to the civil administration. The health and sanitary conditions of the town had deteriorated and cholera broke out. The Bengal Provincial Committee and Cachar and Karimganj Congress Committee came forward to help the distressed labourers.... By the help of Congress volunteers, the labourers departed from Karimgang. The alien government had natural sympathy for the management. So, when the strikers reached Chandpur, the authorities resorted to cruel action against them. They were prevented from crossing the river by the Civil SDO. Mr. Macpherson, a representative of the European Tea Association arrived at Chandpur and pressurized the strikers to go back to their respective tea gardens. But the labourers refused to return back. While boarding a steamer, the authorities ordered for the removal of the gangway. In the process hundreds were drowned. Finding no other alternative, the strikers took shelter in the railway station with the hope of boarding a steamer whenever next available. In the mean time, the authorities indented some contingents of Gurkha Riffles from Narayanganj (Bangladesh). On May 21, 1921 the authorities along with European planters decided to clear up the assembled labourers from the station plateform with the help of armed police and Gorkha regiment. In the darkness of the fateful night the Gurkha soldiers were let loose on the labourers. It was not exactly known how many lost their lives, how many were injured and how many were drowned in the river. It was, however, estimated that about 500 persons died by the cruel process of clearance by the armed men" (Chakraborty 1992).

From the above evidence, it is now clear that the human rights situation was very worst in the tea gardens of Assam during the colonial period. The uprooted tea garden labourers were exploited not only by the contractors on their way to the tea districts in various forms but also by the planters and their staffs. More or less this situation of human rights prevailed in the tea gardens of Assam till Independence.

Human Rights and Development in Post Independence Period

After Independence, the scenario has been changed to some extent in the tea gardens of Assam as most of the tea gardens were sold to Indian entrepreneurs. But there was very little improvement in the condition of the tea garden labourers. They were continuously subject of exploitation by their Indian masters. There have been very few empirical sociological studies about their social, economic and cultural life. Some of the important studies in this area are conducted by Kar (1980; 1981; 1998); Chattopadhyay (1972); and others. The human rights situation in the tea gardens of Assam can be analysed in terms of the the social structure, class structure and power structure of the tea garden society and by analyzing the status of the development indicators such as education, health and communication which reflect the actual working conditions of the labourers in the tea garden society.

Social Structure

The caste constitutes the core of Indian social stratification system. The tea garden labourers had been brought from different linguistic and cultural zones of the country. But one similarity among them was that most of them belonged to the lower stratum of the caste hierarchy of their respective region. The major problem before them was of maintaining their caste identity as well as their linguistic identity. Due to physical isolation of these people from the people of other gardens, in initial period the marriage relations took place within the same garden. In this process they made certain adjustments in order to maintain caste endogamy. The rigidity of sub-caste blurred and kinship ties between the people of different sub-castes of the same region and equivalent castes of the different cultural zone took place. The empirical evidence from Dargakona tea garden reveals the stratification system of tea garden society.

The caste system here is comprised of five strata: *Brahmins* are at the top in caste hierarchy. However, they are very few in number and have not been associated with manual work in the tea garden. In fact, they were brought to perform rituals by the planters in order to maintain cultural identity of the labourers who came from different regions. They can be divided into two sub-strata - Bengali Brahmins (Chakraborty, Bhattacharjee, Mishra) and Brahmins from Northern India (Pandey, Mishra, Tiwari, Trivedi etc.). The second stratrum is of Kayasthas/ Kshatriyas, which is again divided into Bengali (Dutta, Deb) and Hindi speaking caste groups (Singh or Rajput, Srivastava, Verma etc.). The third stratrum is composed of the castes like Goala, Koiri, Bhar and Pasi from Northern India mainly from U.P. and Bihar and Paul from Bengal. It is followed by the fourth stratrum of the castes like Mala, Bhumij and Dhobi from U.P. and Bihar and Mal, Bagti, Roy and Bouri/ Ree from Bengal. The lowest stratum is composed of the castes like Rabidas, Dusad, Dom etc. from U.P. and Bihar and the caste groups like Majhi, Malakar, Sukalbaidya,Chanda etc. from Bengal. Thus, there are two parallel caste-hierarchy in the tea garden, one of those who speaks Bengali and the other of those who came from Hindi speaking belt of Northern India. In the tea garden society, both groups maintain their separate identity and are locally known as *Bengali Samaj* and *Hindustani Samaj*. Thus, linguistic identity of these groups bifurcate the tea garden society into two linguistic groups. The Bengali Samaj identifies itself with Bengali population of the region who were immigrated from East Bengal before the partition of the country but mainly after the partition of the country in 1947 and thereafter at the time of the formation of Bangladesh in 1971. In fact, the process of immigration of Bengali families is a continuous process in this region. The members of Bengali Samaj consider themselves superior in comparison to the members of Hindustani Samaj because they think that they are local and the members of Hindustani Samaj are outsiders as they speak a language which is not spoken in this part of Assam. Thus, linguistic politics of the region played an important role in the degradation of Hindustani Samaj.

Although, in the eyes of town people, the tea garden labourers have no status. For them, they are just *coolie*, whether they belong to Bengali Samaj or to Hindustani Samaj. The term coolie which was used by the British planters for tea garden labourers who were treated by them as slaves is still in usage and is highly politicized. Sometimes it is used to humiliate the tea garden people by some town dwellers in order to show their superiority over the tea garden people. In an another study of a village, it was found that the persons or families out-migrated from tea garden area are given lowest status in the village hierarchy and are addressed as coolie as a social stratum even if they had never been engaged in any kind of plantation work. Thus, there is a great violation of human rights not only in case of tea garden workers of a particular linguistic group by another linguistic group. The use of 'coolie' term as an abuse in this region reflects the condition of human rights situation in the tea gardens of Barak Valley of Assam.

Class Structure

The economic condition of the workers in tea garden can be analysed in terms of class structure, and their standard of living. The land ownership and occupational status may be taken as indicators of class position. The pattern of ownership is very typical in tea gardens. In the sense, that the workers have only cultivation right. They have no right to make any permanent structure or even a temporary structure without the permission of the garden authority. Most of the people used to cultivate the land themselves but in case of the large area of the land they used to lease out the land. They usually grow crop only once in a year due to the occurance of flood in monsoon season and draught in the winter. They are mainly dependent on local variety of seeds and used traditional techniques of cultivation. Although, the labourers have no ownership right on the land, still they can sell the land in their possession by transferring the possession right to the purchaser. Thus, in the tea garden, the land is legally belonged to the garden but the workers have cultivation right on the land and they can transfer it to some other person as well. The empirical evidence collected from Dargakona tea garden (a sub-tea garden of Silcoori Tea Estate) suggests that 67.16 per cent of the workers had less than 4 bigha of land, 19.4 per cent 4-8 bigha of land and 13.44 per cent have more than 8 bigha of land. Most of the families, who possess more than 8bigha of the land, are of non-tea garden workers. Thus, about 67 per cent families in the tea garden area have cultivable land, but a majority of them (87 per cent) are having below marginal level of land. The permanent workers have more land than the temporary workers. This typical pattern of ownership pattern in the tea gardens of Assam gives an upper hand to the garden authorities in controlling the affairs of tea garden society. Whenever they feel a threat from a person they take back the land from such a person. Thus, a person in the tea garden whether he is working in the garden or not tries to maintain good relation with garden authorities. Thus, the land is used as a means to control the affairs in the tea gardens of Assam. In other words, the land can be used as a tool of exploitation and manipulation by the garden authorities whenever they like. It becomes more important in the conditions when the garden has engaged only 165 permanent workers (86 male and 79 female) and only 25 temporary workers (all male) from a total of 535 households with a population of about 3000 persons. Of them about 1800 persons constitute the working population of the garden. In such a situation, it is important to understand that in what type of economic activities this remaining working population is engaged?

The occupational distribution of 342 working persons of 106 households suggests that about half of them (50.58 per cent) are engaged in agriculture and related activities while a little less than one- fourth (23.09 per cent) of them are semi-skilled and unskilled workers. A few of them (3.51 per cent) are engaged in small or petty-business activities within or outside the garden. About one-fifth of them are involved with production process of the tea garden. Remaining 3.81 per cent are in service occupations out side the tea garden. It can be noted that the Dargakona tea garden has a number of locational advantages as it is located on Silchar- Hailakandi road only about 19 kms. away from the main township and just outside the recently established central university, namely, Assam University. The condition of the workers is worst in those gardens, which are located in remote areas of Barak Valley.

Power Structure

There are three major political institutions in tea garden society: (i) Caste Panchayat (ii) Bagan Panchayat and (iii) Gaon Panchayat. The caste panchayat in a tea garden is composed of some reputed persons of a particular caste. This institution is mainly functional among the workers, who migrated from U.P. and Bihar and to some extent among those workers who were recruited from West Bengal. But among those who had migrated from East Bengal for trade and business or some other jobs in the tea garden areas do not have caste panchayat. At present caste panchayat is formed at the village level by the people of the same caste. These village level caste panchayats from different gardens of the region together constitute a district level caste organization. In case of those castes who have only few family in a particular tea garden associate themselves with the neighbouring caste panchayat or with district level body. Thus, the caste panchayat plays an important role not only in regulating the behaviour of its members but at the district level it takes the shape of an interest or pressure group and try to influence the political processes. The caste leadership sometimes is also engaged in bargaining with the leaders of different political parties as they have the command over their caste fellows. But gradually it is loosing its importance particularly among the youth. In a personal conversation the youth of Dargakona tea garden disclosed that during the meeting of samaj they obey the verdict of caste leadership but at the time of casting their vote they do not follow the command of their leaders. It is not because they have high level of political afficacy but they did it just to deny the decisions of the elders. In fact, it is due to their ever increasing exposure to mass media communication and urban exposure and gradually improving educational level.

The Bagan Panchayat is an organization that only looks the interests of the tea garden labourers. The Bagan Panchayat is composed of the parmanent labourers of the garden. It is formed in the presence of the members of Cha Shramik Union. mass media communication and urban exposure and gradually improving educational level.

The Bagan Panchayat is an organization that only looks the interests of the tea garden labourers. The Bagan Panchayat is composed of the parmanent labourers of the garden. It is formed in the presence of the members of Cha Shramik Union. Its executive body is consists of President, Vice President, Secretary, Assistant Secretary and five tosix executive members. This body takes up the problems of the plantation workers and also recommends to the garden authority about the various schemes for the welfare of the tea workers. But this body is highly politicized. In Dargakona tea garden only Congress supported Shramik Union is in existence. The owner of the garden is also a supporter of the Cogress Party. Therefore, at most of the occasions this body works for the benefit of the management who in turn looks after thr interests of the political party for which they work. Therefore, whenever the workers raised any issue against the management the office bearers of Bagan Panchayat interfere and settle the issue by providing various lucrative which rarely go against the garden authority. Thus, the Bagan Panchayat serves the purpose of garden authorities rather than the workers for whom it is constituted. In fact, it helps the Garden authority in manipulating the situation in its favour and hardly serves the interests of the tea workers.

The institution of gaon panchayat, introduced in post-independence period, which is supposed to ensure people's participation in developmental activities on the one hand, and inculcation of democratic values at the grass root level no the other, also failed to create any significant contribution in the tea gardens of Assam. The major problem in functioning of gaon panchayat is that it has to take permission from the garden authority for every kind of developmental activity which they rarely get. Thus, here also the garden authority has its upper hand. Therefore, it can be said that in one way or the other garden authority is capable to control and manipulate the garden affairs in its favour and continues to exploit the tea workers.

Education

During the colonial period, the labourers were illiterate as they had no scope of exposure to education. Although, in some tea gardens L. P. Schools were started by garden authorities, but this facility was mainly used by those families, who were not engaged in plantation work. The plantation workers could not take advantage of school because they were in the clutches of poverty and were discouraged by the garden authorities. After Independence, some improvement in their educational level has taken place. But still the level of education is very low in the tea gardens of Assam. It will be clearer from the empirical evidence collected from Dargakona tea garden.

In Dargakona, there are two lower primary schools (L. P. School). One is Nutun Tila L. P. School established in 1976 and got grant in1982. Another school, Dargakona L. P. School, which was established during the British period in 1902 got government grant in 1971 only. Till 1971 there was only one teacher in this school. In 1976 one more teacher was given to this school. By 1996-97, school got 5 teachers. It shows the condition of schools in tea garden areas of Assam. Another interesting fact in this garden is that in 1993 the villagers established one M. E. School (Middle Elementary School). It continued up to 1998 and due to non availability of land from the garden authorities the school was closed.

The level of education in this tea garden is improving gradually. In a sample of 106 families it was found that out of 134 person of 6-14 age group, only 28 persons were illiterate (37.52 %). Of them, 75 per cent were girls. Among the remaining 106 children of this age group, only 14 students (5 male and 9 female) discontinued their study (11 with 4 standard and 3 with 7 standard). However, 79 per cent children from this age group are continuing their study. Of which 86.67 per cent are from garden workers' family and 86.89 per cent from non-garden workers' family. But, in the age group of 15-25 years 63.55 per cent are illiterate (85% female). Out of 46 males, 15 (32.61%) had dropped with 4 standard, 14 (33.33%) by 7 standard and 7 at high school level. Others are continuing their study at different levels (1 at under-graduate level, 2 at higher secondary level, 4 at high school level, 1 at middle level and 2 at primary level). Among the females of this age group, rate of drop out was slightly low at primary level (31.81%) in comparison to the males. Both at metric and high school level, it was 13.51%. Among the age group of 26-50 years 42.22 % were illiterate (47.12 % male and 58.59 % female). Amog the literate males of this age group, 50 % are primary educated, 21.73 middle level, 15.21 % high school, 6.52 higher secondary, 2 per cent graduates and 4 per cent post-graduates. Among the female literates of this age group, 56.66 per cent could reach up to primary level, 20 per cent up to middle level, 16.66 per cent up to high school level, 3.33 per cent up to higher secondary level and 3.33 per cent at under-graduate level. Among the age group of 51-75 years, 52 per cent males and 96 per cent females are illiterate, 32 per cent males are primary educated, 8 per cent middle and 8 per cent high school. Among the females of this age group only one lady could reach up to high school level. Among the more than 75 years of age out of 4 males only 2 have primary level of education while both the females of this age group are illiterate? It is clear from the above analysis that there is a gradual improvement in the educational level of the tea garden workers both among the males and females. But due to their poor economic condition there is heavy drop out at different levels. Moreover, discouraging attitude of tea garden authorities is also responsible for this kind of situation in the tea gardens.

Health and Communication

From the people of interviewed 106 households only 31 people i.e., only the permanent workers out of total 564 population of the interviewed household gets the medical benefits from the garden authority. Rest of the people takes the medicine mainly from the Ramkrishna Mission's Mobile clinic once in a weak or from local pharmacy. If it is necessary enough, they visit Silchar Medical College, otherwise for minor health problem they do take any medicine or take herbal medicine on which they dependent earlier. Thus, a shift of belief from the herbal medicine or traditional practice to modern health care measures is seen clearly.

As far as communication is concerned, Dargakona is nearest to the Assam University Campus. Before the establishment of this university this road had not much importance though three decades back this road was a major link road for the neighbouring state of Mizoram. But the location of Dargakona got its importance after establishment of the university. Before that it was just a periphery of Silcoorie. Only 3 sets of televisions are found in the studied 106 households. More than 50 per cent people are not the viewers of TV and those who watch are mainly using it as a source of entertainment. Newspaper readers are also very less, of course, availability of news paper is also one of the factors. This means that most of the people are out of flow of direct information. Whatever information they are getting either through two-step flow method or directly whenever they go outside the village, particularly, in the weekly market. When they were asked whether they visited outside the district, the minimum of them told no but a major portion of them particularly male members (mainly young generation) often comes in Silchar town. So they get little exposure, impact of which also be seen in their interaction pattern within the society.

Conclusions

On the basis of above empirical evidence, we can draw following conclusions about the human rights situation in the tea gardens of Assam:

1. The human rights situation in the tea gardens of Assam was worst during the colonial period. The plantation workers were exploited not only by the contractors in various ways during their journey to tea districts of Assam from their place of origin but also by the planters who kept them like slaves and treated them inhumanly. The planters were having full support of the colonial government in these acts.
2. After Independence, the scenario in the tea gardens of Assam has been changed to some extent with the change in the ownership of the gardens which is now in the hand of the Indian entrepreneurs. But there is very little improvement in human rights situation. They have been continuously subject of exploitation by their Indian masters.
3. The prevailing class structure and typical pattern of land ownership are major factors which contribute in a significant manner in perpetuation of poverty in the tea gardens of Assam and provide avenues for their exploitation by the garden authorities in various ways. The land is legally owned by the planters who continue to allow the workers and ex-tea garden workers to cultivate it but whenever they find that a particular person may challenge their authority in the garden they take legal action to evacuate that person from the garden land. Here it is important to note that even the land of workers residence is legally owned by the garden authority. This is the reason that even those who do not work in the tea garden are also bound to maintain good relations with garden authorities and can not raise their voice against them. Moreover, they cannot move away from the garden as they have in their possession a piece of cultivable land which they would not like to loose which fulfils their basic need of food and shelter to some extent. Thus, legal owner ship of land is the major instrument with the planters which is used by them in manipulating and controlling garden affairs and

allows them even to deny the genuine demands of the tea garden people.

4. The tea garden people have lowest place in social hierarchy of the region. They were called 'coolie' by their European masters and non- tea garden people and were living like slaves during the colonial period. This colonial term is still in usage but in a derogatory sense and sometimes used as an abuse bythe local people. In Barak Valley of Assam this term is deliberately used by non-garden population, who themselves immigrated from various parts of East Bengal (now Bengladesh) at different points of time, in order to dominate on tea garden workers. Although, the Bengali tea workers try to identify themselves with non-garden population of the region but for them a tea garden worker is just a coolie. It reflects not only the lowest status of a tea garden worker in regional hierarchy but also the status of human rights situation in the tea gardens of Assam.
5. Most of the population in tea gardens is of marginal farmers. During the off-season they use to do agricultural work. In the plantation season, some of them work as temporary workers in the garden while others work as semi-skilled or unskilled worker within or outside the garden. Thus, economically most of them are very weak and are continuously in the clutches of poverty, which is also one of the reasons, which allows the garden authorities to exploit them and restrict their human rights.
6. The literacy rate in the tea gardens is low. In Dargakona tea garden it is 44.34 per cent, which is considered as a developed one. The female illiteracy is relatively high (56.8 per cent) in comparison to their male counterparts (30.53 per cent). In the adult working population illiteracy is high with 61.27 per cent. The female literacy among the adults is 73.94 per cent. As most of the workers in plantation work are women they can be easily exploited by the garden authorities. Moreover,

the garden authorities always try to restrict the process of education among the tea garden people by taking certain measures such as by not providing the land for school building etc.

7. The health facilities are limited to permanent workers only. However, majority of the villagers depend on the weekly service of an NGO or take medicine from the pharmacy available in the neighbouring village (at a distance of one Km.).
8. The villagers have low media exposure as modern mass media have yet to fully penetrate the territory of the village.
9. The garden authorities are also capable in manipulating and controlling the political behaviour of the tea garden people by influencing traditional caste leaders by giving them some personal benefits and office bearers of Bagan Panchayat through their party linkages and by hampering developmental activities of gaon panchayat which has to take permission from the garden authorities particularly in those schemes in which some land is required.

Thus, in the tea gardens of Assam the human rights situation has been worst from the very beginning. Even after more than five decades of independence situation is not much improved. The planters are violating the human rights of the present tea workers and ex-tea garden workers in various ways: by restricting the right of education and developmental activities for their welfare, by giving low wages to the workers through certain techniques of manipulation, by exploiting them politically with the help of their leaders. In this process, they also take advantage of the local level linguistic politics. The tea garden workers are generally called 'Coolie' which is now a derogatory term. The Bengali workers can easily mixed with the out side Bengali population and they can also escape their identity of tea workers. But, the non-Bengali tea workers due to their language are unable to do so and, therefore, prefer to stay in the tea garden area, in an environment which is highly exploited but with which they are familiar for more than a century.

Note: *The author is thankful to Mr. Sanjoy Chakraborty for his help in collection of data for the present paper.*

References

Bose, N. K. (1954), *Culture and Society in India*, Bombay: Asia Publishing House.

Chakraborty, S. B. (1992), "Exodus of Tea Garden Labour," Paper Presented in National Seminar on *History and Society of Barak Valley*, Nov. 9-11, Sreehatta Sammilani, Delhi.

Chattopadhyay, K. L. (1972), *Slavery in British Dominion*, Calcutta.

Cotton, Henry (1911), *Indian And Home Memories*, London:

Dey, N. B. (1998), "Revival of Weak and Sick Tea Gardens: A Study of Barak Valley Districts," Paper Presented in Regional Seminar on *Society and Development in the Tea Garden of North East,* Feb. 2-3, Department of Sociology, Assam University, Silchar.

Dey, R. (1998), "Ex-Tea Garden Labourers in the Barak Valley," Paper Presented in Regional Seminar on *Society and Development in the Tea Garden of North East,* Feb. 2-3, Department of Sociology, Assam University, Silchar.

Kar, R. K. (1980), "Tea Labour in Assam," *The Bulletin of the Department of Anthropology,Dibrugarh University,* Vol. 9, 25-39.

Kar, R. K. (1981), "Tea Industry in Assam: A Chronological Account," *Man and Life,*Vol. 7, No. 3-4, 131-150.

Kar, R. K. (1998), "Tea Plantation and Its Labourers in Assam: An Overview," Paper Presented in Regional Seminar on *Society and Development in the Tea Garden of North East*, Feb. 2-3, Department of Sociology, Assam University, Silchar.

Maithani, B. P. and V. P. Singh (1987), "Planning and Implementation of NREP in Arunachal Pradesh", *Journal of Rural Development,* Vol. 6, No. 4, pp. 366-385.

Mazumdar, A. (1998), *Statistical Profile of Barak Valley & An Agenda for Research on the Valley's Economy, Silchar*: North Eastern Centre for Advanced Research.

Sanjaoba, N. (1994), Human Rights: Principles, Practices & Abuses New Delhi, Omsons Publications.

Singh, S. N. and Kumar Amrendra Narain (1998), "Socio-economic and Political Problems of Tea Garden Workers of Barak Valley," Paper presented in Regional Seminar on *Society and Development in the Tea Garden of North East,* Feb. 2-3, Department of Sociology, Assam University, Silchar.

Singh, V. P. (2005), Human Rights Situation and Poverty in the Tea Gardens of Assam in S. N. Chaudhary (edited) Human Rights and Poverty in India: Theoretical Isssues and Empirical Evidences, New Delhi, Concept Publishing Company.

4

Paradigms of Human Rights Awareness

Diwakar Singh Rajput

Human Rights, Natural Justice, Social Awareness, Social Environment, Juvenile Delinquency, Social Deviance, Human Resource Management, Crime-Prevention, Victim – Offender Relationship,, Women Empowerment, Social Development, Social Justice.

In the present changing scenario, the social awareness is one of the major tools for the promotion of human right and for the creation of climate of public opinion. Human rights, Democracy, Good Governance & Healthy Social Environment with social. Awareness is the major steps & supporting tools of social justice, national justice & social development. The present study has been undertaken to investigate the relationship between level of education and awareness of the human rights, and the balancing of approach between human rights & social control.

The study shows that most of people do not have the knowledge about laws on human rights; they only have the general idea about the human rights. In comparison to female, male members are more informed about the rights & duties. People learn their rights power through education and awareness. They take the various ways of awareness, action & equality.

By the study & classification of primary data & secondary data/literature. I want to discuss on paradigm known as "KANPUR" paradigm & on one action frame called as "ERPA" Model.

"Kanpur" Paradigm for Human Rights Awareness

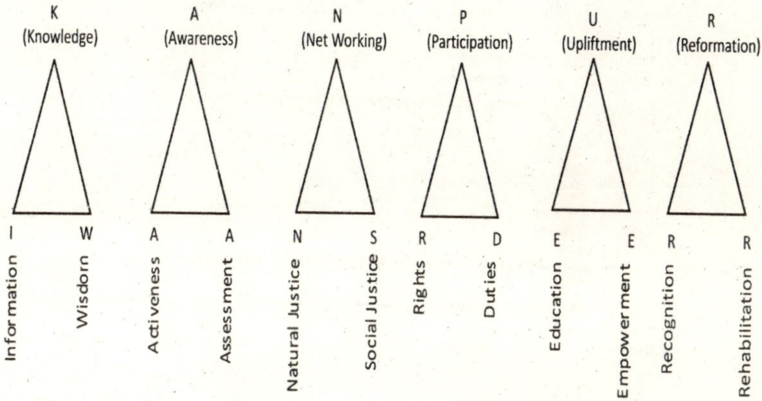

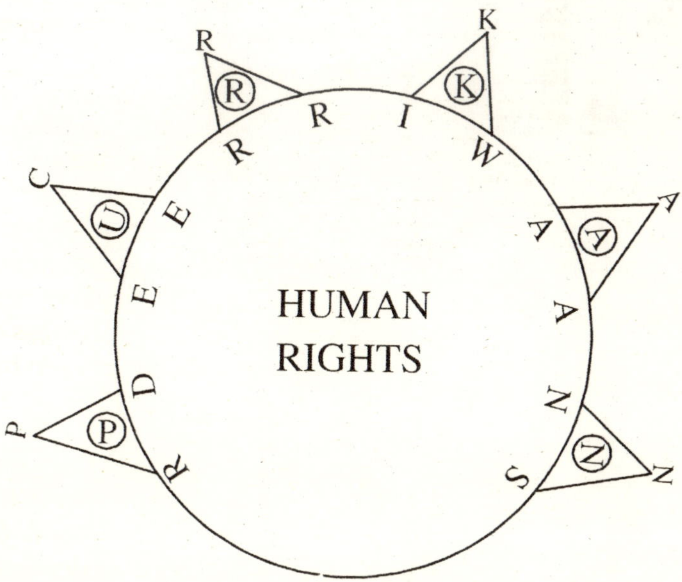

Action Frame for Human Rights Awareness and Social Development Through Human Resource Management

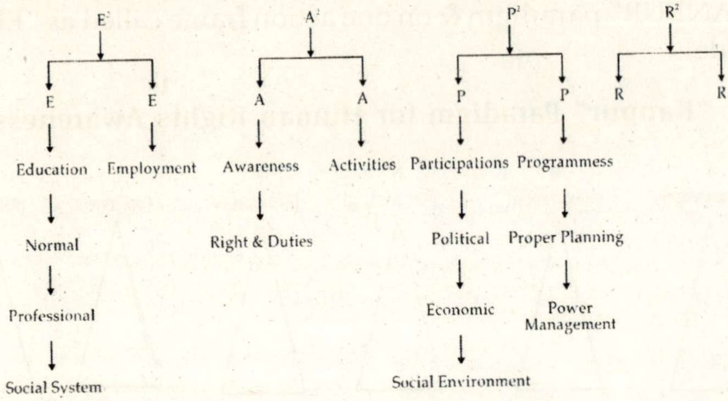

Human Resource Management Through

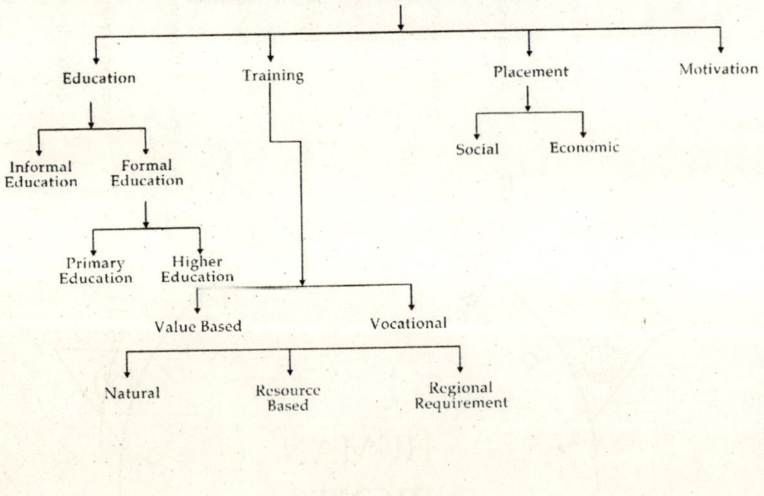

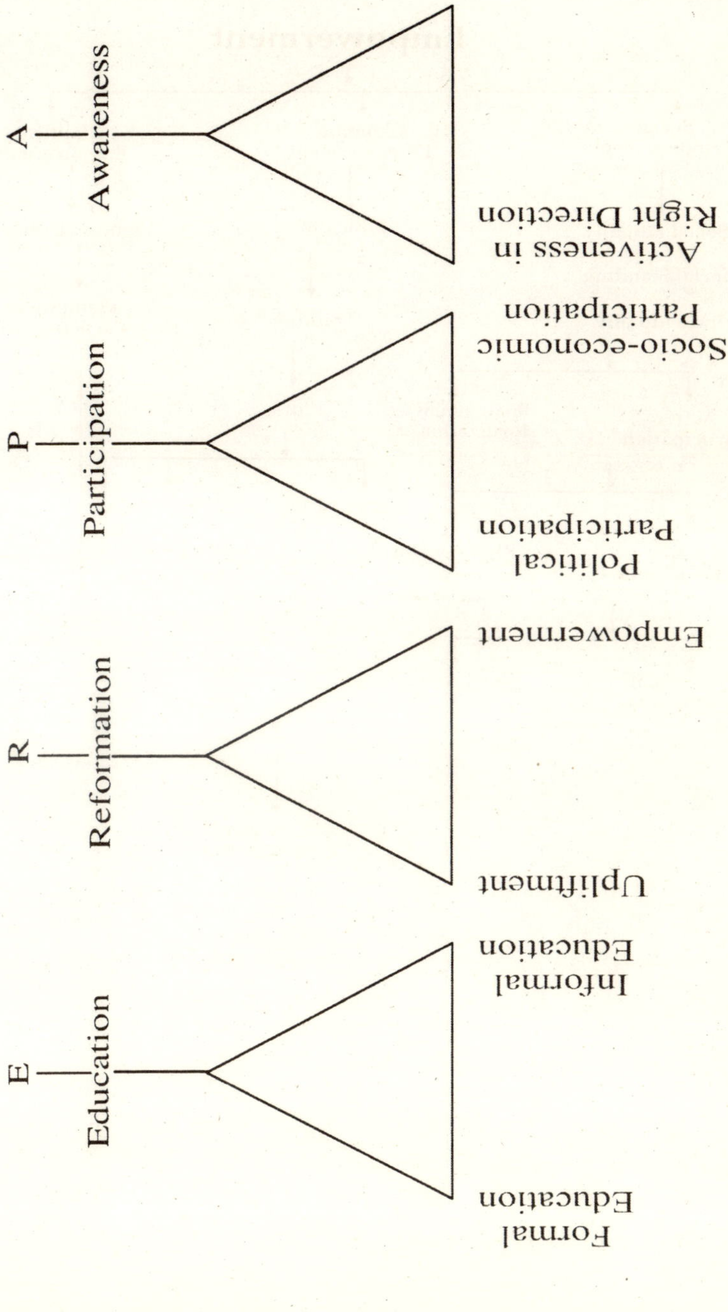
E
Education
Formal Education
Informal Education
R
Reformation
Upliftment
Empowerment
P
Participation
Political Participation
Socio-economic Participation
A
Awareness
Activeness in Right Direction

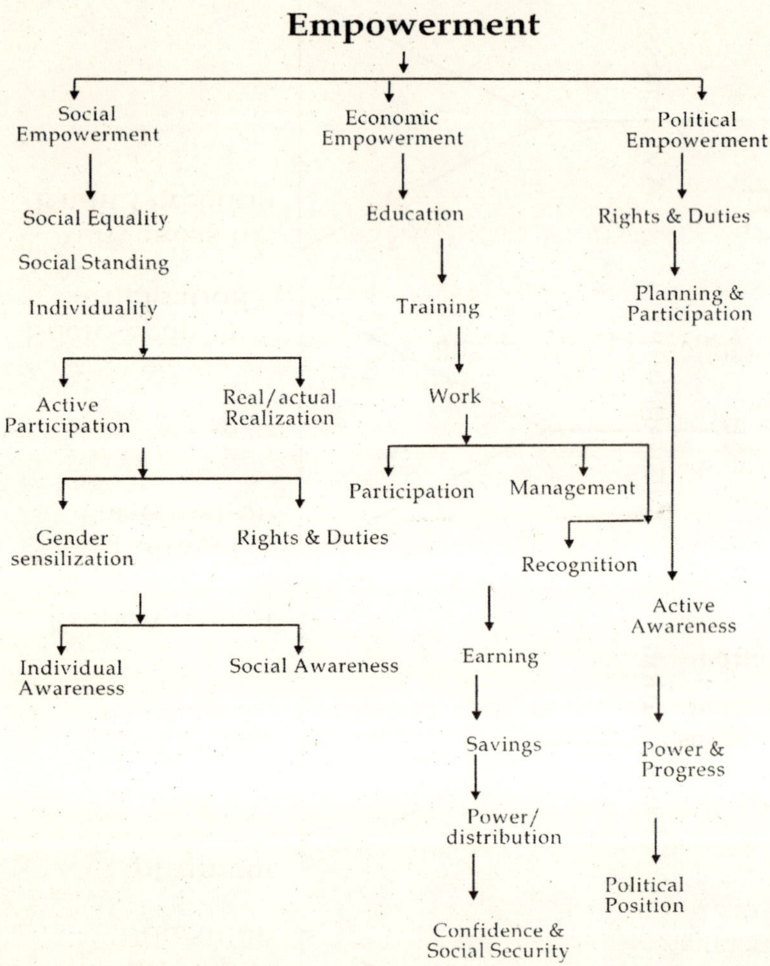
Empowerment
Social Empowerment
Economic Empowerment
Political Empowerment
Social Equality
Social Standing
Individuality
Active Participation
Real/actual Realization
Gender sensilization
Rights & Duties
Individual Awareness
Social Awareness
Education
Training
Work
Participation
Management
Recognition
Earning
Savings
Power/ distribution
Confidence & Social Security
Rights & Duties
Planning & Participation
Active Awareness
Power & Progress
Political Position

5

Violation of Human Rights Among Indian Tribal Communities

UDAI PRATAP SINGH & VIJAY KUMAR

Introduction

Human Rights are "basic rights and freedoms to which all humans are entitled". The doctrine of human rights aims to identify the necessary positive and negative prerequisites for a "universal" minimal standard of justice, tolerance and human dignity that can be considered the public moral norms owed by and to individuals by the mere virtue of their humanity. Such prerequisites can exist as shared norms of actual human moralities, as justified moral norms or moral rights supported by strong reasons, as legal rights at a national level, or as a legal right within international law.

The general idea of human rights has widespread acceptance, and it has been argued that the doctrine of human rights has become the dominant moral doctrine for regulating and evaluating the moral status of the contemporary geo-political order. Indeed, the Charter of the United Nations which has been signed by virtually all sovereign states recognises the existence of human rights and calls for their promotion and respect. However, debate and disagreement over which rights are human rights, and about the precise nature, content, justification and appropriate legal status of those rights continues. The Universal Declaration of Human Rights has acted as the predominant modern codification of commonly accepted human rights principles and many national many international documents, treaties and instruments that have expanded on its principles and act as a collective expression of widespread conceptions of human rights by the international community. The Article 1 of the United Nations Universal Declaration of Human Rights (UDHR) Attempts to harness that all human beings are born free and equal in dignity and rights. They are endowed with reason and conscience and should act towards one another in a spirit of brotherhood.

Examples of rights and freedoms which have come to be commonly thought of as human rights include civil and political rights, such as the right to life and liberty, freedom of expression, and equality before the law; and economic, social and cultural rights, including the right to participate in culture, the right to be treated with respect and dignity, the right to food, the right to work, and the right to education.

Modern international conceptions of human rights can be traced to the aftermath of World War II and the foundation of the United Nations. Article 1(3) of the United Nations charter set out one of the purposes of the UN is to: "[t]o achieve international cooperation in solving international problems of an economic, social, cultural, or humanitarian character, and in promoting and encouraging respect for human rights and for fundamental freedoms for all without distinction as to race, sex, language, or religion". The rights espoused in the UN charter would be codified in the International Bill of Human Rights, composing the Universal Declaration of Human Rights, the International Covenant on Civil and Political Rights and the International Covenant on Economic, Social and Cultural Rights.

The Preamble to the Universal Declaration of Human Rights, (1948) says that recognition of the inherent dignity and of the equal and inalienable rights of all members of the human family is the foundation of freedom, justice and peace in the world.

The Universal Declaration of Human Rights (UDHR) is adopted by the United Nations General Assembly in 1948, partly in response to the atrocities of World War II. Although the UDHR is a non-binding resolution, it is now considered to be a central component of international customary law which may be invoked under appropriate circumstances by national and other judiciaries. The UDHR urges member nations to promote a number of human, civil, economic and social rights, asserting these rights are part of the "foundation of freedom, justice and peace in the world." The declaration was the first international legal effort to limit the behaviour of states and press upon them duties to their citizens following the model of the rights-duty duality.

The drafters of the Covenants initially intended only one instrument. The original drafts included only political and civil rights, but economic and social rights were added early. Western States then fought for, and obtained, a division into two covenants. They insisted that economic and social right were essentially aspirations or plans, not rights, since their realization depended on availability of resources and on controversial economic theory and ideology. These, they said, were not appropriate subjects for binding obligations and should not be allowed to dilute the legal character of provisions honoring political-civil rights; states prepared to assume obligations to respect political-civil rights should not be mitments. There was wide agreement and clear recognition that the means required to enforce or induce compliance with socio-economic undertakings were different from the means required for civil-political rights.

Because of the divisions over which rights to include, and because some states declined to ratify any treaties including certain specific interpretations of human rights, and despite the Soviet bloc and a number of developing countries arguing strongly for the inclusion of all rights in a so-called *Unity Resolution,* the rights enshrined in the UDHR were split into two separate covenants, allowing states to adopt some rights and derogate others. Though this allowed the covenants to be created, one commentator has written that it denied the proposed principle that all rights are linked which was central to some interpretations of the UDHR.

Violations of Human Rights

Human rights violations occur when any state or non-state agency or an individual breaches any part of the UDHR treaty or other international human rights or humanitarian law. In regard to human rights violations of United Nations laws, Article 39 of the United Nations Charter designates the UN Security Council (or an appointed authority) as the only tribunal that may determine UN human rights violations.

Abuses of Human rights are monitored by United Nations committees, national institutions and governments and by many independent non-governmental organizations, such as Amnesty International, International Federation of Human Rights, Human Rights Watch, World Organisation Against Torture, Freedom House, International Freedom of Expression Exchange and Anti-Slavery International. These organisations collect evidence and documentation of alleged human rights abuses and apply pressure to enforce human rights laws.

Only a very few countries do not commit significant human rights violations, according to Amnesty International. In their 2004 human rights report (covering 2003), the Netherlands, Norway, Denmark, Iceland and Costa Rica are the only (mappable) countries that did not (in their opinion) violate at least some human rights significantly.

Wars of aggression, war crimes and crimes against humanity, including genocide, are breaches of International humanitarian law and represent the most serious of human rights violations.

Human Rights in India

The situation of *Human Rights in India* is a complex one, as a result of the country's large size and tremendous diversity, its status as a developing country and a sovereign, secular, democratic republic, and its history as a former colonial territory. The Constitution of India provides Fundamental rights, which include freedom of religion. Clauses also provide for Freedom of Speech, as well as separation of executive and judiciary and freedom of movement within the country and abroad.

As per The Protection of Human Rights Act, 1993 (Amended vide Protection of Human Rights (Amendment) Act, 2006:

> "Human Right means the rights relating to life, Liberty, Equality and Dignity of the individual guaranteed by the constitution or embodied in the International Covenants and enforceable by courts in India."

('International Covenants refer to the International Covenants on Civil and Political right and the International Covenants on Economics, Social and Cultural Rights adopting by the General Assembly of the United Nations on 16 December 1996).

It is often held, particularly by Indian Human Rights groups and activists, that members of the Dalit or Untouchable caste have suffered and continue to suffer substantial discrimination. Although human rights problems do exist in India, the country is generally not regarded as a human rights concern, unlike other countries in South Asia. Based on these considerations, the report Freedom in the World 2006 by Freedom House gave India a political rights rating of 2, and a civil liberties rating of 3, earning it the designation of free.

The *Scheduled Castes and Tribes (Prevention of Atrocities) Act, 1989* was enacted by the Government of India, in order to prevent atrocities against Scheduled castes and scheduled tribes. The purpose of the Act was to help the social inclusion of Dalits into Indian society, but the Act has failed to live up to its expectations.

At the time of independence the Indian Government inherited a large tribal population. The Govt. of India has made a number of plans to protect the rights of the tribals and to integrate them into national developmental planning. The Minority Commission, the National Human Rights Commission etc., are there to prevent atrocities against them and to bring their plight to national lime light. Above all, in the Constitution of India the rights of the tribal's were explicitly recognized and clauses were included to permit positive discrimination in their favour.

The Constitution of India, Article 366 (25) defines Scheduled Tribes as "such tribes or tribal communities or part of or groups within such tribes or tribal communities as are deemed under Article 342 to the scheduled Tribes (STs) for the purposes of this Constitution". In Article 342, the procedure to be followed for specification of a scheduled tribe is prescribed. However, it does not contain the criterion for the specification of any community as scheduled tribe. An often used criterion is based on attributes such as:

- Geographical isolation - they live in cloistered, exclusive, remote and inhospitable areas such as hills and forests.
- Backwardness - their livelihood is based on primitive agriculture, a low-value closed economy with a low level of technology that leads to their poverty. They have low levels of literacy and health.
- Distinctive culture, language and religion - communities have developed their own distinctive culture, language and religion.
- Shyness of contact–they have a marginal degree of contact with other cultures and people.

But the evaluation reports have pointed out that these special provisions have so far failed to bring about any positive gains to the tribal population. As per the Planning Commission Document 1973, "Reviewing the policies and programmes of the proceeding Five Year Plans we are of the opinion that the efforts so far made for social and economic development of the scheduled tribes have not brought an appreciable change in their condition." There can be a number of explanations for the failure of the governmental programmes for tribal development. However, the oppression and appropriation of the tribal people by the economically and politically more powerful groups have led to tribal movements or tribal unrest. For instance, the Santal rebellion, the revolt by Birsa Bhagwan, the Praja Mandal Movement, the Tana Bhagat Movement, the

Naxalbari Movement, the Jharkhand Movement etc., are all attempts by the tribal people to shake off the yoke of exploitation.

In recent times the traditional territories of the tribal people have been subjected to incursions. Their lands are taken away in the name of economic advancement of the country. But in return they receive landlessness, impoverishment and long term degradation of the environment on which they totally depend. For almost two centuries now, tribal communities, like many other non-tribal peasants and forest dwellers, have been witness to the collapse of their multiple relationships with the land, the forest and among themselves. The basis of their cultural ethos, their systems of meaning have faced the collective unslaught of outsider exploiters, the disruptive impact of proselytizing Christianity, and of foreign models of economic betterment which have been conceived without their participation and implemented without their consent. Laws like Land Acquisition Act and the Indian Forest Act legitimise the continuing decline in access and control over forest resources that are the basis of their subsistence economy.

Initiatives from the Bharat-Jan-Andolan, Shosit Jan Andolan, the Indian Council of Indigenous and Tribal Peoples, Adivasi Sangamams in South India, PUCL, PUDR etc., are indicative of these modest attempts to raise - fundamental issues and define an alternative political agenda that frontally challenges the institutions and structures of our bourgeois democracy.

Denotified Tribes

British India notified specified tribes as 'criminal tribes', with all members of the tribe tarred by the same brush, and all of them classed as criminals or potential criminals. The Indian Parliament passed a law in the early years after independence repealing this categorisation of tribes. The 'ex-criminal tribes' are now referred to as 'denotified tribes'. While the status of these tribes has changed in law, the prejudices attaching to treatment of these tribes seems relatively unchanged. The attribution of criminal characteristics to a tribe has not abated. That they continue to be called 'denotified tribes' freezes their status. Rampant discrimination, and criminalisation (different from criminality) was reported. The neglect of land reforms, and of improving their conditions of life, was reportedly allowing for the perpetuation of stereotypes about these communities. The very construction of identity was said to be responsible for the human rights violations that they faced, and was acknowledged as a violation on its own.

The term Criminal Tribes Act (CTA) applies to various successive pieces of legislation enforced in *India* during *British rule;* the first enacted in 1871 as Criminal Tribes Act (Act XXVII of 1871) applied mostly in *North India.* The Act was extended to *Bengal Presidency* and other areas in 1876, and finally with the *Criminal Tribes Act 1911,* it was extended to *Madras Presidency* as well. The Act went through several amendments in the next decade and the finally the Criminal Tribes Act (VI of 1924) incorporated all of them.

The Act came into force, with the assent of *Governor-General of India* on October 12, 1871. Under the act, ethnic or social communities in India which were defined as "addicted to the systematic commission of non-bailable offenses" such as thefts, were systematically registered by the government. Since they were described as 'habitually criminal', restrictions on their movements was also imposed; adult male members of such groups were forced to report weekly to the local police.

At the time of *independence* in 1947, there were thirteen million people in 127 communities who faced constant surveillance, search and arrest without warrant if any member of the group was found outside the prescribed area. Eventually the Act was repealed in August 1949 and former "criminal tribes" were *denotified* in 1952, when the Act was replaced with the *Habitual Offenders Act* 1952 of Government of India, and starting 1961 state governments started releasing lists of such tribes. Today, there are 313 *Nomadic Tribes* and 198 *Denotified tribes of India,* yet the legacy of the Act continues to haunt majority of 60 million people belonging to these tribes, especially as their notification about a century ago has meant not just alienation and stereotyping by the police and the media, but also economic hardships. A large number of them can still only subscribe to a slightly altered label, "Vimukta jaatis" or the Ex-Criminal Tribes.

Denotified tribes (DNTs) are the tribes that were originally listed under the *Criminal Tribes Act* of 187, as *Criminal Tribes* and "addicted to the systematic commission of non-bailable offences." Once a tribe became "notified" as criminal, all its members were required to register with the local magistrate, failing which they would be charged with a crime under the *Indian Penal Code*. The Criminal Tribes Act of 1952 repealed the notification, i.e. 'de-notified' the tribal communities. This act, however, was replaced by a series of *Habitual Offenders Acts*, that asked police to investigate a suspect's criminal tendencies and whether his occupation is "conducive to settled way of life." The denotified tribes were reclassified as habitual offenders in 1959.

The creation of these categories should be seen in the context of colonialism. The *British* authorities listed them separately by creating a category of castes or tribes labelled as criminal.

The name "Criminal Tribes" is itself a misnomer as no definition of tribe denotes occupation, but they were identified as tribes being their primary occupation. The first Census was in 1871 and at that time there was no consensus nor any definition of "tribe". The terms "*Tribe*" and "*Caste*" were used interchangeably for these communities. In this colonial context, the term "Tribe" connoted the notions of primitiveness and backwardness and hence the assumption that these tribes needed to be civilized or transformed.

Indigenous Cultures

The indigenous and ethnic people of the world have learnt to live in most hostile environmental condition in this universe. The most interesting feature associated with these indigenous and ethnic has been found that, they live in localities which are immensely rich in biodiversity. It is estimated that about 300 million indigenous people are living in world, out of which nearly half i.e. 150 million are living in Asia, about 30 million of which are living in Central and South America and a significant number of them are living in Australia, Europe, New

Zealand, Africa, and Soviet Union. A list of some of these prominent ethnic and indigenous people is presented in table -1. These ethnic and indigenous people have played a vital role in conservation of environmental management and development process as they posse's traditional knowledge which has been useful in Eco-restoration. It has been noticed that these people know how to live with harmony in nature.

Indigenous Tribes in India

In India, 68 million people belonging to 227 ethnic groups and comprising of 573 tribal communities derived from six racial stocks namely-Negroid, Proto-Australoid, Mongoloid, Mediterranean, West Breachy and Nordic exists in different part of the country (Pushpgandhan 1). These ethnic people mostly the indigenous tribals live close in the vicinity of forests and have managed and conserved the biodiversity of their localities since long time. These tribals take shelter from forest and utilize wild edible plants both raw and cooked. The flower and fruits are generally eaten raw where as tubers, leaves and seeds are cooked. Tribals utilize forest produce, forest timber and fuelwood. These tribals are living in forest since ages and have developed a kind of affinity with forests. India is a country with large ethnic society and has immense wealth due to which it is rich in biodiversity. There are 45,000 species of wild plant out of which 9,500 species are ethnobotanically important species. Of these 7,500 species are in medicinal use for indigenous health practices. About 3,900 plant species are used by tribals as food (out of which 145 species comprise of root and tubers, 521 species of leafy vegetables, 101 species of bulbs and flowers, 647 species of fruits), 525 species are used for fiber, 400 species are used as fodder, 300 species are used in preparation and extraction of chemicals which are used as naturally occurring insecticides and pesticides, 300 species are used for extraction of gum, resins, dyes and perfume.

Indigenous Culture and Religions

In addition to these a number of plants are used as timber, building material and about 700 species are culturally important from moral, cultural, religious, aesthetic and social point of view of. Indian sub-contient is one of the twelve mega-centres of biodiversity representing two of the eighteen hotspots of biological diversity one occurring in Western Ghat and another in North- Eastern Himalaya (Zeven and Zhikovsky 3). Floristically 141 endemic genera belonging to over 47 families of higher plant occur in India In India 11.95% of the world's biodiversity has been conserved by ethnic people in many ways(Arora,4). Botanical survey of India has reported 46,214 plant species are found in India of global flora of these 17,500 represents flowering plants. Thirty seven of these are endemic and found in North -East of India.

Indigenous Human Rights

One Indigenous Perspective of Human Rights, Irene Watson, an Indigenous lawyer and academic, provides a uniquely Indigenous view of "rights" with particular reference to the Draft UN Declaration on the Rights of Indigenous Peoples and the stonewalling that surrounds acceptance by some member states of the meaning and intent of the term "self-determination" as proposed by Indigenous Peoples. An especially significant element of Watson's chapter is the movement backwards and forwards between her strong Indigenous voice and her articulation of the law in the international human rights arena. Perhaps most appealing to this writer is her frank discussion in a footnote (p. 40) of the misconstruction and misperception surrounding the term "Aboriginal leadership". This discussion should rightfully be developed as a chapter in its own right.

The word *Nomadic Tribes* refers to the people who were forced to live a wandering life by the *Indian Caste System*. The Nomadic and *Denotified Tribes* constitutes of about 60 million in *India,* out of which about five million lives in *Maharashtra.* There are 313 Nomadic Tribes and 198 Denotified Tribes.

Due to wandering traditions of over hundreds of years without any good means of life under the influence of caste system, they are forced to live under sub human conditions. The large section of this tribes is known as *vimukta jatis* or 'ex-criminal castes' because they were branded as criminals by birth under the act *Criminal Tribes Act 1871*, enacted by *British rule in India*.

After independence of India, this act was repealed by *Government of India* in 1952. However, they have been deprived from the status of *Scheduled Tribes* because of some historical circumstances. A large section of these people has converted to *Buddhism* under the leadership of *Laxman Mane*.

The Bhils, Gonds, Santhal, Nahals, and many such ancient tribes of India are the most Adi and the indigenous peoples of this country. They have known with many generic names as autochthons, sons of the soil, Deshaj, Adi Nivasi, Adi Vasi, Adivasi but not vanvasi. They lived here from the time immemorial, even before coming of the Aryans, to these subcontinents, at least to their adi nivases of home lands, or to their deshes. In the context of the Bhils, Gonds and Santhals, their present home land, was not the one in which they are living present times. In many cases and areas of the Adivasis, they were forcefully treated by armed and aggressive peoples who invaded their lands. The Adivasis never invaded or did atikraman (encroachments) of alien territories in history but shared and sheltered others in their land and with their own resources to the incoming peoples, a hospitality matchless with any ethnic groups in India today. But these, in the course of Indian history deprived them of their total resources, forcing them to take shelters in the remotest parts of hilly gorges calling them with derogatory terms such as vanvasis and others as well, prohibited by Atrocity Act of India. Thanks to the Indian Government today for this legal protection. The Bhils, Gonds, Santhals, Mundas, Bhilas and many others are the original peoples of the past. Some of whom have lived in the valley of Ganges even from where they were unseated.

When their ancient geographical space is so badly shrunk socially, culturally, linguistically and politically today, in context of their dear Adivasi/tribal cultures, languages, religions, art, music, songs, myths, legends, folktales, games, indigenous knowledge, world views and values which is vastly influenced over the period of more than 20 centuries, and they are totally subjected today for everything and in everything, then how their overall human rights can be respectfully upheld........? On the contrary they have to learn Sanskrit at the cost of their own tribal languages. When all take English education, excelling in higher studies, in English, only tribals are forced to learn in Hindi and regional languages by state education boards. What a discrimination...? Already in the first stage itself. It is a prime time to revive the ancient tribal histories, cultures, languages, religions, art, symbols, and unite them under tribal geographical regions the Bhils in Bhilanchal, Gonds in Gondwana, Santhals in Santhal Desh, etc., for the preservation, protection and integration of the ancient denied overall human or Adivasi tribal rights. Or else even their names shall be conveniently wiped out from the antique pages of ancient Indian tribal and other histories as the attempts are being done all over India in connection with the tribal/Adivasi names and surnames who shall be rendered soon as Dalits/ Shudras or Chandals.

Would any tribal or the indigenous peoples like their presence be wiped out from the face of ancient and present day history...? If we do not protect ourselves according to the rights given by the Constitution of India, the Bhils and other tribals shall be vanished for ever from the face of ancient Nishad Desh and present Bhilanchal and similarly other tribes in the same way. In order to protect our tribal/Adivasi humanity in the Bhilanchal and other tribal respective regions, for the overall Bhil or tribal/Adivasi rights of their ancient origin, ancient Adivasi regions prehistory, history, culture, ancient Nishad Deshes, encounter with other peoples, look into the transferring of their land into the hands of incoming aggressive and militant peoples, suppression and oppressions of their ancient sublime Adivasi cultures and societies, exploitations today, diminishing of their developmental opportunities, inappropriate division the Bhil, Gond, Santhal and other Adivasi lands in four or more present states of these respective tribes, they should be meticulously studied in equal justice and social eaqualities. If these rights are not protected according to the rights and privileges given in the 5th and 6th Schedules of the great constitution of India, according to the great vision for the indigenous peoples of the country seen by our country's Constitution maker Baba Saheb Bhimrao Ambedkar, then their total rights shall appear to be systematically denied, and we shall appease ourselves eating only crumbs. Many minor tribes have been given with their own tribal states. Then why not Santhals with Santhal Desh, Gonds with Gondwana and the Bhils with BHILANCHAL for the protection of their tribal/ Adivasi human rights in dignified way of national integration....? In the present political scenario, only one party seems to be respecting the human rights of the indigenous peoples. But many media persons are awakened to look into these issues. The tribal intellectuals and other scholars have begun to enlighten the nation. We suppose the dawn of Tribal/ Adivasi human rights is appearing gradually.

State Policy and the Tribals

The edifice of colonial forestry was inherited by the Government of Independent India and immediately put to work in the service of the State's primary goals of repaid industrialization. The National Forest Policy 1952 underlies continuity of the colonial policy. It reinforced the claim of the State to exclusive control over forest protection and production. Significantly this policy identifies shifting cultivation as one of the main threats to State forestry. But in turn this affects the basic rights of the tribals to be dependent on forest resources. Hence, many tribal groups mounted a sustained challenge to the continuing denial of their rights. The Khanwar tribes of Madhya Pradesh protested in 1957 against revenue collection and called upon the people to defy forest laws which violated their customary rights. Their slogan, "Jangal Zamin Azad Hai", (forest and land are free gifts of nature) succinctly expressed the opposition to external control and commercial use. Another concept of conflict is the 'Contractor System' which is the modus operandi of forest working in India. The State's unwillingness to replace the contractor system has given rise to militant movements. Naxalite movement is one of the results of this type of exploitation.

Tribal people's rights being a part of the broad human rights a phenomenon has acquired significance in recent times. As human beings the people who live in tribal lands acquire a similar set of rights like others. Being citizens of the country they are entitled to a number of privileges as well. From time immemorial there have been violations of their fundamental rights. In contemporary society the state comes to their rescue to some extent. The increasing awareness of the concept of human rights under the aegis of the UNO, world media, NGOs etc. proves beneficial to the victims.

Human rights are those conditions which are inherent to nature and without which one can not live as a human being. These rights and fundamental freedoms allow one to develop fully and use one's human qualities, intelligence, talents and conscience to satisfy one's spiritual, physical, social and other needs. They are based on human kind's increasing demand for life in which the inherent dignity and worth of each human being will receive respect and protection.

Human rights constitute a variable category as is adequately demonstrated by the history of the last few centuries. The list of human rights has been modified and continues to be modified in changing historical circumstances. Thus rights may not be fundamental by nature. That which appears to be fundamental in a given historical era or civilization is not fundamental in other era or civilization. Since the time of Hobbes and Locke, liberal political theorists have made it their primary purpose to explore relationships between the individual and the State.

It is not enough to think in terms of two level relationships, the individual at one level and the State at another nor is it enough if the nation is added. Considering the heterogeneity of mankind and of the population of virtually every existing State it is also necessary to think of ethnic communities and certain other kinds of groups, and to include them among the kinds of rights and duties bearing units whose inter relationships are to be explored.

Rights that belong to individuals may go them either as human beings or as members of a group. The Universal Declaration of Human Rights enumerates rights of the first sort;

they go to, "everyone.... without distinction of any kind, such as race, colour, sex, language, religion, political or other opinion, national or social origin, property, birth or other status".

With regard to the legal rights of groups, ethnic communities are sometimes treated as political units within countries, both through territorial delimitations and through the use of separate electoral rolls. Ethnic communities in many countries are differently treated with respect to rights of property and residence; it is not only a question of territorial reservation for the indigenous but also a question of special measures designed to make it possible for the communities to preserve their distinctive identify. In case of less advanced groups that have suffered discrimination, it is now not uncommon to give them a right to expect special measures (affirmative action) designed to promote their quality, e.g. in the educational and economic realms.

Human rights are often held to be inter-related and mutually complementary. According to this view the 'first generation,' civil and political rights form the bedrock of 'second generation' economic, social and cultural rights, while collective and solidarity rights, such as the evolving indigenous rights constitute a 'third generation' of human rights. Further human rights are often said to be compatible with the rule of law and representative democracy. As per Stig Toft. Madsen's (State, society and Human rights in South Asia) hypothesis, "some instances of human rights do not form an integrated whole but are rights in intergenerational conflicts."

The conflict according to Madsen is between the presently dominant 'first generation', civil and political rights professed and guaranteed by a liberal State accepting the ideals of democracy and rule of law and the rights of legal and political, cultural and economic autonomy enjoyed by tribal groups. The outcomes of the conflict between the two incongrous orders of rights has been a working understanding or compromise. While this compromise has guaranteed the survival of tribal cultures, it has also meant that the tribal in question have been denied many of the rights enjoyed by others. So the question is how the tribal autonomy or collective right to autonomy including legal autonomy have circumscribed first generation rights, democracy and the rule of law.

The recent international thinking on indigenous rights is exemplified by the draft of Universal Declaration on the rights of indigenous peoples. According to this draft, "indigenous people have the right to participate fully in the political, economic, social and cultural life of the state while maintaining their distinct political, economic social and cultural characteristics".

The Rio de Janerio Declaration on Environment and Development, adopted on 14th June, 1992 by the United Nations conference proclaims that states should recognize and duly support indigenous peoples' identity, culture and interest and enable their participation in the achievement of sustainable development.

Indigenous people and their communities have an historical relationship with their lands and are generally descendants of the original inhabitants of such lands. They have developed over many generations a holistic traditional knowledge of their lands, natural resources and environment. According to the Rio Declaration, they shall enjoy the full measures of human rights and fundamental freedoms without hindrance or discrimination. Their ability to participate fully in sustainable development practices on their lands have tended to be limited as a result of factors of an economic, social and historical nature.

The International Labour Organisation also in its convention No. 169, year 1989, on "Indigenous and Tribal Peoples", suggested that governments must consult with indigenous and tribal peoples within their countries on development projects and other activities effecting them. It provided for respect for their land rights. This right include protection of their lands and right to refuse displacement form their lands except in exceptional circumstances and against compensation.

Alienation was defined by Hegel and was used by Marx to describe and criticise a social condition in which man far from being the active initiation of the social world seemed more a passive object of determinate external processes. Marx says, alienation is fundamentally a particular relation of property, involving involuntary surrender to autagonistic 'other'.

Alienation is inherent in exploitative relations of production and its nature varies with that of exploitation. Hence alienation's manifestations also differs among societies based on slavery, serfdom and capitalism etc. Thus the concept of alienation may be interpreted to understand a specific problem of the tribals where land becomes the primordial source of exploitation and results in the creation of a society where exploitative production relations exit.

Gender Inequality

Gender is seen as the "psychological, social and cultural aspects of maleness and femaleness" (Kessler and Mckenna 1978). The system of gender virtually organized every realm of our life. It is sometimes difficult to see it in operation because it is universal in nature. It operates as a set of hierarchically arranged roles which makes masculine half of the equation positive and stronger and the feminine negative and weaker. The operation of gender in our society take up these sets of meaning, organizers them as masculinity or femininity, and matches them with male and female body. The feminine behavior is the projection of feminine identity.

Gender discrimination begins even before the birth of girl child. The census data showing the declining female ratio at national level speaks about the gravity of the situation. The practice of sex determination through ultrasound largely started dominating the from late 1970s and early 1980s. Female feticide has become popular with the spread of amniocentesis, a medical technique evolved to discover birth defects. A part of the test involves establishing the sex of the foetus. It is known to us how this test has been misused to kill the female foetus. In this sense, prenatal sex determination tests are basically Human Right violations. It is an extreme manifestation of gender discrimination and violation against women.

In the Indian patriarchal system, women suffer more because they are considered biologically weaker then man. Their status is low in the society and they are victims of all types of deprivations, discriminations, exploitations, oppressions and violence. The convention of the Elimination of All forms of discrimination against women (CEDAW) adopted in 1979 by the UN General Assembly is often described as International Bill of Rights for Women. Consisting of a Preamble and 30 Articles, it defined what constitutes discrimination against women and sets up an agenda for national action to end such discrimination. According to the Convention, discrimination against women is:

> Any distinction, exclusion or restriction made on the basis of sex which has the effect or purpose of impairing or nullifying the recognition, enjoyment or exercise by women, irrespective of their marital status, on a basis of equality of men and women, of Human Rights and fundamental freedom in political, economic, social, and cultural civil or any other field.

Thus, Human rights are everybody's minimal rights. Wherever there is deprivation, discrimination, exploitation and injustices; there is need for Human Rights awareness. In the case of women, Human Rights are doubly required because of overall gender insensitivity in our society.

Sexual Violence in Tribes

Under domestic violence, one of the most common forms of violence that is seen in the country and throughout the world is sexual violence. Few important Researches that were done in Indian Tribes suggest that nearly one in four women may experience sexual violence by an intimate partner, and up to one-third of adolescent girls report their first sexual experience as being forced. In India, sexual violence during first night after wedding is very common especially with the submissive nature of Indian women and the dominance of Indian men. Sexual violence has a profound impact on physical and mental health of an individual. Not just that it also has both immediate and long term consequences. It can have an impact on mental health as on physical as well. Sexual violence can also profoundly affect the social life of the victim.

Sexual violence, especially in domestic violence, is usually a result of the expression of power and dominance of one sex over another in most cases, dominance of the husband over his wife. The problem aggravates when men think that their actions are legitimate just because they are married and that they have full control and power over their wives. Also in our country, women really do not talk about domestic sexual violence because they too think that their husbands have a right to torture them and rape them and that all they can do is shed some tears. This is seen in remote rural areas of the country. Many of the women and men are also be raped when in police custody or in prison. The common consequences of sexual violence are those related to mental health and social wellbeing being disrupted.

Violation of Land Rights

The question of land is not just result of the existing situation but its origin may be traced to the periods of deprivation of tribal lands or to periods of the withdrawal of their rights to exploit forest. Gradually, due to various structural changes within and outside the tribal systems, the more advanced groups forced the tribals either to retreat to the nearest jungles or to become landless labourers. Though land is the only source of their livelihood, as their other assets being extremely meagre, tribals were severally deprived. Basically, moneylenders, traders, the feudal lords, or the rich peasants exploit the tribals most. It is an established fact that there is a large scale alienation of lands which belong to the tribes and grabbers invariably in all cases are the non-tribes. This phenomenon has further been ruined by the emergence of new forces of production. Commenting on this, the National Commission on Backward-Areas Development (1980) says, "In a number of areas new industrial and mining complexes, many major irrigation projects were located in the tribal areas resulting in the submergence of extensive lands belonging to the tribals".

Also in the operations of denudation of forest on a massive scale tribal labour had been used to a great extent to clear off the forest area which was a method of the land lords to alienate the tribals from the forests. This further widened the gap between the tribal landless and landed gentry of the non-tribal communities.

Commenting on the problem of land alienation in tribal areas, the Committee on Plan Projects, Planning Commission, presented a report on the Tribal Development Programmes in 1969. The committee noticed that tribal lands in many areas passed into the hands of non-tribals, the legal prohibitions against such transfers notwithstanding. Sample studies in Andhra Pradesh, Orissa and some other States have shown that transfers have taken place on large scale without the permission of the collector or other competent authorities as required by law. The loopholes were exploited by the money lenders and others and they continue to circumvent the legal provisions by entering into 'benami' or other clandestine transactions with the native tribals. The impotency of legislation to arrest this growing menace to the economic advancement of the tribal in such a situation is thus obvious.

Forms of Land Alienation

The first and foremost is the manipulation of land records. The unsatisfactory state of land records contributed a lot to the problem of land alienation. The tribals were never legally recognized as owners of the lands which they cultivated.

The second form of land alienation is reported to have taken place due to 'benami' transfers. The report of the study team of the Union Home Ministry (May 1975) pointed out that large scale transfers of ownership of the Adivasis' lands are being allowed to go out of hands through illegal and benami transactions, collusive civil proceedings etc., in which land remains to be in the names of the original owners who are reduced to the level of share croppers.

Another form of land alienation is related to the leasing or mortgaging of the land. To raise loans for various needs the tribals have to give their land as mortgage to the local moneylenders or to the rich farmers.

Encroachment is another form of dispossessing the tribals of their lands and this is done by the new entrants in all the places where there were no proper land records. Bribing the local Patwari for manipulating the date of settlement of land disputes, ante-dating etc., are resorted to claim the tribal lands.

Concubinage or marital alliance is another form to circumvent the law and grab tribal lands at no cost at all.

Fictitious adoption of the non-tribals by the tribal families is also another method to snatch the lands of the tribals.

Also the slackness in the implementation of the restrictive provisions encourages the non-tribals to occupy the tribal lands. Lands alienation which takes place in various ways has assumed alarming proportion threatening the right to life of the tribal population. Though the problem lies elsewhere, it is being unfortunately always interpreted as the handiwork of certain individuals like the moneylender, traders, land lords, etc, without understanding the class connection of these individuals. The unsystematic land record of the pre-colonial and colonial periods was followed by the present State. There was collection of 'taxes-(a strange phenomenon for the natives and it was the beginning process of alienation) in the tribal areas.

In the name of protecting the interest of the tribals stringent laws were enacted by the government but the non-tribals found the loopholes to their advantage. This double edged nature of State policy in one of the facets of the existing contradictions in the Indian Tribal Society. The process of land alienation is not an accidental one, but it has arisen because of the concerted efforts of the antagonistic class interest that are operating in the tribal areas. This is not just migration of the non-tribals into tribal areas rather there is a history behind this migration and the State has supported the migrant non-tribals to the settle down in the tribal lands.

However, being the natural owners of forests and its adjoining lands the tribals are being deprived of their rights to own them. They have been relegated from their earlier 'self-reliant' status to a 'dependent' one. Coupled with the exploitation by the non-tribals, the State legislations also proved detrimental to their interests. Therefore to understand the root causes of the land alienation process of the tribal communities its relationship with the changes in the socio-economic structures have to be understood properly.

Religious Violence in Tribes

In Orissa refers to civil unrest and riots in remote forest region surrounding *Kandhamal* in *Orissa* in *India*. Parts of Kandhamal are tribal reservations where only tribal people can own land. Tribals and tribal land are protected by "The *Scheduled Caste* and the *Scheduled Tribes* (Prevention of Atrocities) Act". The largest community in Kandhamal is the Kandha tribe. Most Kandha tribal people follow tribal religions or *Hinduism*. They respect all religions. However, the socio-economic and political landscape is dominated by the second largest community non-tribal Panna who are mostly *Christian*. The region is also home to a *Maoist* terror group which is the largest terror group operating against India and responsible for 3338 deaths in India in five years from 2004 to 2008. Maoist has proclaimed *Hindu nationalist* organizations to be their natural enemy and many local Kandhamal terrorists are Panna-caste-Christians. Major Issues in Kandhamal are Violation of "The Scheduled Caste and the Scheduled Tribes (Prevention of Atrocities) Act" like forcible occupation of tribal land, fake issuance of tribal certificates, illegal building of places of worship mostly churches on tribal land etc, *religious conversions*, re-conversions and terrorism. This has also resulted in Civil unrest and tensions in 1986, 1994 and 2001.

Domestic Violence

In locating domestic violence in the terrain of human rights, one point of view was that it is not the identity of the perpetrator alone which can be allowed to determine whether a victim has been subjected to a human right violation or not: that it is a man or his family who exercises their power to harass, assault and injure a woman, and not the state which is the perpetrator, should then make no difference to the place for this violence in human rights discourse. Also, it is state practice, and endorsement, of patriarchy that keeps such violence in the home-

- Crime against women cells in police stations
- Counseling centres

- Help lines
- Short stay homes - which, though, are few in number have been set up in many cities. There has also been a concerted effort to bring in a law to deal with domestic violence. A Bill prepared, debated and presented to the government by a women's organisation has been adopted by Parliament for discussion, which is a significant step in a non-governmental role in law making. S.498 A was introduced into the Penal Code in 1983. It makes cruelty to a woman within the matrimonial home punishable with imprisonment up to three years and fine. It is a cognisable, non-bailable, offence. Widespread violence against women, and increasing evidence of women dying unnatural deaths in the matrimonial homes provoked the women's movement to demand a change in the criminal law. The offence is non-bailable, that is a complaint under s.498 A, once registered as an FIR, would result in the arrest of the members of the matrimonial family of the woman. They would have to be granted bail by a court before release, and this could keep them in custody for varying periods of time. In matters of remission of sentence, too, offenders convicted under s.498 A may be excluded.

On the one hand, there have been complaints of the misuse of this provision, and the consequent harassment, often incarceration, of many members of the family complained against. On the other, there is little scope to deny that the incidence of cruelty, including physical cruelty, which leads even to death, is extraordinarily high. This is an issue yet unresolved; the Domestic Violence Bill may have some impact on it. In the meantime, an activist lawyer asserts that the phenomenon of violence and death in the matrimonial home should not need to be linked invariably with the phenomenon of dowry; violence and cruelty are independent entities within many homes. An activist also told us: when a man beats his wife regularly, and the wife gets him soundly thrashed by the police, civil liberties groups are sometimes confused on what stand to take.

Child Marriage

Though a law prohibiting child marriage has been in the statute books since 1929, it is still performed in many parts of India. For instance, the practice of performing child marriages in Indian Tribals is occurred. Many tribal's in India who performed the polygeny system of family they practices such type of marriage. In case of Rajasthan, Uttarakahnd, Uttar Pradesh, Madhya Pradesh and Bihar it is reported, has not stopped in tribal community.

Child Labour

Apart from the employment of children in work, including those classified as hazardous, it was reported that:

- Children continue to be sold into labour. The parents of a young tribal's girl from Assam were paid a sum of money for the girl to be brought to Delhi as a domestic worker. Her plight came to light when she ran away from the ill-treatment she suffered, and she was given shelter by a social activist.
- Child workers employed in homes and in commercial workplaces were subjected to ill-treatment. The chaining of bonded child labour in the carpet industry near Varanasi so that they could not escape was reported. In Maharashtra, a civil liberties organisation took the state and a contractor to court when the latter ill-treated, resulting in death, one of the young boys he had brought with him from Tamil Nadu. These manifestations of violence against the child disguised as child labour calls to be addressed. The vulnerability of the child has also been seen in Delhi, for instance, where child domestic workers have been accused of killing their employers, or in being accomplices to outsiders. The 'social clause' on child labour does not result in doing away with child labour, we were told, but causes segregation. There were dissenting voices on the ILO Convention on the Elimination of the Worst Forms of Child Labour. The provisions which speak of child prostitution and child

> pornography as labour are unacceptable, they said. 'These are crimes, not labour,' we were told. Further, when Indian law is so strict that it says that non-payment of minimum wages amounts to bonded labour - a provision that is not found in any international convention – what use is one more convention, we were asked.

In 1993, the Supreme Court declared that education is a fundamental right till a child reaches the age of 14 years. Education for the child has got tangled with the issue of child labour; sending the child to school is projected as a necessary step to ending the practice of child labour. In Andhra Pradesh, an organisation working in the area of education for children has done away with the uncertainties of definition by working on the premise that every child out of school is child labour. They have therefore arrived at a non-negotiable: that every child must belong in a school. In this view, NFE (non-formal education) centres, for instance, would be a means of perpetuating child labour. So, too, with the adjusting of school timings to accommodate the working child. In the meantime, this 1999 Convention is being canvassed for signature, and ratification by the Indian State. The convention defines 'the worst forms of child labour' as comprising:

(a) all forms of slavery or practices similar to slavery, such as the sale and trafficking of children, forced or compulsory labour, debt bondage and serfdom;

(b) the use, procuring or offering of a child for prostitution, for the production of pornography or for pornographic performances;

(c) the use, procuring or offering of a child for illicit activities, in particular for the production and trafficking of drugs as defined in the relevant international treaties;

(d) work which, by its nature or the circumstances in which it is carried out, is likely to jeopardize the health, safety or morals of children.'

This is in consonance with the recent trend among UN organizations (e.g., WHO) to directly involve human rights in standard-setting, and the creating of binding obligations of states in their area of operation.

Child Abuse

There has been increasing evidence of child abuse, and more particularly child sexual abuse, being pervasive. The perpetrator is often a near relative or someone close to the family. This adds to the vulnerability of the abused child, and, apart from the confusion and sense of shame which the child experiences, it is also that there is a problem with a refuge which the child can access. The dependence on the family as a support structure in times of abuse breaks down when the offending event occurs in the home.

Following what is widely considered as a useful intervention in the Supreme Court in the *Vishaka* guidelines regarding sexual harassment in the workplace, the matter of child abuse has also been taken to the court, and the Law Commission has been inducted into setting the parameters for care and action in cases of child sexual abuse.

The 'Unwanted' Girl Child

The declining sex ratio, particularly the declining juvenile sex ratio, even in Kerala which is celebrated in economic writings and in state policy for having achieved a high rate of literacy and negative population growth, has begun to seriously engage, among others, researchers and women activists. The low status of women continues to be reflected in:

- The practice of infanticide including in some parts of Tamil Nadu,
- foeticide,
- Sex-selective abortion which the amniocentesis technology has made common, and
- Mal-nourishment among girl children.

In Usilampatti Taluk, reportedly, the ratio of female: male is 879:1000. Since 1986, the issue of female infanticide has been in focus in this area. More recently, scanning centres have mushroomed in the area, and female foeticide is rampant among those who are able to afford it. We were told that, in Tamil Nadu, there are around 2000 scan centres, most of which are unregistered.

A researcher reported his encounter with the sale of girl children by communities in Andhra Pradesh to persons who then placed them for adoption. He drew attention to the astonishing fact that there is, as of now, no law to control, or punish, the sale of children. The involvement of adoption agencies in A.P. in what is allegedly the sale of children has since come to public attention, in April 2001.

Abortion in the context of Women's Health and Sex Selective Abortion

When Parliament passed the 1971 law legalising abortion under certain conditions, the statement of objects and reasons listed three reasons for passing the law:

- As a health measure - when there is danger to the life or risk to the physical or mental health of the woman;
- On humanitarian grounds - such as when pregnancy arises from a sex crime like rape or intercourse with a lunatic woman, etc.; and
- Eugenic grounds - where there is substantial risk that the child, if born, would suffer from deformities and diseases.'

By 1995, when the Maternity Benefit Act 1961 was amended, the insertion of population control provisions into the law was being acknowledged, and resisted. The 1995 amendment, however, did give a renewed emphasis to placing the onus for family size on the woman when it incorporated 'leave with wages for tubectomy operation' as a 'maternity benefit', even as it gave medical termination of pregnancy the same position in law as miscarriage. This is a statement of the adoption of abortion as state supported policy.

The question of abortion as a right, and abortion as a population control measure may need to be re-visited.

There was also a proposal to limit the provision of maternity benefit under the Act to women workers up to the second child;

this however seems to have been dropped, perhaps because of the protest that met the proposal at almost every turn. The Pre-natal Diagnostic Techniques (Regulation and Prevention of Misuse) Act 1994, which was modelled on an earlier Maharashtra law, was enacted expressly 'to prohibit pre-natal diagnostic techniques for determination of sex of the foetus leading to female foeticide. Such abuse of techniques is discriminatory against the female sex and affects the dignity and status of women. The punishment for transgressing the prohibition of the law is intended to be deterrent. Yet, in the seven years since the law was enacted, there have been no prosecutions of which any of our respondents made mention. The conflict inherent in asking for abortion as a matter of right, and believing that sex selective abortion needs to be curbed requires to be squarely addressed.

Women Trafficking (Prostitution)

The fear of AIDS, it is perceived, has given the issue of prostitution a visibility. This has; however, led to attributing to women in prostitution the trait of being a 'high risk group', even as it has been contended that it is high risk behaviour and not high risk groups that should be targeted. It appears that patterns of funding have impacted on this identification of the prostitute woman as belonging to a high-risk group. The demand for prostitution to be recognised as 'sex work' has been raised, with dignity of the woman in prostitution as its basis.

There are differing perceptions about prostitution - one which sees it as exploitative of women, and another that views it as representing the 'agency' of the women in the profession. There are various shades of meaning given to 'exploitation' and 'agency' which lies in the spaces between these two positions. Decriminalisation is also proposed, and disputed, on differing understandings of what decriminalising will mean, and do. Most of the people we spoke to on the issue of prostitution, however, felt after a discussion emphasizing the difference, that the practice of prostitution should be delinked from the issue of trafficking. In this context, trafficking is seen to be the sale and purchase of women and girls, and, more recently, boys, into prostitution. While 'voluntariness' is a term with graded meanings, especially since economic compulsions and social exclusion are not uncommon causes for entering into the practice of prostitution, it is the distinctly involuntary nature of trading in human beings that is at the hub of trafficking. Trafficking in minors is a scourge that is commonly referred to as a crime to be curbed. We encountered the issue of organising women in prostitution in two different ways. In Calcutta, a 'samiti' of sex workers are articulating their position, and taking a pro-active lead in matters of preventing the entry of minors into the profession in their area of operation. They also said that, if trafficking be seriously dealt with, they be allowed to, legally, participate in curtailing trafficking - for who else was more likely than the people already in the profession to know when women and girls were bought and sold, they asked.

In Mumbai, a respondent working among prostitute women for over a decade, advocated 'collectivisation' but had a problem with adopting the norm of forming unions of women in prostitution. While she did find that the state was doing very little about trafficking, she was convinced that if sex work were seen as 'real work' under the law, all efforts to curb trafficking would cease. It was also suggested that 'sex work is real work' is a funderdriven agenda, and, that those who do not adopt this line were being deliberately excluded.

In Kerala, however, a different perspective emerged where a distinction was drawn between the demand that persons in sex work should get all labour rights and the rights based approach. As a feminist, our respondent espoused the rights based approach. There was recognition that most feminist ideologies oppose commercial sex workers coming together; the commercialisation of the body was identified as the problem. Also, most people do not believe in the agency of commercial sex workers, it was explained. There was an opposition to licensing since that would only lead to further exploitation. The issue has been invisibilised over the years, and with people in high places being involved, it has helped to send it further underground. The *Surinelli* and *Vidhura* cases have however increased confidence to complain; and people are now listening differently. Another women's activist opposed the use of the term 'commercial sex worker': prostitution is not productive work, she said. But her main problem was that she saw prostitution as reinforcing patriarchy, and that endorsing prostitution as work would fall into the snare patriarchy has set for the women's movement.

In the matter of trafficking, it was pointed out that proposals for checking all women travelling on their own, particularly across borders was a move detrimental to the interests of women and could end up curbing their right to free movement and achieve little else.

Bonded Labour

Though the Bonded Labour Act is of 1976 vintage, it was not till the Supreme Court's judgment in December 1983 that the recognition of bonded labour acquired a national reach. As the champion of the bonded labour said it, it is:

- Minimum wages
- Minimum guarantees of employment
- Child labour
- Land rights and
- Alcohol

That needs to be dealt with to get people an experience of human rights. Identification, release and rehabilitation of bonded labour have happened essentially by court supervision. In Tamil Nadu, Uttarkahnd, Uttar Pradesh there is a separate ministry that has been set up to deal with bonded labour; this was following a report given to the Supreme Court of the extent of bonded labour prevalent in the state.

The issue of bonded labour has been handed over by the court to the NHRC, which has set up a committee including activists, advocates and bureaucrats with experience, to find a means of dealing with the issue. We watched while a political activist working among bonded labour discoursed with a body of bonded labourers from Rajasthan. They were seeking his help in getting free, and getting land which could help them retain their liberty. The advice was that they get together a mass of similarly positioned people before launching a campaign in their district. The confidence they exuded that bringing together 25,000 people in the district would not be an unmanageable task was an indication of the dimensions of the problem of bonded labour.

Case Studies

Tribals of Mayurbhanj District in Orissa

Orissa occupies a special position in the tribal map of India. In the State the Scheduled Tribes Constitute 22.21%. There are 62 different types of tribes in the State. Mayurbhanj is one of the most tribally dominated districts, lying at the Northern border of Orissa. This district was formed in 1949 out of the ex-State of Mayurbhanj. The percentage of Scheduled Tribes in the district in nearly 58.56%. The district is extremely important from anthropological point of view. It is inhabited by almost all the important tribes found in the eastern region of India through it is a fact that only a few of them have a concentrated settlement here e.g. the Santals, Hos, Bhunyas, Bhumijas, Bathuris and Gonds etc. The basic tribal population of the district is therefore formed by these six principal tribes.

As it has happened in other tribal parts of this country, the tribals of Mayurbhanj are also not spared off. Land alienation is rampart here. Due to poor economic conditions and illiteracy the tribes have not been able to understand the vicious circle thrown by their non-tribal exploiters. The Tribal Research Bureau conducted surveys and studies to analyze the relationship between the tribals and non-tribals who settled down in tribal areas e.g. an untouchable caste, Dom and Pano, the first non-tribals to settle down on the hills, live in intimate relationship with the Kandhas and Saoras of South Orissa. Similarly milkmen oilman and others live with the Juangs and Paudi Bhunyas of North Orissa. Many researchers put this relationship of the tribals with the non-tribals as parasitism but sometimes a symbiotic relationship is also found between them. Indebtedness among the tribals is a chronic malady. Schemes by the State Government have been bogged down in bureaucratic red-tapism. According to the Tribal Research

Bureau the original purpose of these schemes is lost sight of. The two major steps by the Govt. of Orissa to prevent land alienation of the tribals are,

(i) Orissa Scheduled Areas Transfer of Immovable Property (by STs) Regulation, 1956, provides for the control and check of the transfers made by the scheduled tribes to the non-scheduled tribes in the Scheduled Areas.

(ii) Also outside the Scheduled Areas, alienation of land of the scheduled tribes has been restricted under Orissa Land Reformed Act, 1960.

Though Mayurbhanj possesses enormous forest wealth, the tribal people have no freedom to enjoy its benefits. Even for making agricultural implements they have to seek permission of the authorities. Permission to cut fire wood is available on payment of a stipulated amount. Sardari system of collection of land revenue gave enough scope for the feudal practices to survive. In the Colonial revenue administration Sardars, Tehsildars and Lakrajdars were the intermediaries. Notwithstanding various welfare measures introduced by the Colonial Government, there seemed to be a deep-seated unrest among the peasants of Mayurbhanj which provided congenial atmosphere for the growth of Prajamandal Movement during 1930s and 40s.

The tribal composition of Mayurbhanj is another important aspect of its history. The tension between the tribals and non-tribals often resulted in violent outburst leading to direct intervention by the Govt. The Kol insurrection and the Bamanghaty disturbances were instances which speak of tribal's refusal to accept a alien system.

However, in order to understand the present tribal problem of land alienation in Mayurbhanj a general background of the land structure of the district is to be analyzed starting from the pre-colonial phase. Also an analysis is to be made to understand the changing pattern of the land structure in Orissa's plains and its effect over the neighboring forest regions that lead to the fast depeasantisation of the tribal communities. As this depeasantisation has emerged as criteria of the class antagonisms, its effects are to be examined in the district. Above all, the failures of State Govt.'s policy and the result of such failures are to be found out.

However, there is an imperative to project the land alienation of the tribals as human rights violation and to bring to attention of the government as well as non-government agencies. Nowadays the awareness of human rights brings about a certain awakening and often generates courage of tribals to stand up for their own rights. As far as the concept of tribal rights are concerned the challenges are to make the tribals aware of judicial systems, prepare them for political participation, create opportunity for equality, prepare them for self-governance to guarantee rights to traditional natural resources, provide them land rights etc.

Also the Tribal - Sab-Plan, the Bhuria Committee Recommendations, the Constritution's 73rd and 74th Amendments etc., are the recent endeavours by the State to remove socio-economic backwardness of the tribal population and to integrate them into the national mainstream of development and progress.

This book written by B. Janardhan Rao in based on empirical studies of tribal areas in Andhra Pradesh, particularly of Warangal district. Very aptly he discusses the concept of alienation in the beginning. Starting from Hegel to Marx he points out the structural functionalist approach to it. Then he gradually proceeds to examine the existing land laws and administrative arrangements of Andhra Pradesh Govt., as far as the tribal areas are concerned. The process of depeasantisation has also been highlighted. He identified the agents who reign in the regime of exploitation in tribal areas.

Though he has pointed out the causes of land alienation yet he fails to give possible solutions to prevent it. Moreover, he has not dealt with the bigger aspect of human rights violation of the tribal population as a result of land alienation.

Tribals of Meghalaya

The *Khasi* are a tribe in Meghalaya, formerly part of Assam in north-eastern India and in parts of Bangladesh, who call themselves *Ki Hynñiew trep* which means "the seven huts" in the *Khasi language*. Their language, also called Khasi, was essentially oral until the arrival of European missionaries, and particularly significant in this regard was the Welsh missionry *Thomas Jones*, who transcribed the Khasi language into the Roman Script. The *Khasi* people form the majority of the population of the eastern part of Meghalaya. Most Khasi are *Presbyterian*, Anglican, *Roman Catholic*, or followers of the original Khasi religion *Ka Niam Tynrai*, although there is a tiny *Unitarian* presence, as well. Some Khasi reside in the hilly areas of *Sylhet*, Bangladesh. The Khasi tribes are usually dependent upon *jhoom* cultivation in which the vegetation is left to grow totally under the care of nature. In Bangladesh, one of the main products produced by the Khasi using *jhoom* cultivation is *betel*

The Khasis consist of four sub-tribes, Khynriam, Pnar, Bhoi and War, the Khasis or Khynriam inhabiting the Khasi Hills proper, the *Pnar* or *Syntengs* the Jaintia Hills and the steep southern slopes leading to Bangladesh. The Bhoi live in the lower hills to the north and north-east of the Khasi and Jaintia Hills towards the Brahmaputra valley. The Lynngam people who inhabit the western parts of the Khasi Hills display linguistic and cultural characteristics which show influences from both the Khasis to their east and the Garo people to the west. The *Wars* inhabit the precipitous slopes and deep valleys to the south of the district.

Khasi from different regions have small, but noted differences. They are descendants of *Mon-Khmer* speakers who migrated probably from *Mongolia* to Meghalaya. Most Khasi have brown to light yellow skin, epicanthic folds, high nasal bridges and aquiline noses. The Khasis have a *matrilineal* and *Matrilocal* society. Descent is traced through the mother, but the father plays an important role in the material, mental life of the family and social welfare. According to Khasi laws, a woman cannot be forced into marriage, she owns the children and properties. In Khasi tradition, the youngest daughter will also inherit the property. A woman may end a marriage at her will with no objection from her husband. The Khasi have an unusual dedication toward matrilineal customs, most notably similar to the *Minangkabaus.* These are various sort of violation of Human Rights which can be viewed as in the Table 1.

Table 1
Forms of Attrocities Among Khasi Tribals

Attrocities	*Khasi (Meghalaya)*
Land Alienation Cases	23
Police Torture	2
Rape	3
Women Attrocities (Domestic Volilenec)	12
Forest Attrocities	26
Robbery	2
Murder	14
Child Marriage	5
Total	87

Tribals of Uttaranchal

Bhoksa or *Buksa* are *indigenous people* living mainly in the Indian states of Uttarakhand (Foothill Bhoksas) and Uttar Pradesh (Tarai Bhoksas). They are most concentrated in the Nainital district in the *Kumaon foothills* of the outer Himalayas. The Bukshas are inhabitants of the Terai, although their locality falls in the Western fringes of Nainital (now Udham Singh Nagar) and borders that of the Tharus. Buksa is the second major tribes in Uttrakand. Although they claim descent from Rajputs (like the Tharus they are of Tibetan descent), the Bukshas have merged all their castes and even today, observe only *septs* (family names) among their people. Bukshas still worship Hindu gods, though also accept the existence of spirits and eat meat. In addition, a *Seyana* (literally, "Wise One") also administers to their medical/spirit needs. Bukshas build their houses in two rows, with the space in between serving as a courtyard. As shifting cultivators, the Bukshas made the best of the protection afforded them by the inhospitable and malarial marshes of the Terai. However, since the *coming of migrants* from other states throughout the 1950s and 1960s, the Bukshas have lost much of their land. Many have ended up as labourers for the new masters who gained their land through foul and unlawful means.

The law generally prohibits the transfer of land from a tribal to a non-tribal in agency areas, or scheduled areas, except for reasons recognised by law, and by procedure prescribed therein. While this is usually respected as fair and legitimate protection extended to scheduled tribes, and to prevent exploitation of the tribal by the non-tribal, the situation in Uttarakand has been somewhat complicated. The state legislature enacted the Uttarakhand Scheduled Tribes Restriction on Transfer of Lands and Restoration of Alienated Lands Act. The law has had a chequered career, with the government attempting to dilute the effect of the law, by amendment, and the courts demanding its implementation. The question of alternative land rather than restoration has also been mooted – but it is not clear that such alternative land exists. While tribal activists have been campaigning for enforcing the law, others have been muted in their reactions. The reason, our respondents say, is because the land appears to have been transferred for a price to settlers who are themselves only marginalised populations. It would be unjust and iniquitous to dislodge them from lands for which they have paid as much as they can afford, it was said. This was represented as a case of conflicting interests, but of two equally, if differently, affected communities. Rehabilitation of the already displaced adivasi community appears to be one way of resolving the issue - a view with which tribal activists do not concur, considering it as an erosion, even a denial of the right against alienation of land.

Various forms of atrocities are noted during the study in the last calendar year. Such atrocities are a form of violation of Human Rights found in Uttarakhand (Foothill Bhoksa) and Uttar Pradesh (Tarai Bhoksa). Table 2 depicts the ststus of Human Rights violation in the two groups of the Bhoksa tribe:

Though the Bonded Labour Act is of 1976 vintage, it was not till the Supreme Court's judgment in December1983 that the recognition of bonded labour acquired a national reach. In Uttakahand, there is a tribes namely Jaunsari. They are work as bonded labours whole life, because during the ceremony

Table 2
Form of Attrocities Among Bhoksas

Attrocities	*Tarai Bhoksa (Udham Singh Nagar)*	*Foothill Bhoksa (Dehradun & Haridwar)*	*Total*
Land Alienation Cases	7	12	19
Police Torture	2	1	3
Rape	3	2	5
Women Attrocities (Domestic Volilenec)	19	11	30
Forest Attrocities	21	26	s47
Robbery	2	–	2
Murder	2	1	3
Child labour	2	4	6
Women Trafficking	5	7	12
Total	63	53	116

they took lots of many to Sahukar. After that they are bounded for ever separate ministry that has been set up to deal with bonded labour; this was following a report given to the Supreme Court of the extent of bonded labour prevalent in the state. The issue of bonded labour has been handed over by the court to the NHRC, which has set up a committee including activists, advocates and bureaucrats with experience, to find a means of dealing with the issue. We watched while a political activist working among bonded labour discoursed with a body of bonded labourers from Rajasthan. They were seeking his help in getting free, and getting land which could help them retain their liberty. The advice was that they get together a mass of similarly positioned people before launching a campaign in their district. The confidence they exuded that bringing together 25,000 people in the district would not be an unmanageable task was an indication of the dimensions of the problem of bonded labour.

Tribals of Uttar Pradesh

The Tharu people mainly live in the *Surkhet Valley* in the west mountain region, Chitwan Valley, Dang Valley,Deukhuri

Valley,Sindhuli and Udyapur in *Inner Terai Valleys of Nepal* and the *Terai plains* on the border of Nepal and India. The population of Nepal is 28,287,147, of which the Tharu people make up 6.6%. A large number of Tharus live in India, mostly in Champaran District of Bihar and in Nainital District of Uttarakhand, Pilibhit, Lakhimpur, Bahraich, Gonda, Shrawati, Mahrajganj and Gorkhpur districts of Uttar Pradesh.

Tharus social system of resource prevails in hunter-gatherer and shifting cultivation. In these system Tharus control a certain land area, its territory as community property. The pattern of resource use on this land, including allocation of plots exchanges with the outside, for instance, honey and ivory for mental. However, such exchanges are quantitatively insignificant. This meant that the tribal population has a real stake in the security of resource base of their territory and evolve a number of cultural traditions to ensure its sustenance. These not only included long fallows in the cycle of rotation of shifting cultivation, but also selective retention of valuable trees. But after the making of Forest law numbers of restrictions enforced by the Governments. So they are left the forest and forest land. Due to this they face livelihood problem.

The first and foremost is the manipulation of land records. The unsatisfactory state of land records contributed a lot to the problem of land alienation. The Tharu tribe have no own land they are only work in agricultural land as a worker. Because, tharu are very poor and they take lone to local moneylender or rich farmers for various needs. After few months their lone is more than the original amounts. In this situation, moneylenders are takeover their land. Such form of land alienation is related to the leasing or mortgaging of the land. Tharu tribes are never legally recognized as owners of the lands which they cultivate. Therefore socio-economic structures of the tharu peoples are very low. The situation of Human Rights is also not plausible. Various atrocities may be encountered if the five endogamous groups are observed closely. The reperted cases of attrocities are given in the following table.

Table 3
Forms of Attrocities Among Tharus Tribals of Uttaranchal & Uttar Pradesh

Attrocities	*Rana (Naninital)*	*Jogia (Naninital)*	*Katharia (Gonda, Bahraich)*	*Donguria (Gonda, Bahraich)*	*Pachhimaha (Mahrajganj)*	*Total*
Sexual Harasment	–	3	5	8	–	16
Abuse	5	1	3	4	4	17
Bounded labour	2	–	1	1	–	4
Robbery	5	9	10	2	3	29
Domestic Voilence (Women Atrrrocities)	1	2	1	1	1	6
Police Harrasment	2	1	5	8	1	17
Land Alienetion	–	5	21	27	–	53
Forest Attrocities	6	4	7	3	5	25
Women Trafficking Child Marriage	7	4	6	3	9	29
Total	28	29	59	57	23	204

Patharkatta/ Kanjars or Grihar

Patharkatta/ Kanjars or *Grihar* are nomadic people who were recognized as a tribe by William crook (1891). In this computer age they are still living with their primitive stones. Their economy is based on stone work, hunting and food gathering. They generally live in form of groups and lives in huts with their pets. They settle temporarily around cities or close to the village and move from place to place to sell their products. Their facial feature subscribe to some Mongoloid strains. But they ascertain there origin from Rajputana land (Rajasthan). Carving stone grinding states and wheels and weaving ropes and making brooms, brush, flower, pots etc. are there major profession. They also hunt brides and animals and gather fruits and tubers and honey too. All of them are mostly landless. Mostly about are 95% illiterate. They basically worship Mata Allahabadin and Mata Maharani as their Principal deity. They bury as well as cremate their dead.s Because they are nomadic Kushabadiya/Patharkatta can be compact to Routes. The only differences in those routes roam in Jungles where as Patharkatta go around they vicinities of settlements. Recently however they have started to settle at one place. The main areas of Patharkatta are U.P., Rajasthan, Uttarnchal, Karnataka, Chattisgadh & Mid Western terai region in western development region. They have there won dialects. They have distinct rites for birth, marriage & death. They slaughter Pig worship family deities and drink wine/sprit when a son is born in the family. They prefer marriage with won closed relatives but not of same Kuri. They have there won social organization. There is always a community Chief present in between who control them.

They practice group endogamy but clan is exogamous. They marry their son/daughter with the members of other clans. It shows clan exogamy but they never marry their won son/daughter outside of Patherkatta community.

There is a rule of marriage that is they at ways marry their Son/Daughter with other Gotra (Kuri) and that Kuri should be higher than their won Kuri or they marry in other Kuri which is equal to there won Kuri. In marriage they practice bride wealth payment instead of dowry.

Reported cases of attrocities in Pattarkatta Tribe are given in Table 4. It shows that women attrocities are many as compared to other cases found in the tribes.

Table 4
Reported Cases of Attrocities among Patharkatta Tribals

Attrocities	*Patharkatta/Kanjar (Uttar Pradesh)*	*Patharkatta (Rajasthan)*	*Total*
Child Labour	18	9	27
Child Marriage	7	5	12
Police Torture	32	21	52
Rape	23	26	49
Women Attrocities (Domestic Violence)	52	43	95
Women Trafficking	14	7	21
Robbery	14	9	23
Murder	18	12	30
Total	178	132	310

Tribals of Jharkhand and Madhya Pradesh etc.

Tribals in India constitute around eight per cent of the total population. Oraon is one of the tribal communities found in India, which *mainly depends on agriculture* for earning their living. They are also known as Kurukh tribes. These tribes are mainly found in the states of Jharkhand, Bihar, West Bengal and Orissa. In the ancient days, Oraons used to make their living by chopping timber and selling forest products. Majority of the population of Oraons can be found in Northeastern states engaged in the occupation of tea cultivation.

The *Oraon* or *Kurukh* tribe (*Kurukh*), also spelled *Uraon, Oran,* or *Oram,* inhabits various *states* across central and eastern India as well as Bangladesh. Traditionally, Oraons depended on the forest and farms for their ritual and economic livelihood, but in recent times they have become mainly settled agriculturalists. Small numbers of Oraons have immigrated to the northeastern part of India, where they are mainly employed in tea estates. A number of educated Oraons have settled down in metros like Kolkata, Delhi, Mumbai,Chennai and many other cities of India including Patna, Bhopal, Bhubaneswar,

Hyderabad, Allahabad, and Lucknow. Today a large number of Oraons live in Jharkhand, Orissa and parts of Chhatisgarh, Bihar, West Bengal. During the colonial era, the Tana Bhagats, led by their Tana saint Turia Bhagat, protested against the imperialists by not paying the 'chaukidari' tax while the Bishnu Bhagats under Bhikku Bhagat.

The Oraon language, *Kurukh*, belongs to the *Dravidian family*, and is most closely related to *Brahui* and Malto (Paharia). Kurukh language is being taught in Ranchi University in Jharkhand. A Kurukh Literary Society have been formed after the first Kurukh Conference held in Ranchi in October, 2006. Many Kurukh language magazines are being published from various parts of India.

The Oraon people have a rich and vast range of *folk songs, dances* and tales, as well as traditional *musical instruments.* Both men and women participate in dance, which are performed at social events and festivals. Mandar, Nagara and kartal are the main musical instruments.

A sizable numbers of Oraon have immigrated to the northeastern part of India, where they are mainly employed in tea estates of West Bengal, Assam, and Tripura. A sizable numbers of Oraon have settled down in North Bihar and in Nepal. Many have settled down in the lower part of Bhutan (Samchi district).

Kartik Oraon, who was a highly educated Oraon, an Indian Congress leader and former state communication minister of India, *Albert Ekka,* the Paramveer Chakra awardees, and the *Roman Catholic Archbishop* of Ranchi, *Cardinal Telesphore Placidus Toppo and Dilip Tirkey,* former Captain of the Indian Hockey Team are all Oraons.

The Oraon people have a rich and vast range of folk songs, dances and tales, as well as traditional musical instruments. Both men and women participate in dance, which are performed at social events and festivals. The majority of Oraon write their *gotra* along with their name. However, those who follow Tana Bhagat principle or Sarna Dharma write the *Bhagat* in place of their gotra. Many prefer to write Oraon as a second name in place of a gotra. Majority of oraon write their gotra

(Kerketta, *Xalxo*, Xaxa, Xess, Tirkey, Toppo, Tigga, Kujur,Minz, Ekka Barla, Barwa, *Indwar* or *Ind*, Lakra, Beck, Dhanwar, Baghwar, Kachhap, kindo, Kispota, kanda, Kokro, Gaddi, Khoya, Chermanko,Dadel, Niya, Panna, Bakula, Basa, Bando, Bhagat, Binko, Beck, Munjni, Runda, Linda, Son, Rawna, etc.) with their name. However, those who follow Tana Bhagat principle or Sarna Dharma write Bhagat in place of gotra. Many Oraon who have converted to Chritianity have opted new names in place of gotra like some Toppo clan writes their second name (gotra) as Marjec. Some oraon write Mody and Rath in place of oraon traditional gotra systems, specially in Orissa. Oraon prefer to marry a oraon only. However, Christian Oraon often marry other caste and community (Munda, Kharia, Santal)due to influence of Christianity. However, Sarna Oraon prefer marriage with a oraon only with full traditional fashion.

In the heartland of West Bengal, quite a number of tribes reside in great freedom and independence. According to the census report of the year 1971, Oraon tribes are one of the biggest tribes in the whole of south Asia numbering 1,702,663 persons. These Oraon tribes converse with each other in Kurukh, a popular language belonging to the family of Dravidian family. Due to their amiable nature, these Oraon tribes live in close association with their adjoining tribes like Munda. In fact the chief of the Oraon tribes is called as Munda.

If one dissects the Oraon society, it can be segregated into several sub castes. These include Kudas ("navvies") and Kisans ("cultivators"), having their diverse occupations, tend to marry among themselves. Beyond this, Oraon tribes abide by the village and clan exogamy. The patrilineal extended family is the supreme residential unit, and also nuclear families are also prevalent. On the average a family contains five to seven co resident members.

Following the practice of several tribes of India, these Oraon tribes follow the trend of sending these Oraon youths to the dormitories. These dorms are called dhumkuria. Boys are marked on the arm before being allowed in to this establishment. The dormitory also gives a supply of farming labor that can be employed when and where necessary. Thus needs no mentioning that most of the Oraon tribal communities have taken up the profession of cultivation, mainly the shifting just like their ancestors used to adapt in the earlier times. Although hunting profession was given due importance, later it has become only an affair as part of the ceremonial event. Moreover, now days, a special hunting ceremony also is feted exclusively for women folks of Oraon society .It is observed every twelve years.

Those anthropologists who have conducted surveys on Oraon tribes and its various aspects of Culture and tradition, have unanimously came to the conclusion that these tribes are religious minded mostly following the customs of Hinduism. Their foremost gods and goddesses are indigenous, mostly non-Sanskritic, namely, Chandi, Chauthia, Dadgo Burhia, Gaon Deoti, and Jair Budhi. What is interesting to note that nowhere else in India these deities are being worshipped. Only a small section of people, near about twenty five percent, follow Christianity.

There is a significant feature of this Oraon tribal society for which they are being widely known. In fact Oraon society is amongst those few handfuls of tribes in the whole world who till date carrying on the age old custom of doing human sacrifices. All the Oraon tribes regard this practice of this human sacrifice as otanga or orka. Even in the records of during the nineteenth century, British officials accounted about these Oraon tribes including some other tribes including Munda, Oraon, Gond, Kond, and Santal tribes.

As per the police records show that even as late as the 1980 and onwards there were a couple of sacrifices every year among Oraon tribes and others like Munda and Maria. The human sacrifices by and large take place in distant places around the beginning of the sowing season and the associated festival of Sarhul. Sometimes blood of the sacrificial victim is amalgamated with seed grain before it is sown. In former centuries the whole body was probably cut up and parceled out to the various fields around a village.

The sacrifice is as a rule presented to a malicious goddess in order to appease her and also control the lushness of the soil. However, when these Orean tribes could not find any of the human beings for offering at the time of sowing ceremony, the usual practice is to use hair, sputum, or some other human bodily leavings instead. These are blended with the blood of a hen as a token offering to this deity.

The *Gond* (Gôndi) are a people in central India. They are spread over the states of Madhya Pradesh, eastern Maharashtra (Vidarbha), Chhattisgarh, northern Andhra Pradesh, and western Orissa. With over four million people, they are the largest *tribe* in Central India. The *Gondi language* is related to Telugu and other *Dravidian languages*. About half of Gonds speak Gondi languages, while the rest speak *Indo-Aryan languages* including *Hindi*. The Gonds are traditionally agriculturalists; some practice shifting cultivation, while others raise cereals or herd cattle. Gond society is highly stratified and does not conform to the usual image of egalitarianism among tribals. The Gonds belong to a category of very large tribes (also including *Santals* and *Bhils*) that have traditionally dominated the regions in which they have lived. The Gonds state that their rulers descend from a Naga king of Ceylon. However, like other *Adivasis,* the Gonds have suffered from increasing landlessness since the 1960s. Traditional Gond religion involves a distinct pantheon of gods and spirits, which many Gonds practice along with *Hinduism*. *Gondwana* or "land of the Gonds", is a loosely-defined area of southeastern Madhya Pradesh, eastern Maharashtra, and parts of Chhattisgarh, Orissa, and northern Andhra Pradesh. The region was home to several *Gond kingdoms* from the 15th century to the mid-18th century, when the *Marathas* expanded into the region from the west. In an ancient time, the Gonds were megalith builders, and some cultural-continuity of this practice survives, with the erection of smaller standing stones. Remnants of an archaic 'dual society' still survive. The region gave its name to *Gondwanaland,* the ancient southern supercontinent which comprised present-day Africa, Madagascar, South America, Australia, the Indian subcontinent and Antarctica.

The Gonds of Andhra Pradesh effectively lost their only advantage in trying to protect their lands when the Banjaras, a group of nomadic cattle herders that had been settling in Gond territory, were classified as a Scheduled Tribe in 1977. Their newly acquired tribal status made the Banjaras eligible to acquire Gond land 'legally' and to compete with Gonds for reserved political seats, places in education institutions, and other benefits. Because the *Banjaras* are not scheduled in neighboring Maharashtra, there has been an influx of Banjara emigrants from that state into Andhra Pradesh in search of better opportunities.Some of the major groups derived from the principal professions they follow or the crafts they practice, for example, the cattle-breeding group takes the significant name of *Gawli*, derived from a *Sanskrit* word for cow. The names of the shepherd castes seem to be derived from words meaning sheep. Such is at least the case with Gadaria from 'gadar', on old *Hindi* word for sheep. Many others of these major groups called castes bear merely tribal or ethic names. Such are for example: *Arora, Gujjar, Lohana, Bhatia, Meena, Bhil, Dom, Oraon, Munda, Santal, Koch, Ahir, Mahar, Nayar, Maratha, Gond, Khond,* etc.

Over the years, several of the tribal communities have settled down in safe haven ievery corner in quite large numbers. Also the Gond tribes identify themselves as 'Koytoria'. . Majority of these Gond tribes are adapted to the religion of Hinduism and are mainly concentrated in the rural areas. If one traces out the origin of the word Gond, one finds it no difficulty to find out the fact that this has been taken from the Telugu word 'Konda' which signifies hill. Also there are several surveys that have been carried on the region, which has thrown some light on the total population of the Gond tribes. It has been enumerated to be more than four million thus making the Gond tribes the largest tribal community of the Central India. In order to carry on conversation, these Gond tribes have developed fluency in the beautiful Gondi language. Quite a handful of these Gond tribes also converse with each other in numerous dialects of the Indo - Aryan language family. Hindi is also quite popular amongst these Gond tribes. Following the tradition of several other tribal communities of the Indian subcontinent, these Gond tribes too have adapted certain occupation in order to meet the basic necessities of their day-to-day living. In general these Gond tribes are the cultivators Some of these Gond tribes even exercise shifting cultivation till date. Other chief occupations of these Gond tribes are namely gathering forest products, hunting, fishing, and devising metal goods in cottage industries and other prime arenas of the Gond society. When one loses her husband, the Gond widow can get married to the younger brother and it is also not necessary, he need to be always married. She also can marry the elder brother of the deceased husband or any one else. Dowry system is also prevalent amongst this Gond tribal community. Gond tribes acquired the knowledge of making medicine from several herbs and plants, which also down the years, have been passed on to the next generation. In fact till today due to the absence of health amenities of the modern times, this Gond tribal community follows the customary medicinal system. Utilization of the plants and herbs are made in order to cure several diseases. The whole of the Gond society has a rich heritage of culture as highlighted in several of cultural elements. If one dissects the whole of the Gond tribal society, one can find the presence of few sub castes . Important ones are namely Maria, Muria and Dorla. Like any of the Hindus, these Gond tribes practice the system of social hierarchy. In fact the Gond society is considered to be highly stratified and not conform to the values of equalitarianism amongst themselves. However, whatever traditions this Gond tribal community is following has gained high acclamation amongst all the researchers and anthropologists of the whole country. In the matters of marriages, these Gond tribes have a preference for going for blood relations as per rules of several of the rituals and practices of Hindus. At times 'mock elopements' are also approved. Other common practices of these Gond tribes are divorce, remarriage, widow marriage, marriages with the wives of the brothers and between brothers and sisters. The Gond tribal community has exercised a special rite. According to this ritual, the groom has to pay bridal price to the father of the prospective bride. This is a mark of showing respect to the females of the Gond community. There are also some other unique systems that have been developed by the Gond tribes. 'Ghotul' system is a famous one that has been widely accepted by most people of this Gond tribal community. As per the norms of the system, although the unmarried young men and women of the Gond community reside in separate houses, they have got the permission to mingle and do everything they want. During this whole period they interact and take pleasure in dancing, music, local story telling and much more in quite a frenzied mood. Interestingly, if they find themselves to be compatibly and can nicely gel with each other, these Gond male and female can get out of the Ghotul and go for marriage. This practice is specially prevalent amongst the Muria Gonds and the origination of the whole system is connected to the goddess 'Lingopan', whom these Gond tribes revere in great veneration.

These are hundreds of cases of attrocities among Oraons and Gonds noted during five year i.e. from June 2004-2009. All of them are shown in Table 5. They utter a miserable situation of Human Rights which are incapable to protect the livelihood and fundamental rights of these tribal groups in few states.

Table 5
Reported Cases of Attrocities Among Oraon and Gond Tribals

Atrocities	*Oraon (Madhya Pradesh)*	*Gond (Madhya Pradesh)*	*Oraon (Bihar)*	*Oraon (Jharkhand)*	*Total*
Land Alienation Cases	8	7	15	13	35
Police Torture	14	12	21	10	57
Sexual Harrasment	17	4	19	11	51
Women Attrocities (Domestic Volilenec)	31	17	43	19	110
Forest Attrocities	12	8	16	21	57
Robbery/Loot	8	5	14	12	39
Murder	24	6	17	9	56
Abortion	4	7	5	3	19
Total	118	66	150	98	424

Tribals of Tamil Nadu

There are 36 Scheduled Tribe communities in Tamil Nadu. As per the 2001 census, the Scheduled Tribe population in Tamil

Nadu was 6.51 lakhs. Out of the 36 Scheduled Tribe communities, 6 Tribal Communities namely Toda, Kota, Kurumbas, Irular, Paniyan and Kattunayakan have been identified as so called 'Primitive Tribal Groups'. The other Tribals living in scattered areas were classified as Dispersed Tribes. The area where the population of Scheduled Tribes exceeds 50% of the total population was declared as Integrated Tribal Development programme area. A separate Directorate, Directorate of Tribal Welfare, has been functioning for the Welfare of the Tribals since 1 April 2000.

In some of the tribal villages in the State, the closest Public Health Centre is nine Km away and tribal schools have no teachers. Sickle cell anaemia and malnutrition were the most common health problems among tribals. There were also pending backlog vacancies in the state. There were an estimated 595 vacancies for SCs/STs in 1998. 100 of them were filled by December 1998. The rest of the posts were still vacant as of July 2007.

The Tamil Nadu Government sanctioned Rs. 61.96 lakh, including Rs. 34.4 lakh allotted on 3 November 2007, to compensate victims of 'Vachathi violence' The violence relates to an event in which forest officials, police and revenue department officials attacked the tribal hamlet of Vachathi in June 1992. However, out of 475 persons, the government had identified only 349 persons as eligible to claim compensation.

The provisions of the Scheduled Tribe and Forest Dwellers Act (Recognition of Forest Rights), 2006, stipulate that nobody who has been living on forest lands prior to December 13, 2005, can be evicted. Yet, in October 2007, forest officials harassed and evicted the dwellers of Suriyur village in Salem district on the pretext that the village was in the jurisdiction of the reserve forests. The National Human Rights Commission also sent its senior member Tsering Samphal to the village on 17 October 2007. The officials had even allegedly filed legal cases against villagers. The villagers had been living in the village for generations, tilling lands and raising crops.

The Todas are found only in the Nilgiri district. They follow pastoral life and live in 64 settlements called munds. The munds consist of a few half-barrel shaped living quarters, a temple for worship, cattle pen huts and grasslands for their buffaloes. The residential huts have a small living space and are provided with small doors supposedly to stop stray animals from entering them. Physically, the Todas are tall in stature and well proportioned. They are fairly colored and thus a contrast from the general Tamil populace. They can be easily recognized by their traditional dress which has an impressive work of embroidery and their distinctive hairstyle. They are traditional lacto vegetarians, their main diet being milk and its products.

Throughout recorded history the Toda community has been small. In 1603, a Jesuit priest who visited them wrote that the Toda numbered "about a thousand." The first government of India census in 1871 counted 693. In 1952 the parent, non-Christian community reached probably its all-time low of 475, and then it began slowly to increase. In August 1988 the author counted 1,042 Toda traditionalists (all but 35 living in Toda hamlets) and another 4 persons, born traditionalists but made outcaste for marrying non-Toda. The three Toda Christian settlements accounted for a further 133 people, but only 38 could claim pure Toda Descent; kin and affines of these Toda Christians, living elsewhere in India and abroad, numbered at least 150, but only 35 were of pure Toda descent. Traditionalists, together with Christians and Outcastes of pure Toda descent, therefore totaled 1,119. Female infanticide (officially prohibited in 1819, but continuing sporadically for several decades) probably accounted for ancient population limits. More recently, venereal infections kept numbers low until a drive to eradicate these diseases, begun in the 1950s, succeeded in raising the birthrate.

The Toda community is divided into 2 endogamous clans-the thartheroll and the Tevelioll. The Exogamous clans include the peiki, the pekkan, the kuttan, the kenna and the todi. The word Toda is definitely a name they came to acquire. As they became known to the South Indian populace living around the Nilgiris, they must have been called 'Tudavar' by the Kannada people. It means 'those who live on top'. It must have seemed an apt description for the tribe who occupied only the highest summits in the mountains of the Nilgiris. Alternatively, it may be that the name comes from the Tamil word Toruvan or toran which means herdsman. For the Todas themselves they are just o.l, 'the men'.

Regarding their place of origin, the Todas insist that God created them in the Nilgiris and that they were its oldest inhabitants. The study of ancient history however reveals the presence of a race that was markedly different in its culture. This led to speculation regarding their origin and migration. Scholars opined that the Todas migrated from the West, based on the fact that most settlements of the Todas are concentrated on the western slopes of the Nilgiris. Linguistically, their language resembles Tamil but is strikingly different in pronunciation of certain phonemes. The Toda tongue is assumed to have branched off from the pre-Tamil about 2000 years back.

Among the interesting rituals, there are the marriage rites. The suitor has to prove his worth to the girl's family by lifting a heavy stone to his shoulders. The marriage ceremony itself is a celebrated event among all Todas. The members of the clan assemble at a customary place, mostly a tree. A group of settlements of clans might regard a single tree as their place of marriage. The particular tree has a hole which is made to accommodate the lamp, which is has a very important role in

Table 6
Cases of Attrocities Among Todda, Paniyan and Kota Tribals

Attrocities	*Todda (Tamil Nadu) thartheroll*	*Kota (Tamil Nadu)*	*Paniyan (Tamil Nadu)*	*Total*
Land Alienation Cases	4	7	14	25
Police Torture	8	6	4	18
Rape	2	5	1	8
Women Attrocities (Domestic Volilenec)	32	37	19	88
Forest Attrocities	5	8	14	27
Robbery	–	–	–	–
Murder	2	7	1	10
Child Marriage	7	5	3	15
Total	60	75	56	191

rituals. Child-marriage is prevalent with the actual consummation being delayed until maturity. The lady has her husband's name tattooed over her left hand.

When the girl is pregnant they come across the 'bow and arrow' ceremony in which the girl is presented with the bow and the arrow. This particular rite may suggest an aspiration for a brave boy. In spite of the commitment shown by the girl towards her husband, we find that a marriage that does not produce children is dissolved and the girl remarries. In the records various sort of violation of Human Rights are found in three groups of Toda, Kota and Paniyan of Tamilnadu. These cases are shown in table 6 which futher reveal that the fundamental rights are not well protected indicating deformity in implementation of Human Rights Act.

Conclusion

Thus, in view of the facts of the preceding pages, it is obvious that the Adopted Human Right Act protects the livelihood rights of tribal People apart from fundamental rights cited in the Indian Constitution. The major aims of these Rights are to universalize the doctrine of "live and let to live". Since the tribals are the inhabitants of backward areas maintaining indigenous culture, endogamy, definite territory and specific dialect, their dependency on forest produces, agriculture, animals, fishes etc. is nowadays challenged due to exploitation and encroachments of non tribals. Country's immigrants and landlords impel them to become landless. Tribal societies which were of egalitarian type in older days are emerging unequal under the influence of modernization and urbanization. Their interrelations within the community are now guided by the motives of profit and loss Poverty, indebtedness and illiteracy are the riders in the life of them. It is evident that practices of child labour, bounded labour, Land grabbing, sexual harassment, molestation, rape, women trafficking, girl kidnapping, head hunting and so on, are the major evils prevailing in the tribal community. Such sort of violation of Human rights multiplies the livelihood miseries of Indian Tribes.

Although certain issues have been raised by the social welfare agencies and media (press) too supported with letter and spirit, but the political leaders & elite class by which these tribals are surrounded could not come forward in the movement. Tribal leaders too, discourages their ward to report such cases. So, various forms of attrocities are confined either in the vicinity of the hut and house or mild penalties are imposed to the culprit. If culprit is influential and well off, he attempts to manipulate allegations. If such convict does belong to the community, he employs the power of money and impact over their common mass. In these condition victims are left at lurch as they are mostly down trodden among tribal communities.

The government too was not serious about establishing strong commission, it is hardly surprising that there are many deficiencies in the establishing Act itself. Numbers of tribes like Bhokasa, Tharu, Toda, patharkatta/kanjar, Gond, Oraon etc. are facing the problem of their rights which can be viewed as the violation of Human Rights like deforestation, Identification, Land Alienation, Gender inequality, sexual harassment, labour exploitation, bounded labour, Domestic Violence, Sexual Violence etc. It takes a wider view of human rights. This helps one in recognising and acknowledging some of the parameters within which the commission has to operate. This is also indicative of the fact that sometimes task of the commission is onerous particularly in those conditions where the political will is lacking; the state is not serious about fulfilling its obligations. Menno T. Kammingo in his book 'Inter State Accountability for Violations of Human Rights' distinguishes the term 'accountability' and 'responsibility'. Accountability is claimed to involve a duty to provide an explanation or account for an act apparently contrary to an international obligation. Responsibility involves a duty to provide appropriate reparation for an internationally wrongful act. Responsibility can be a means of discharging accountability, but accountability is a wider concept because a state may be able to explain an act of apparent violation of international law in a way that does not involve its responsibility can be understood as a limited sub-category of accountability. This definition of accountability mandate to ensure the protection of rights enshrined in the two covenants and the Indian Constitution can help to some extent in understanding and evaluating the performance. Particularly in the area of holding the government accountable by making the government conscious of the fact that it is the primary duty bearer and it has an international and constitutional obligation to discharge this duty.

References

Aurora Sneh (2001), 'Balancing the Scales: Gender Composition of Commonwealth National Human Rights Institutions', Commonwealth Human Rights Initiative.

Bareh, H. (1994), People. Encyclopaedis of India: Meghalaya. New Delhi, Rima Pub. House, pp. 50.

Bate, Crispin (1995), (PDF). *Race, Caste and Tribe in Central India: The Early Origins of Indian Anthropometry.* Edinburgh: Centre for South Asian Studies, School of Social & Political Studies, *University of Edinburgh. ISBN 1-900-795-02-7. http://www.csas.ed.ac.uk/fichiers/BATES_RaceCaste&Tribe.pdf.*

Branded by Law: 2(2001) Looking at India's Denotified Tribes, by Dilip D'Souza. Published by Penguin Books,.

Cook, Rebecca J., Mahmoud F. Fathalla (September 1996), "Advancing Reproductive Rights Beyond Cairo and Beijing". International Family Planning Perspectives, 22 (3), 115–121. doi:10.2307/2950752.

Crooke, W. (1975), The Tribes and Castes of North Western India, Vol. III.

Das, J.C. (1990), Socio-economic and Cultural Profile of Himalaya in: S.K. Biswas (ed.) Strategy of Development in the Himalayas. Institute of Social Research and Applied Anthropology, Calcutta.

Dayal Virendra, 'Evolution of the National Human Rights Commission, (1993-2002), A Decennial View', in *Journal of the National Human Rights Commission,* India, 2002, p. 45.

Desai, Mihir (1999), "Civil Laws Affecting Gays and Lesbians", *cf.* Bina Fernandez Ed., Humjinsi, Indian Centre for Human Rights and Law, Mumbai.

Durham, H (2004), "We the People: The Position of NGOs in Gathering Evidence and Giving Witness in International Criminal Trials", in Thakur, R, Malcontent, P, *From Sovereign Impunity to International Accountability*, New ^ "The Concept and Foundations and Objectives of the CCASG". *http://gcc-sg.org/Foundations.html*. Retrieved.

Earle Patrick, Human Rights Council of Europe, National Human Rights Institutions and the Human Rights Approach to Development.

Ember, M., C. R. Ember (1971), The Conditions Favouring Matrilocal Residence. *American,Anthropologist*, Vol. 73, pp. 571-94.

Freeman, Michael (2002), *Human Rights: An Interdisciplinary Approach*. Wiley-Blackwell, p. 15-17.

Gupta, M. L. & Sharma, D.D. (2000), Social Anthropology, Sahitya Bhawan Publication.

Kannabirân, Kalpana; Ranbir Singh (2008), *Challenging the Rules of Law: Colonialism, Criminology and Human Rights in India*. SAGE Publications Inc. p. 22. ISBN 0761936653.

Kessler, Suzanne J. and Wendy Mekenna (1978), Gender: An Ethnomethodology Approach. Chicago, II: University of Chicago Press.

Louis Henkin, The International Bill of Rights: The Universal Declaration and the Covenants, in International Enforcement of Human Rights 6-9, Bernhardt and Jolowicz, eds., (1987).

Louis Henkin (1981), Introduction, The International Bill of Rights, 9-10.

Majumdar D. N. (1980), *A Study of Culture Change in Two Garo Villages of Meghalaya*. Guwahati, Gauhati University.

Malli, Gandhi, (2008), Denotified Tribes: Dimensions of Change, by Malli Gandhi. Kanishka Publishers, 2008.

Narula, S. (1998), *"Broken People" Caste violence against India's Untouchables*. Human Rights Watch.

National Commission for Scheduled Caste and Scheduled Tribes. India, 2000.

Nickel, James (2009), "The Stanford Encyclopedia of Philosophy", in Zalta, Edward N.

Nickel, James. *Making Sense of Human Rights: Philosophical Reflections on the Universal Declaration of Human Rights*, pp. 521.

Quadri, N. A. F. and Singh, U. P. (2007), Patharkatta/Kanjar Janjati: ek Nrijati Vaygayanik Adhyan, *The Asian Man,* Vol. 1, No. 1&2, Asian Institute of Human Science and Development, Lko.

Ravi Nair, *The New York Times*. Cited in Norchi, 'The National Human Rights Commission of India,' p. 114.

Samal, P. K. (1993), The Status of Women in Central Himalaya: A Cultural Interpretation, *Man in India,* Vol. 73, No. 1.

Sahoo, Alka (2008), Human Rights Movement: Towards Gender Equality, The Eastern Anthropologist, Vol. 61, No. 3, p. 411-418.

V. Vijayakumar (2000), "The Working of the National Human Rights Commission: A Perspective," in C.J. Nirmal, ed., *Human Rights in India: Historical, Social and Political Perspectives* (Oxford: Oxford University Press, 2000), Chapter 12, p. 215.

6

Ground Reality of Human Rights Declaration

Ravi Prakash Yadav, Ragini Deep & Puja Roy

"All human beings are born free and equal in dignity and right."
–U.N. Declaration of Human Rights (Article 1, 1948)

"Every state is known by the rights its maintains."
–Harold Laski, *A Grammar of Politics*

Introduction

Our planet 'Earth' now carrying the burden of about 700 crores human beings, uncountable number of animal, birds and other beings. The life of the resident of beautiful earth is governed by the 'laws of nature'. There are certain rights are essential for the normal development of their lives. After the 'origin and development, society and state became the provider, maintainer and protector of all types of related to human beings and other beings. Human rights are the set of civil, political (Protection rights/Negative rights), economic, social, cultural (rights to adequate wage, food, clothing, healthcare, education, entertainment/positive rights) and solidarity rights. Different institutions of the society are trying continuously that every member of the society can enjoy and make his life beautiful with the help of such rights.

The maintenance of human rights is the indicator of how free the society is from 'exploitation', 'injustice', 'inequality', 'oppression' and restrictions' on the continuity of the growth of a man leading to his development to the fullest. The denial of (any category) human rights affects the physical, social, economic, psychological and cultural development of the human beings. The life is not a grand harmony, subjugation, domination, exploitation, injustice, inequality, oppression and restrictions also exit. Subjugation, domination, oppression, exploitation and so on of the weaker sections of the society are 'inherent features' of human society ever since its existence.

Weakers are always sufferer and sufferers are always weaker. Weakers and sufferers of many society of the world are deprived from human rights. 'Violation of human rights' in human society created a situation of 'social instability'. It is an inevitable outcome of denial of human rights.

It is the responsibility of state and society to prevent such types of atrocities on the weaker and vulnerable sections by the powerful. It is the duty of state to ensure a life with full of dignity, liberty, security and equality for ever member (weaker and powerful) of the society without any discrimination. It is closely associated with 'universal rights of all human beings' regardless of their caste, creed, colour, nationality, status, religion, age, sex or race. Human rights are the 'birthright' (inherent rights) of all human beings. It is automatically granted by the society just after the birth of an individual. All human beings get such rights by the virtue of their birth. These are 'inalienable rights' of an individual. An individual cannot give up them. These are the 'non transferable' rights. Human rights, generally described as 'universal, inherent and inalienable' rights of man. These are the 'minimal rights' for any individual as human being. Virtually such rights specify the minimum conditions for 'human dignity' and a 'tolerable life'. These rights are essential for the over-all-development of the personality of man as human being. Human rights are the exclusive rights and prerogatives of any individual. Such rights are the natural demands and pre-requisite for his self-development.

Human Rights: From First to Third Generation

After birth every human being are entitled for civil, political, economic and cultural rights (privileges and opportunities). There are three phases (categories) of human rights. Which are as follows:

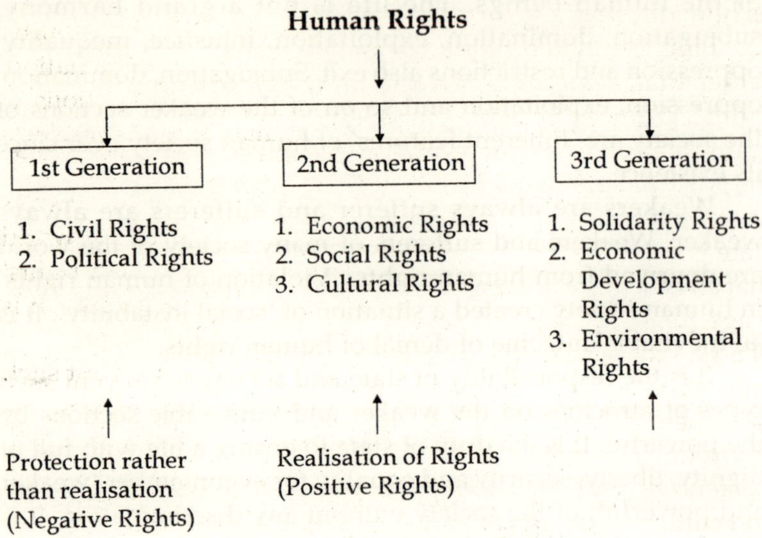

The civil and political rights (i.e. First Generation rights) are exclusively related with the rights to adequate wage, food, clothing, education, health care as well as rights to life, liberty, free trail, free speech free movement etc. The economic rights are associated with rights to social security, Medical care, employment, social services and so on. One thing should keep in mind that one human right does not contradict with other right. So on one have right to beat, to slave, to excessive profit, to trafficking any one etc. In this situations any one have the full right to realise his full potential as human beings.

Now the question of one million is related with 'protection and violation' of human rights. The history of both protection and violation is very old. The violation of human rights by both state institution and powerful individuals is a 'universal phenomenon' (Mausmi Majumdar, 2009). It is the duty of the state to eliminate all forms of dominance and discrimination from the society. So every member of the society have the right to dignity, right to equity, right to security and fight to liberty. These are well known as 'universal rights' of all human beings regardless sex, age, race, caste, religion or nationality. Because there are inherent rights (Birth right) for all just after the birth as human being.

First generation rights are mainly related with protection rather than realisation. Therefore, they known as 'negative rights'. Whereas 'Second generation rights' are concerned with realisation of economic, social and cultural rights ensure by the government for the people. It is the duty of the government to ensure these rights to mass. In order to ensure these rights, state is responsible to provide social provisions or services. So that all human beings can enjoy these right related to adequate wage, food, clothing, health care, education etc. As per the view of S.W. Pinto (2004), the 'third generation' or 'solidarity rights' only make sense if defined as a collective level. The further says these rights include the right to economic development, environmental rights, peace, humanitarian etc. For the sake of existence human beings want to enjoy civil, economic, political and cultural privileges and opportunities. No wonder the term 'human rights worker' every today conjures up images of people working for the protection 'first-generation' human rights abuses like political prisoners, torture, violence by the police and the security forces and so on.

The concept of human rights is to old and deep rooted. Basically is developed as a device for controlling the use of 'Autocratic power' by power and rich person of group in the society. The deep rooted history of human rights can be trace out from Magna Carat (1215), The Glorious Revolution (1698), The American Revolution (1776), The French Revolution, The Russian Revolution (1917) and so on. The 'Modern State' is more serious about rights of human being than 'Medieval State' in term of quantity and quality aspects of human rights. The universality of human is a clear reaction to the universalisation of the 'Modern State' as the dominant from of political and social organisation (S.W. Pinto, 2004). Modern State is more particular on the issue of human rights. The democratic countries played an instrumental role in this regard.

Universal Declaration of Human Rights (UNO, 1948)

On 10th December 1948 the General Assembly of the United Nations adopted the *'Universal Declaration of Human Rights'*. It is indeed a historic and remarkable document in this regard. Virtually it is recognised by international level. This declaration has been ratified by all most member country including India. After the rectification, it is obligatory for member countries to ensure such conditions so that all human being can enjoy these rights for their fullest development. At the same time it is the duty of the state in the case of violation person concern should be punished. Some important articles are mentioned below:

1. "Every one has the right to life, *liberty* and security of person." *–U.N. Declaration (Article-3).*
2. No one shall be subjected to *torture* of cruel, inhuman or degrading treatment or punishment. *–Article-5.*
3. Everyone has the right to recognition everywhere as a person before the law. *–Article-6.*
4. All are equal before the law and are entitled without any *discrimination* to equal protection of the law. *– Article-7.*
5. Everyone has the right to an effective *remedy* by the competent national tribunals for acts violating the fundaments of granted him by the constitution or by law. *– Article-8.*
6. Every one has right to education. *Education* shall be free at least in the elementary and fundamental stages. Elementary education shall be compulsory. *–Article-26.*

The Human Rights Commission (HRC) in India was formed in 1993. In the same year the *Human Rights Act 1993*, was passed by the house. According to section 2(d) of the Human Rights Act, 1993, 'Human Rights' means following rights well guaranteed by constitution or embodied in the international covenants ratified by India:

1. Right relating to *life* of individual;
2. Right relating to *liberty* of individual;
3. Right relating to *equality* of individual and
4. Right relating to *dignity* of individual.

For the preservation and protection of human rights many commissions has come into existence like-National Commission for *Minorities,* National Commission for *Scheduled Caste and Scheduled Tribes,* National Commission for *women,* National Child Rights Commission and so on. Similarly at state level many commissions were formed by different states. The basic objectives of these commissions are to provide safeguard every people against any kind of discrimination.

The *ground reality* of Human Rights all over the world however presents not a good picture. Despite of the rectification and formation of HRC, the social, political, economic and cultural status of women, SC. ST. OBC, Labour and Minority Community (Deprived Section) ares more or less remained unchanged. Virtually till today they are deprived section of the society. However, 56 years from the adoption of the declaration, we are still faced with a situation where the vast majority of the people of the world are still deprived from several important human rights contained in the Universal Declaration (Shanti Bhushan, 2004). The human rights in our society are being constantly and systematically violated by all agencies without any qualms, be they Government or non-Governmental (Devika Paul, 1994). But we know 'every state is known by the rights it maintains (Laski Harold). There are huge number of cases of the violation of human rights in our society at different level and different forms. Many sections of the society and many categories of the workers (i.e. weaker section) are still stand for away from their basic and minimum right as a human.

The 39 articles in the Declaration include various rights like right to equality, free speech, life, liberty, free trail, free movement as well as economic rights such as right to employment, social security, food, clothing, housing, medical care, education and other social services. But what is the ground reality of these rights? About 25 crores in the world and 2 crores in India children are deprived from their child right. They are working as child labour. Billion of people are living below poverty line. As one estimation, out of 180 crores workers of the world, Women are only 54 cr. (30%) Million of women are out of employment. Majority people of Third World Country (Asia, Africa, South America) are still deprived of basic economic rights such as employment, housing, medical care, education and even food (Shanti Bhushan, 2004).

According to a study FAO study, at the beginning of this new millennium 791.4 million people remain hungry in the developing world; of the 283.9 million are in South Asia alone (Asit Mishra & Panchali Sen, 2002). There are 386.6 million poor in India, who do not get adequate food to meet their daily consumption needs (A.N. Bose, 2002). 87 percent of women in our country suffer from 'anemic a and Iron deficiency'. They give birth to under-weight babies (Asit Mishra & Panchali Sen, 2004). Implications of violation of human rights are more dangerous at various levels. Billion of people do not have access proper house. They are compelled to live in a house, which is not fit for human habitation.

Human Right Declaration: An Introspection

Children

United Nations Convention for the *'Rights of Children'* was ratified by India in 1992. According to the 'Charter of Child Rights' (CCR), "All children are born with fundamental freedom and human beings have some inherent rights". As per the Charter Children of all over the entitled for following rights:

1. Right to *survival* - to life, health, nutrition, name and nationality
2. Right to *development*- to education, care, leisure, recreation
3. Right to *protection*- from exploitation, abuse, neglect
4. Right to *participation*- to expression, information, thought and religion.

The ground reality is quite different as far as the matter of human right related to children's concern. Despite of the declaration, the reality provides a different story. The conditions of the children's are not very good in this regard. Millions number of children's stand away from their basic and minimum rights as human beings. They are in unhuman conditions. As per one report, 2 millions Indian babies die before they celebrate their first birthday. More girl children are killed at birth. Despite of this presently, India has second largest 'educational system' in the world after China, with 6.27 Lakhs primary, 1.90 Lakhs upper primary, 79.65 thousands high schools, 28.49 higher secondary schools (Nayar, 2000). About 35 millions children aged 6-14 years do not attend school (out of school).

As per the UN declaration every children have the right to survive, develop, be protected and participate in decisions that impact their lives. But what is the ground reality?

According to latest estimates, about 70% Childhood mortality in developing countries is due to five major conditions: diarrhea disease, acute lower respiratory tract infections, malaria, mealer and mal nutrition (Kavita Sharma, Raju Jain and Uma Iyer, 2008). In India, malnutrition in children is a major concer, as about 53% of children under five years are under weight and 52% are stunted (Unicef, 2000). Every fourth child is affected by 'protein Energy Malnutrition' (PEM) with 150 million children being under weight and 182 million stunted. Under-Nutrition is measured as the prevalence of under weight, stunting or wasting. It is clear that under weight, stunted and wasting situation is worst especially in developing countries (see Table 1).

Table 1
Region Wise under Weight, Stunted and Wasting (in %)

Region	*Under Weight*	*Stunted*	*Wasted*
Latin America & Caribbean	6	12	2
Africa	24	35	8
Asia	28	30	9
India	47	45	16
Bangladesh	48	45	10
Pakistan	40	36	14

Source: ACC/SCN/2004

Further without child labour (2002) and 'Every child counts' are the latest report of I.L.O. regarding child labour. As per the report, more than 21.10 crores children's are economically active all over the world in the 5-14 age category. The Asia-Pacific region labours the largest number (12.13 crores) of child labour followed by sub-sharan Afric (4.8 cr.) and Latin America & Caribbean (1.74 cr.). There are approximately 24.60 crores children in child labour all together (5-17 years). The region wise break-up is given below:

Table 2

Regional Estimates of Economically Active Children (Aged 5-14) 2000

Region	*No. of Children (in crores)**
Developed Economies	0.25
Transition Economies	0.24
Asia and the Pacific	12.73
Latin America & Caribbean	1.74
Sub-Saharan Africa	4.80
Middle East of North Africa	1.34
World	21.10

Source: '*Every Child Count:* New Global Estimates on Child Labour, I.L.O., Geneva, April, 2002, p. 17.
*Converted from millions to crores.

It is clear from above mentioned Table 2 that 'every one is necked in HAMAM '. It is clear that about 25 crores children's are not in school but engaged as child labour. This way and that way they are deprived from their basic and minimal rights. Is it not the matter of violation of human rights? As the matter of fact 25 crores children's as Child Labour are deprived from rights to education, entertainment, Self-Development and so on.

Right through history, children's have been abused and exploited. Child Labour Problem is an alarming one and constitutes an 'egressions violation' of child rights. This situation is in worst form particularly in Asia and Pacific, Sub-Saharan Africa and Latin America & Caribbean (See Table 2.)

Out of 24.55 Cr. Child Labour (5-14 aged) about 70% (17.05 Cr.) children's were working in 'hazardous conditions/ situations' (see Table 3).

According to I.L.O. (2002), "Hazardous Work by children is in any activity or occupation which, by its nature or type has, or ideas to adverse effects on the child's safety, health (physical or mental), and moral development." ILO further said that Hazards could also derive from excessive workload, physical conditions of work, and or work in terms of the duration of hours of work even where the activity or occupation is known to be 'non-hazardous or 'safe'.

Table 3
Age Wise Child Labour in the World, (No. in Cr.)

Age group	*Child Labour*	*Child labour in Hazardous work*
5-14	18.63	11.13
15-17	5.92	5.92
Total (5-17)	24.55	17.05
%	100	70

Source: Ibid, p. 20.

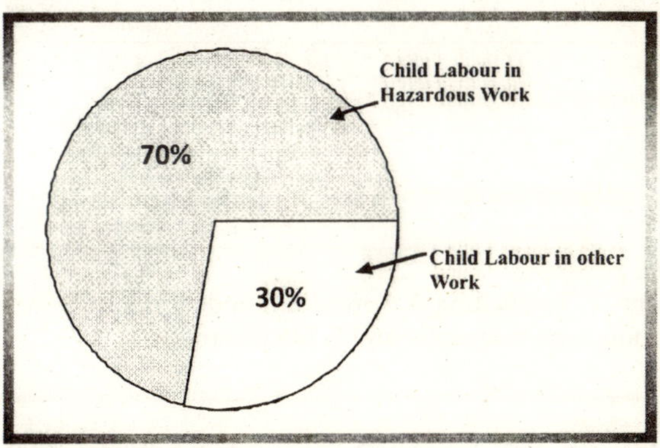

So when ILO conversion No. 138 (1973) and No. 182 (1999) define 'hazardous work' as "likely to jeo pardize/harmful for the health, safety or morals of children" and prohibited such type of 'employment of children' than such type of employment is matter of 'gross violation' of human rights. Nerra Burra and other eminent scholars found children engaged in Match, Glass, Silk, Beedi, Zari, Brick-kilns, Brass ware, Lock-making, Slate-Pencil, Diamond-cutting, Gem Polishing, Power loom, Cotton hosiery, Carpet weaving, Pottery, Textile, Knives, Handicrafts,

Circus, Handloom industry that is unsafe and unhealthy. Virtually millions of childrens are working with potassium cyanide, Trisodium phosphate, Sodium silicate, Hydrochloric acid, Sulphuric acid (Lock industry) and so on. In these hazardous conditions they have bound to inhale noxious fumes. Not only this they are exposed to electric shocks. And ultimately suffer from tuberculosis, bronchitis, asthama, joints pain, fault related to eyes, skin disease etc. These are most 'Notorious Industries'. As far as the matter of violation of human rights is concerned.

In addition to 17.05 Cr. Children's (Hazardous work), there are about 84 Lakhs children's are involved in work form all over the world well defined by I.L.O. convention No. 182 (Article 3, 1999). As per the C.N. 182 they are defined as unconditional worst forms of child labour. There are five categories of such type of child labour (see Table 4).

Table 4
Region wise Child Labour in Worst Forms

Region	*No. (Lakhs)*	*%*
Asia & Pacific	64.30	76.55
Latin America & Caribbean	10.43	12.42
Africa	3.80	04.52
Transition Eco.	0.05	00.59
Developed industrialized economies	5.31	6.32
World	84.00	100.00

Source: Ibid, p. 207

*Worst form- 1. Trafficking 2. Forced & bonded labour 3. Armed conflict 4. Prostitution & pornography and 5. Illicit activities

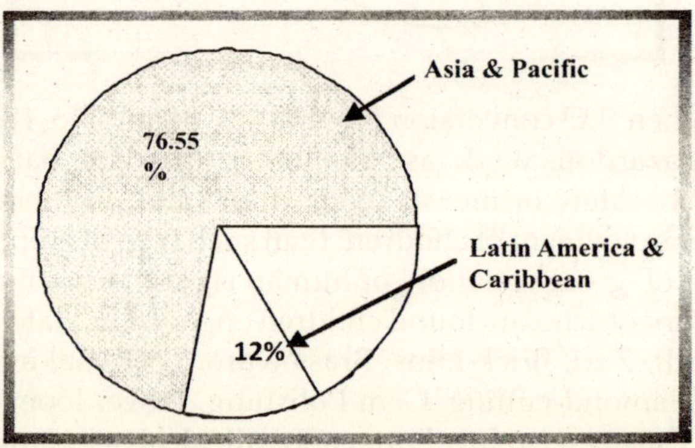

Now the question arises has the charter on Human Rights any meaning for such childrens? Child labour in clearly detrimental to individual children, preventing them from enjoying them physical or psychological damage; it is also detrimental to families, to communities and to society as a whole (A future without child labour, 2002). This represent a 'global consensus' to end the 'most severe' forms of the violation of Human Rights.

Women

The educational status, employment status of females compared to male is quite discouraging. The 'Sex Ratio' is also an important indicator to check the real situation of violation of human rights. It reflects the matter of 'gender based inequality'. In every field 'gender based disparities' are still large. In education field this disparity has been increased from 9.23% in 1901 to 22% in 2001 (see table). In India, in the 0-19 age group, the death rate of girls is higher than boys. Studies on 'Intra-house holds distribution' with gross mal nutrition and nutritional deficiency, the deficiency among girls and women was 25% more than men (Vibuti Patel, 2007). National family Health Survey, 2006 has revealed that 'Anemia' among Indian women is around 50-60%.

Table 5
Sex Ratio and Female Literacy Rate in India (1951-2001)

Year	*1951*	*1961*	*1971*	*1981*	*1991*	*2001*
Sex Ratio(Per thousand female)	946	941	930	934	927	933
Female literacy (in %)	9	15	22	30	39	54
Male-female literacy gap (in%)	18	25	24	26	24	22

Source: Census 1951-2001, Govt. of India.

Millions of people are still struggling for drinking water. Every on can see this situation in their town city.

Rape

Despite of the charter a huge no. of women are raped and murdered. The numerous cased in rape in 'police-custody' are a reminder of 'stark reality' that the protectors of law in many countries are the worst offenders. (S.W. Pinto, 2004, 44). So many notorious rape cases like Mathura case (1972), Maya Tyagi Rape case (1980), Piparia Rape case (1988), Bhumika-Assam Rape case (1988), Gumta Bahn Case (1987) and so on are the important examples of violating the human rights regarding women. Tyagi Rape Case and Mathura Case was the instance of police brutality. In most of cases the victims were belonged to Scheduled castes and Scheduled Tribes. Yearwise 'Reported rape' situation in given in table 6. It is clear from this table that the rape incidents against women shows upward trend. It moves from 10,068 (in 1990) to 14,849 (in 1996). It reveal about 40% enhancement in rape cases (see Table 6).

Table 6
Year wise incidents of rape in India

Year	*1990*	*1991*	*1992*	*1993*	*1994*	*1995*	*1996*
Rape incidents	10,068	10,425	11734	12,223	13,218	13,774	14,849

Source: 1. Crime in India, 1994, p. 235.
2. Statistics on children in India, p. 235, National Crime Records Bureau, 1996, p. 88.

Table 7
Reported Rape Incidents in Selected Countries

Country	*America*	*Canada*	*Australia*	*France*	*Japan*	*Spain*	*Sweden*
Reported Rape	90,400	20,500	2300	2900	1800	1500	100

Source: Samaj Kalyan Ministryu of Women & Child development, GOI, New Delhi, July, 2000, p. 18.

Rape of women is not only a national phenomenon but also global phenomenon. Rape incidents among developed countries are more than developing countries. High rape incidents can be seen table 7. Rape, violence, domestic violence, dowry murder, sexual harassment at the wonk place all are related the violation of human rights.

However, after the nationwide 'anti-rape movement' in 1980, cases of 'violence against women' issues for parties to score points against contends in electoral battles as well as in the local power struggles (Vibhuti Patel, 1994). But the rape incidents school and college going girls are still continued.

No. place is safe for the girl and women. The sword of rape is always hanging before their heads. There are so many related cases before national commission for women and state commission for women.

Murder for Dowry

In India, the dowry-murder cases are continuously increased. It is not a good sign for India society. There are a huge no of families who are suffering from this problem. The dowry murder cases were increased from 4836 in 1990 to 5250 in 1996. (See Table 8).

Table 8
Year wise Murder incidents for Dowry in India

Year	*1990*	*1991*	*1992*	*1993*	*1994*	*1995*	*1996*
Murder for Dowry	4836	5157	4962	5811	4935	5151	5250

Source: Samaj Kalyan, Dec. 1998, p. 20.

Women are not safe in any place. A survey conducted by National Commission for women in 1998 on the issue of sexual and other harassment of working women. The report revealed that 68% women were mentaly harassed, 25% physiological (sexual) expolitated and 32% women discriminated on the matter related to salary, promotion & work allocation (see Table 9). Are we ensuring and providing human rights? These are the clear-cut case of violation of human rights.

Table 9
Sexual Harassment of Working Women

Incidents	*Mental Harassment*	*Physiological Exploitation*	*Salary, Promotion, work allocation related discrimination*	*Discrimination related to rules & condition of work*
%	68	25	32	24

Source: Survey by national commission for women (1998) of about 1200 working women in organised and unorganised sectors-selected cities Hyderabad, Mumbai, Nasik, Bhopal, Raipur, Lucknow, Allahabad, Kolkatta, Midnapur.

Conclusion

On the basis of above mentioned facts, it is clear that despite of the UN declaration a large section of the people of the world particularly Asian, African and South American are still deprived from first as well as second generation human rights. Such people are deprived from the right to life (Dowry-murder, Girl Foeticide etc.), liberty (bondage, child labour), free trail, equality (unequal remuneration), employment (million youths unemployed), Food (struggling from hunger), housing (millions people houseless), education (Billion people illiterate), medical care (die due to in availability of M.C.) and so on.

People in general and child & women in particular, are deprived from their basic and minimal human rights. They are still living in Uuhuman conditions, many of them still unable to get two square meals a day. Million of them still compelled to live in unhuman habitation. Out of 155 Cr. childrens, about 24.55 Cr. children are 'out of school'. They are working as 'child labour' in all over the world. Millions of babies die before they celebrate their first birthday. Many girl foticides are killed before their natural delivery. Many girls are killed after birth. This is the real story oh human rights declaration. These are the case of gross violation of human rights all over the world. School going, college going and working women all are raped by the citizen of so called civilized society.

The above analysis proved that not a single article of human rights declaration put down effective effect upon children specially in the case of child labour and many women workers of the unorganised sector. A large sector of unorganised workers are stand for away from the minimum basic human rights in this civil society. Is it the fortunate story of a democratic global society?

It is well recognised by the countries of all over the world that the state is an important player in order to provide the human rights field. But there are so many examples that tell the violation stories by governmental authorities or agencies. But now the 'global society, is more serious in order to implement human rights norms in the world. Many country interfered on the issue of the violation of human rights in the another country. 'Today Human Right Movement' is becoming stronger and stronger.

The concept of Human Rights is fast gaining acceptance both among the activists and the people of large. But we should always remember that mere declaration of rights is not enough. Yes time has come to help the 'Human Rights Workers' honestly and sincerely.

Refrences

Bhushan, Shanti (2004), "Human Rights Challenges in the World Today", Bhartiya Samajik Chintan, Vol. III, No. 3, October-December, Kolkata, p. 155-156.

Every Child Counts (2002), ILO, Geneva, p. 19-23.

Ghatak, Sandip Kumar (2004), "Human Rights and Coalmines Workers", Bhartiya Samajik Chintan, Vol. II, No. 4, January, Kolkata, p. 68-69.

Majumdar, Maushmi (2008), "Women Stone-Breaker: Violation of Human Rights" ed. Women Welfare and Empowerment in India by Rameshhwari Pandya, New Century Publications, New Delhi, p. 577.

Kumar, Ashok (2006), "Educational Status of Girl Child, *Kurukhsetra,* Vol. 55, No. 1, N. Delhi, p. 14.

Patel, Vibhuti (2007), "Globalisation and Women", Bhartiya Samajik Chintan, Vol. VI, No. 2 (New Series), July-September, Kolkata, p. 106.

——(2008), "Women's Struggles & Movement in India", Bhartiya Samajik Chintan, Vol. VI, No. 4, January-March, Kolkata, p. 326-27.

Pinto, Shrithadi Willian (2004), "Human Rights and Democracy", Bhartiya Samajik Chintan, Vol. II, No. 4, January, Kolkata, p. 39-44.

Sharma, Kolkata, Jain, Rajul and Iyer, Uma (2008), "Counselling Mothers in Child Feeding Practices", ed. Rameshwari Pandya, New Century Publications, New Delhi, p. 62-63.

7

Gender Equality in India: Constitutional Provisions and Human Rights

D. K. Singh

The Constitution of India, which came into force on 26th Jan. 1950, with 395 articles and nine schedules, incorporates the most elaborate fundamental rights ever adopted. The preamble to the constitution pledges to secure to all Citizens of India justice-social, economic and political, liberty of thought, expression, belief, faith and worship, equality of status and of opportunity, and to promote among them all, fraternity assuring the dignity of the individual and unity and integrity of nation. The concept of human right implies the respect of all human beings and its absolute worth, regardless of colour, race, sex, religion or other considerations. These rights are essential for the full development of the human personality and for human happiness. Concept of human rights has always been regarded as the backbone of every democratic setup. Democracy is based upon the concept of human rights which are essential not merely to fulfill biological needs of the mankind but also for the dignity of the individual. Without recognizing the concept of human rights no polity can be democratic one. Every democratic constitution tries to recognize the concept of human rights in one way or the other.

Fundamental Rights and Human Rights

The fundamental Rights have been included in the Indian constitution in accordance with the trend of modern democratic thought. These rights were deemed essential to protect the rights and liberties of the people against the encroachment of the power delegated by them to their Government.

The fundamental rights guaranteed to the citizens of India in the Constitution (Articles 12 to 35) constitute the political and civic rights and are justiciable, an aggrieved person can go to a court of law for redress. India has incorporated the Universal Declaration of Human Rights 1948 in its constitution. The following provisions reflect the spirit of protection and promotion of human rights in our constitution:

(i) Article 14 – guarantees equality before law; the state shall not deny to any person equality before the law or the equal protection of law within the territory of India.

(ii) Article 15 – prohibits discrimination on grounds of religion, race, caste, sex or place of birth for access to shops, public restaurants, hotels and places of public entertainment or the use of wells, tanks, bathing ghats roads and place of public resort, maintained wholly or partly out of state funds or dedicated to the use of the general public.

(iii) Article 16 – provides equality of opportunity in matters of public employment.

(iv) Article 17 – abolishes untouchability and forbids its practice in any form and makes the offence punishable in accordance with law.

(v) Article 19 – protects rights of freedom of speech and expression, to assemble peacefully and without arms, to form associations or unions, to move freely throughout the territory of India, to reside and settle in

any part of the territory of India and to practice any profession or to carry on any occupation, trade or business.

(vi) Article 21 – provides protection of life and personal liberty.

(vii) Article 23 – prohibits traffic in human beings and forced labour.

(viii) Article 24 – Prohibits employment of children below the age of 14 years in any factory or mine or any other hazardous employment.

(ix) Article 25 – grants freedom of conscience and free profession, practice and propagation of religion subject to public order, morality and health.

(x) Article 26 – grants freedom to manage religious affairs to every religious denomination.

(xi) Article 28 – derives religious instruction in any educational institution wholly maintained out of state funds.

(xii) Article 29 – grants protection of interests of minorities and their right to establish and administer education institutions.

(xiii) Article 31 – provide fundamental right to property.

(xiv) Article 32 – provides remedies for enforcement of the fundamental right by empowering the Supreme Court to issue directions, orders on writs.

Directive Principles of State Policy

The Directive Principles of State Policy constitute the social and economic rights of the people of India. They are contained in Articles 36-51 of the Constitution in the Government of the country and its shall be the duty of the state to apply these principles in making laws. Articles referring to these principles may be briefly mentioned as follows:

Article 38 – expects the State to secure a social order for the promotion of the welfare of the people. It states that State shall strive to promote the welfare of the people by securing and protecting as effectively as it may, a social order in which justice, social, economic and political, shall prevail in all the institutions of the national life.

The State shall, in particular, strive to minimize the inequalities in income, and endeavour to eliminate inequalities in status, facilities and opportunities, not only amongst individuals but also amongst groups of people residing in different areas or engaged in different vocations.

Article 39 - The State shall, in particular direct its policy towards securing:

(a) That the citizens, men and women equally, have the right to an adequate means to livelihood;

(b) That the ownership and control of the material resources of the community are so distributed as best to sub serve the common good;

(c) That the operation of the economic system does not result in the concentration of wealth and means of production to the common detriment;

(d) That there is equal pay for equal work for both men and women;

(e) That the health and strength of workers, men and women, and the tender age of children are not abused and that citizens are not forced by economic necessity to enter vocations unsuited to their age or strength;

(f) That children are given opportunities and facilities to develop in a healthy manner and in conditions of freedom and dignity and that childhood and youth are protected against exploitation and against moral and material abandonment.

Article 39A - The State shall ensure that the operation of the legal system promotes justice, on a basis of equal opportunity, and shall, in particular, provide free legal aid, by suitable legislation or schemes or in any other way, to ensure that opportunities for securing justice are not denied to any citizen by reason of economic or other disabilities.

Article 41 - The State shall, within the limits of its economic capacity and development, make effective provision for securing the right to work, to education and to public assistance in cases of unemployment, old age, sickness and disablement and in other cases of undeserved want.

Article 42 – The state shall make provision for securing just and humane conditions of work and for maternity relief.

Article 43 – The State shall endeavor to secure, by suitable legislation or economic organization or in any other way, to all workers, agricultural, industrial or otherwise, work, a living wage, conditions of work ensuring a decent standard of life and full enjoyment of leisure and social and cultural opportunities and, in particular, the State shall endeavor to promote cottage industries on an individual or co-operative basis in rural areas.

Article 45 – The State shall endeavor to provide, within a period of ten years from the commencement of the Constitution, for free and compulsory education for all children until they complete the age of fourteen years.

Article 46 – The State shall promote with special care the educational and economic interests of the weaker sections of the people, and in particular, of the Scheduled Castes and the Scheduled Tribes, and shall protect them from social injustice and all forms of exploitation.

Article 47 – The State shall regard the raising of the level of nutrition and the standard of living of its people and the improvement of public health as among its primary duties and, in particular, the State shall endeavor to bring about prohibition of the consumption, except for medicinal purposes, of intoxicating drinks and of drugs which are injurious to health.

The difference between the Fundamental Rights and Directive Principles lies in this that Fundamental Rights are primarily aimed at assuring political freedom to the citizens by protecting them against excessive State action while the Directive Principles are aimed at securing social and economic freedoms by appropriate State action. The Fundamental Rights are intended to foster the ideal of a political democracy and to prevent the establishment of authoritarian rule but they are of no value unless they can be enforced by resort to courts. So they are made justiciable. However, it is also evident that notwithstanding their great importance, the Directive Principles cannot in the very nature of things be enforced in a court of law. But, it does not mean that Directive Principles are less important. than Fundamental Rights or that they are not binding on the various organs of the State. The Fundamental Rights and the Directive Principles constitute the 'conscience' of our Constitution. The purpose of the Fundamental Rights is to create an egalitarian society, to free all citizens from coercion or restriction by society and to make liberty available to all. The purpose of the Directive Principles is to fix certain social and economic goals for immediate attainment by bringing about a non-violent social revolution. Through such a social revolution the Constitution seeks to fulfill the basic needs of the common man and to change the structure of our society. It aims at making the Indian masses free in the positive sense. Without faithfully implementing the Directive Principles, it is not possible to achieve the welfare State contemplated by the Constitution.

Indian Judiciary and Human Rights

Indian Constitution also provides for effective machinery for the enforcement of fundamental rights. If fundamental right is interfered with by an act of the executive or by a Federal or State Law, any person entitled to the right can move the Supreme Court to get the act or law declared unconstitutional. Initially the attitude of judiciary in India towards the Directive Principles was not favourable and it had nullified many important legislation embodying socio-economic reform. However, with the passage of time there has been a shift in the attitude of Indian judiciary towards socioeconomic rights contained in part IV of the Indian constitution. The court felt the necessity of a change in its earlier outlook.Undoubtedly, India has made honest efforts for the protection' and promotion of human rights the world over and is the greatest champion of the Human Rights in the third world.

However, the fact remains that there is a wide gap between theory and practice. Despite extensive constitutional and statutory safeguard, there continues to be significant human right abuse in country due to lack of awareness and sensitivity. The level of awareness and sensitivity even among the elite is very poor. Report of custodial death, violence against women, exploitation of children, excesses by police army and other forces are pouring in daily. In the list of countries where large scale abuse of human right occurs, India has been included by the Amnesty International. In spite of above facts, the Government of India bears enormous responsibilities in ensuring protection and promotion of human right in all their aspects.

The major contribution in this regards the government of India has constituted the National Human Rights Commission for the protection and promotion of human right with power to investigate and recommend policy changes, punishment and compensation. The National Human Rights Commission has the mandate to spread human rights Awareness and sensitivity by available means. The Indian culture is laid on the principles of equality, equity and other egalitarian tenets. All human beings are regarded as the children of God and any kind of disparity among them should be shunned. This is incorporated in the Hindu Vedas, the Babylonian Code of Hammurabi, the Bible, the Quran (Koran) and other religious scriptures.

In Article 1 of Universal Declaration of Human Right 1948, it is said' all human beings are born free and equal in dignity and right. They are endowed with reason and conscience and should get act towards one another in a spirit of brotherhood. At another place in the same document it is stated "all are equal before law and are entitled without any discrimination of equal protection." (Article 7) Human rights are universal. They are the birthright of every member of the human family. They symbolize the basic standards without which people cannot realize their inherent human dignity. No one has to earn or deserve human rights.

Gender Equality

Gender equality means an equal visibility, empowerment and participation of both genders in all spheres of public and private life. Gender equality does not mean gender similarity rather it is the opposite of gender inequality, which is not gender difference. Gender equality is an overriding principle that applies to the enjoyment of all rights: civil, cultural, economic, political and social. Sustainable prosperous and progressive democracy can be achieved only by true equality between women and men.

Gender Inequality In Society

Gender disparity is seen in almost all walks of life in the human society. Nobel Laureate Amartya Sen said that "gender inequality is not one homogeneous phenomenon, but a collection of disparate and interlinked problems". In one of his essays (*Many Faces of Gender Inequality*) Dr. Sen described Seven Types of Inequality in society. Though all the form of inequality can be involved in the broad area of social life, it is better to the social life in general and other types of social life in particular. In social life women tend to have less access than men to resources, opportunities and decision-making. Domestic violence, not doing marriage of divorce and widow are major socio-cultural condition that violates women's human right and shows gender inequality. Inequalities are impediments to the ability of women to develop and exercise their full capabilities, for their own benefit and that of society as a whole. Gender inequality in education leads to inequality in access to decision making positions and to low levels of economic empowerment; inequality in decision making leads to inequality in access to information and technology, ownership of property and to low levels of legal literacy; inequality in property ownership leads to inequality in poverty levels. Following are the main area where gender disparity is seen in society:

Professional Life

Women face Professional inequality greater handicap than men in employment promotion in work. There are two types of Gender disparities, direct and indirect. Direct gender disparity is when a woman is treated less fairly than a man because of her gender or marital status or because she is pregnant while the indirect one is when a requirement, that is the same for everyone, has an unfair effect on some women because of their gender, marital status, pregnancy or potential pregnancy. Fear of violence is a cause of women's lack of participation in activities beyond the home, as well as inside it. Within the home, women and girls may be subjected to physical and sexual abuse as punishment or as culturally justified assaults. These acts shape their attitude to life, and their expectations of themselves.

The persistence of unequal outcomes suggests that women's as well as men's experiences require explicit attention in terms of the protection and promotion of human rights. This is the main thrust of Human Right Education because this only can protest and promote Human Rights.

Educational Life

Education is "one of the most valuable means of achieving gender equality and the empowerment of women." and enrolment ratios for boys and girls at the primary level are approaching equality in most of the places in India but differences persist at the regional level and for different age groups and levels of schooling, especially at higher levels. Two thirds of the world's illiterate adults are women, with illiteracy highest among older women who never had the opportunity to go to school. Differences also persist at retention of girls/ women at different classes because formal education is perceived as of very little importance for girls. Tough it is always found that the pass percentage of girls at different levels is higher than that of their male counterparts.

Economic Life

Although women's participation in various aspects of economic and community life has increased but it still remains less than that of men. Women work in different jobs and occupations than men, almost always with lower status and pay. The female economic activity rate is now nearly 70 per cent of the male rate in developing countries, ranging from 86 per cent in East Asia to 50 per cent in Latin America and the Caribbean. A large part of women work in low paid or unpaid occupations. In agriculture, family enterprises and the informal sector, women have little possibility for savings, credit or investment and limited security. Women's work is poorly measured in official statistics in spite of its tremendous importance for the well being of families. No economic evaluvation is done for the household chores which has indirect impact on the economy of the society in general and family in particular. Women's full enjoyment of their human rights, including those relating to economic development and resources, is essential to any strategy aimed at poverty eradication and sustainable development.

Political Sphere

Women are subjugated in political and other decisions making structures at all levels. The example is the Women Reservation Bill, which could not be even tabled in parliament let alone be discussed.

When policies are designed in the context of respect for, and promotion and protection of, human rights, then unequal outcomes for women in the economic and social spheres oblige governments to design items in a way that would reduce inequalities.

International human rights instruments, the Beijing Platform for Action and the Vienna Declaration and Programme of Action provide a solid basis for promoting women's enjoyment of their human rights, including those related to economic development and resources and the alleviation of women's poverty. The Bejing Platform for Action recognizes the impact of gender on the enjoyment of human rights, including access to rights, opportunities and resources and with regard to treatment in many areas and identified 12 critical areas of concern. They are:

1. Poverty
2. Education
3. Health
4. Violence
5. Armed and other conflicts
6. Economic Participation
7. Power sharing and decision making
8. National and international machineries

9. Human Rights
10. Mass Media
11. Environment and Development
12. The Girl Child

Human Right and Woman

The Human Rights of women and the girl-child are an inalienable, integral and indivisible part of universal human rights. The full and equal participation of women in political, civil, economic, social and cultural life, at the regional, national and international levels, and the eradication of all forms of discrimination on the grounds of sex are priority objectives of the international community. (*Vienna Declaration and Programme of Action* (Part-I, Para 18)).

Gender disparity is seen everywhere as women's human rights have always been violated in almost all countries through political and societal structures, irrespective of the country's economic and political status. Violence against women is a very common feature. There has always been a restriction on their active participation in developmental activities outside their homes. Illiteracy, infanticide, sexual abuse and teenage pregnancies are some of the problems which women are facing.

Equality and equity on the basis of gender is a fundamental principle of international human rights law first recognized by the United Nations in its Charter (1945) and subsequently in the 1948 Universal Declaration on Human Rights.

Recent world conferences, including Vienna (1993), Cairo (1994) and Beijing (1995) have confirmed the strong link between the gendered nature of violations of human rights, and the actual advancement of women's rights. Discrimination against women violates the principles of equality of rights and respect for human dignity. It is also an obstacle to the participation of women on equal terms with men in all spheres of society.

Violation of Human Right of Women

Despite many positive developments in securing women's human rights, patriarchy continues to be embedded in the social system in India denying the majority of women the choice to decide how they live. The over-riding importance of "community" in a patriarchal sense ensures that women rarely have an independent say in community issues.

Crime against women are on the rise whether it be female foeticide, female infenticide, dowary deaths, sexual abuse, molestation, rape, sexual expolitation in work place, disparity in right and duties of men and women employmees etc. the less said in better to describe the present day scenario. Even IAS officers are not spared of gender disparity according to National Commision for Women.

It is a violation of women's Human Rights when:

- female foetus is denied the right to be born because she is a girl.
- married woman are mutilated because she refuses to concede to an undesirable and indecent proposals within the family.
- Girls are denied formal education for want of money and time or security.
- Women are denied to enter the proffesion of their choice
- Women are given name if they enter in political life.
- Women are desserted by husband for his second marriage.
- babies are denied food or drowned or suffocated or their spines broken, simply because they are born girls.
- women and girls are sold into the slavery of prostitution.
- women are burnt to death or physically tortured for dowery.
- individual women are raped in their own communities.
- women are denied the right to plan their own families and that includes being forced to have abortions or being sterilized against their will and going for multiple pregnancies for want of a son.
- An unwed pregnant girl is murdered publicaly or privately in the name of saving the honour of the family.

Human Rights Education

An International Congress of Human Rights held in 1968 at Tehran. International Congress on the teaching of Human Rights convened by United Nations at Vienna in 1988 and later in 1993 drafted a Declaration ultimately inspiring the UN decade for Human Rights Education 1995-2004.

Human rights education, training and public information were essential for the promotion and achievement of stable and harmonious relations among communities and for fostering mutual understanding, tolerance and peace are required for happy and developed society.

"Education shall be directed to the full development of the human personality and to the strengthening of respect for human rights and fundamental freedoms. It shall promote understanding, tolerance and friendship among all nations, racial or religious groups, and shall further the activities of the United Nations for the maintenance of peace" (Universal Declaration of Human Rights, Article 26.2).

Human Rights Education (HRE) is a process whereby people learn about their rights and the rights of others, within a framework of participatory and interactive learning. HRE is concerned with changing attitudes and behaviour, learning new skills, and promoting the exchange of knowledge and information. HRE is long-term, and aims to provide an understanding of the issues, and equip people with the skills to articulate their rights and communicate this knowledge to others.

Human Rights Education is all learning that develops the knowledge, skills, and values of human rights. It includes a varied range of innovative and effective education programs in the formal, informal and non-formal sectors, which are implemented by Amnesty International around the world.

The Expected Outcomes of Human Rights Education

Human rights education teaches both about human rights and for human rights. Its goal is to help people understand human rights, value human rights, and take responsibility for respecting, defending, and promoting human rights.

An important outcome of human rights education is empowerment, a process through which people and communities increase their control on their own lives and the decisions that affect them. The ultimate goal of human rights education is people working together to bring about human rights, justice, and dignity for all.

Education about human rights provides people with information about human rights. It includes learning about universality, indivisibility, and interdependence of human rights and the inherent dignity of all people and their right to be treated with respect. It also includes the way to promote peaceful resolution of conflicts and also history and continuing development of human rights.

Education for human rights helps people feel the importance of human rights, internalize human rights values, and integrate them into the way they live. These human rights values and attitudes include "strengthening respect for human rights and fundamental freedoms" (UDHR Article 30.2), understanding the nature of human dignity, respecting the dignity of others and also non-violence and believing that cooperation is better than conflict

Education for human rights also gives people a sense of responsibility for respecting and defending human rights and empowers them through skills to take appropriate action. These skills for action include recognizing that human rights may be promoted and defended on an individual, collective, and institutional level and realizing that unjust situations can be improved.

Human Right Education and Woman

There must be national and international efforts to strengthen and protect women's rights and to eradicate certain oppressive social/cultural conditions, with special emphasis on empowering all women. Human Rights Education is a tool for peaceful societal transformation with a gender perspective and framework for social development. It aims at the empowerment and the building of capabilities of women, men, youth and children through critical thinking, understanding, applying and claiming all human rights, including civil and political, economic, social and cultural rights and the right to development.

Connecting Human Rights with Women's Life

It is very essential that Human Rights Education must be practical and relevant to women's daily lives because women learn from their own narratives to conceptualize human rights and work towards their fulfillment. Then only it is possible to bring changes in the society in general and in the life of women in particular.

It is imperative that Human Rights Education be free of gender bias, racial and other stereotypes, be sensitive to particular needs and be based on the principles of non-discrimination and equality in the enjoyment of all Human Rights which emphasizes on capacity building for good governance, democratization, accountability and stability.

Intersection of Gender, Class and Caste

Women of all disadvantaged classes are vulnerable to attrocities and symbolise exploitation. Gender and caste status intersect to create violence against women as a symbolic gesture of exploitation and discrimination against the class they belong to. Sexual harassment by landowners, moneylenders, sexual overtures by bosses and incest is common.

Violence against women within the community is often characterized by attacks on the "honor" of women by stripping and parading of women in naked who are believed to have broken the community's norms. In some areas this extends to the killing of women as witches or dayans in order to snactch their property (movable or immovable).

Access to Justice

Unless supported by male relatives or a strong social group, women victims of violence are at a severe disadvantage within the criminal judiciary system. Gender disparity which exists in Indian institutions are often exacerbated by ingrained caste and other biases against members of disadvantaged groups.

Non-registration of crimes is a serious problem. Without a First Information Report (FIR), a case cannot continue. Only a miniscule percentage (5%) of cases of crime against women are registered in police circles. Even women police officers have reported being verbally abused for trying to file a complaint.

Police sometimes acts as a party to accused and often withhold and destroy evidence. Along with poor access to medical facilities in general, police often refuses to institute immediate forensic medical examinations, leading to lack of evidence when finally done. In addition, there is little access to the financial resources, time to pursue a case or legal aid support available to members of disadvantaged groups.

Women's Empowerment

Social activists and women organisations play a very important role in highlighting women's issues and lobbying for changes in the law. Many of the positive initiatives of the state have been taken as a result of forceful arguments of the women's movement in the country. In most of the part of India, the challenge of defending women's human rights is compounded by gender disparity inherent within traditional societies as well as within state structures. Though the enrolment in schools is increased in girls but the quality education in Science and Technology is not given to girls on presumption that this is not a cup of tea for girls as they lack understanding in these subjects.

The Suggested Remedies

Abuses have continued because, for too long, the history of women has been a history of silence. Even today, there are those who are trying to silence their words. Women tolerate unjust behaviour either due to ignorance of their rights or sometimes under social and emotional pressures. When laws, customs, traditional roles, family responsibilities or attitudes and stereotypes provide women with fewer opportunities or place them at a disadvantaged position as they seek to access opportunities, remedial measures are needed to eliminate such disadvantages, and to prevent them from recurring. The objectives to be achieved by social changes are as follows:

1. The subordinate place of women in societies should be replaced by full social and legal equality including their movement and economic and property right.
2. Right to marry a person of her own choice at the age of her choice and right to remain single if she feels so, should be enforced by excersing the social pressure of activist groups.
3. Women should have equal access to education including higher education, and be free to choose their subjects of study.
4. They should be free to choose their own work and should be allowed to fully participate in public life-from politics and sports to the arts and sciences.

The remedies suggested can be listed below:

- To enact a uniform civil code under which men and women have equality of choosing religious beliefs and practices.
- To make law which include the rights of women as set out in the Universal Declaration of Human Rights and the UN Convention on the Elimination of All Forms of Discrimination against women.
- Women should be given reservation in political and policy-making bodies.
- Due recognition should be given to the emotional and familial and non-financial roles of every woman.
- Disparity in food, education, clothes health should be listed as offence.
- Listen to the voices of women in their homes, neighborhoods, and workplaces.
- We must respect the choices that each woman makes for herself and her family. Every woman deserves the chance to realize her own God-given potential.
- We also must recognize that women will never gain full dignity until their human rights are respected and protected.

- No woman should be forced to remain silent for fear of religious or political persecution, arrest, abuse or torture.

In the name of justice, for the sake of human progress, and for the benefit of all the friends, wives, daughters, sisters, and mothers of the world, we call upon all societies to respect the human rights of women.

Women are entitled to equality with men where the enjoyment of all human rights, including those relating to sustainable human development is concerned. They should be made more accessible to rights resources and opportunities. Not only is the enjoyment of rights - including the right to access resources on an equal basis - an end in itself, it is an essential ingredient in achieving the empowerment of women, social justice and overall social and economic development.

Last but not least it can be said that empowering the women does not mean disempowering men because women empowerment draws both men and women them out of the clutches of stereotypes.

References

Diwan P. (1998), Human Rights and Law Universal and Indian : Deep and Deep Publications Pvt. Ltd., New Delhi.

Kapoor S. K. (1999), Human Rights Under International and Indian Law, Central Law Agencey, Allahabad.

Mohanty J. (2000), Human Right Education, Deep and Deep Publications Pvt. Ltd., New Delhi.

http://www.unhchr.ch/html/hchr.htm : The Office of the High Commissioner for Human Rights: Women's Rights are Human Rights: Special Issue on Women's Rights - Spring 2000: Geneva, Switzerland.

http://www.amnestyusa.org/learn/ : Amnesty International USA: 5 Penn Plaza : New York, NY 10001.

WHRnet - Women's Human Rights Net.htm

http://india_resource.tripod.com/social.htm

Vinayak, Ramesh "Victims of Sudden Affluence." *India Today*. December 15, 1997.

http://www.bc.edu/bc_org/avp/law/lwsch/journals/bctwj/21_1/01_TXT.htm

Frontline (National Magazine from the Publishers of *The Hindu*) Volume 18, Issue 22, Oct. 27 , Nov. 09, 2001

8

Development, Forced Displacement and Resettlement: A Human Rights Perspective

A. K. Singh

Displacement is no uncommon in the development process, but it is its expanding size and adverse impact on the quality of life that are now a cause for serious concern. In India development projects in last 60 years are estimated to have displaced roughly 60 million to have displaced naughty 60 million people, most of whom have never been properly resettled. Moreover the fact remains that not all those displaced are able to understand why they should be asked to bear disproportionate costs of economic development and why in the process of development they should be treated as less than citizen and human beings by the developers. The developers, like the developees, form a heterogeneous category. In any event, the outcries of the worst-off developers fall on the hearing-impaired or challenged developmentalist ears. (Baxi, 1969).

In this zodiac the worst-off developees, are perhaps more accurately the next–of–kin (the human rights activist and social movement flocks) proceed to launch a full throated assault on the paradigm of development. In so doing, they run grave risks.

They remain liable to the indictment of being naive romanticist paradigm warriors constantly in need of massive public re-education. Further, it is all too easy to misrepresent and misrecognize them either as these who want cost-free development.

In recent years the private sector has emerged as a major player in the development process, and the govt., obsessed with achieving higher and higher economic growth targets, is trying to attract private investment in sectors as varied as power generation, manufacturing, mining, roads and housing, to name a few. S.E.Z. far large private corporations, including Multinational companies (MNCs), are being set-up to accelerate the development process.

Under globalization pressures, laws are being amended or promulgated overnight in an unseemly haste to create investor friendly conditions, regardless of what happens to the livelihoods of farmers whose lands will be gone for a pittance. The requirement of land for such gigantic development plans is going to be enormous, and this is bound to precipitate displacement on an unprecedented scale.

Worldwide experience with resettlement has shown that people who are displaced do not easily recover, much less improve, their previous standards of living, Resettlement studies have vividly documented the divesting consequences of failed resettlement projects, which creates new pockets of poverty where none existed before (Mathur, 1998, Radhika, 1996) Such displacement not only puts affected people to grove impoverishment risks, but also causes a set back to the entire poverty reduction effort. As one observer put it "Truly, development is a very contradictory affair if it reinforces the very poverty that it aims to eliminate (Black, 2002).

Impoverishment is the most consistently visible impact on the lives of those forcibly displaced. Based on an examination of empirical evidence from a large number of projects and findings of numbers anthropological and sociological studies from all over the world, Cernea (1995) found eight recurrent characteristics that contribute to the process of impoverishment. These are: Landlessness, Joblessness, Homelessness,

Marginalization, food insecurity, increased morbidity and mortality, loss of access to common property, and social disarticulation, These are negative features of development induced displacement that they must be judged, in an empirical sense, as amongst its defining characteristics–things could be otherwise, but they almost never are (Turton, 2002).

Resettlement studies have further shown that it is the poor who are most at risk, ending up poorer than before - on the other hand the affluent groups, come up as winner all time. often they are able to turn even displacement into an opportunity to get richer. Seabrook (1993) provides an example from the Tehri Dam Project where in connivance with the project officials the rich people hurriedly built some 5,000 bogus houses in the submergence area, declared these as long-established family properties, and got away with hefty amounts as compensation claims. The only people who did not benefit were the real oustees, in spite of the resettlement promises.

The poor not only lose from displacement, they are even denied their basic human rights. They are not consulted during the project preening process although it is their lives that are most directly affected by the project.

The affected people never receive any information about the project or how much compensation will they get and when; and where, when and how they will be relocated (MARG, 1986) it needs however to be acknowledged that development often presents very real dilemma to planners ; how to implement urgent development projects designed to promote Commonly agreed goals and promote the realization of human rights at the same time is not easy task, yet it is important that in the pursuit of development goals the fundamental rights are not violated. The WCD (2000:204) noted: 'An equitable and sustainable approach to development requires that a decision to build a dam or any other options must not at the outset, sacrifice the rights of any citizen or groups of affected people'.

Although projects are undertaken to promote wider societal development yet the displaced person is seldom the beneficiary of development projects. The benefits mostly go to an entirely different set of people. For example while electricity generated in the singrauli Region benefits urban centres and industries located hundred of miles away, the poor people in that region who gave up their lands for the erection of power plants have no access to it (Mathur, 1999). Other studies also confirms that those who receive the benefits, usually urban dwellers, Commercial farmers and industries, are typically not the same groups that bear the social cost.

The establishment of large industries in different parts of rural India led to exploitation of vast natural resources, factories were established in (1986). backward areas and have displaced a large number of people from their habitat and occupation.

Costs of Development

Developers maintain that development interventions and projects are designed to service both the immediate and they long - run future of human rights. In this staple discourse, the present production of developmental destruction remains some how directed towards the future amelioration of the worst-off citizen peoples. There exist no easy way out of ways those in which developmental temporalities stand fully state constructed (Baxi, 2007).

There is no doubt that development interventions and projects are presented in terms of many manifest benefits measured in economic term (such as improvement in infrastructure, increased sources of energy, power generation, increased per capita income etc.). The principal costs are those of displacement of affected population when arrayed against, the manifest benefits. The cost presented as 'necessary' and desirable. However in contrast some social historians substantiate' the notion of the hidden costs of development comprising mainly of Demographic factors such as morbidity and mortality rates. The recent growth in the activist and social theorist awareness further point to immediate and long run environmental/ecological costs. typically under disclosed and under esteemed amongst the developmentalist articulations and mindsets; these typically include biodiversity depletion, social erosion, ecological imbalance, deforestation, desertification, contamination of water supplies and most crucially now, climate change concerns.

On this register displacement remains an important issue, but presents no longer any sovereign concern. When broadly non-economic costs are introduced in the discussion, the developers frame the issue in some rather large and formidable discourse of the efficient management of 'negative externalities' of the development enterprise. Put another way, the art and science of development primarily consist in the management of side effects, in the main associated with formidable discourse concerning the 'principle of Double effect'.

The Rule of law Costs and Human Rights Costs of Development

However, even this inventory needs further supplementation going beyond the mutual hostilities between developmentalists, developers, and next of their kin. I may here refer rather all too briefly (for reasons of space) to two kinds of 'non-economic' costs may produce sets of direct and indirect economic effects): The rule of law costs and human rights cost (hereafter respectively ROLC and HRC). Both these expressions are heavily freighted with conflicted meanings and with an overall paucity of rigorous comparative empirical examinations.

ROLC remain eminently measurable in terms of governance transparency and public accountability of the class of developmentalists, though not fully the theory of development which may, and does indeed nun counter to the idea of rule of law. High levels of official corruption often match with patterns of authoritarian and militarized governance of politics of citizen protest.

The not-so-hidden costs of development in the Indian design of developmental governance escalate state investment and dedication of disproportionate resources in police, paramilitary, and related security forces. In turn, these furnish a reason, it not always the cause, for the cumulative acts of destruction of public property and citizen falatitiy in policing. A shared culture of political responsibility amongst the rulers and the ruled here emerges as a prime ROLC.

In any event, under way now in the discourse of development and displacement are no longer constitutionally based notions of development as social justice, but the mimetic, and often wounding 'Good governance, talk inspired by globally hegemonic agencies. The HRC furnish a more reality available register. For ex. The world commission on Dams (WCD) refers us to' an increasingly robust foundation of "International Covenants, charters, declarations and conventions" does indeed suggest a "shaping focus on equity (WCD, 2000, hereafter WCD report), but is remains, at the same time, insensitive to human rights obligations upon nation-states (Baxi, 2001). Overall, its prescriptions for an integrated policy frame concerning development and displacement have almost altogether escaped the attention of the talented Indian policy makers.

The problem of identifying fazing and measuring costs and benefits of development remains imperious for any sensible policy approach/Framework for development interventions and projects Cost, in paradigmatic economist ways of thought must, in order to exist remain measurable when the worst-off developers. Complain that large/mega irrigation projects threaten their right to life as a right to a set of distinctively cultural/civilization lifestyles, they remain insensible to developers every where because lifestyles logics remain altogether immeasurable. Displaced worst-off peoples were not merely arguing for cash are land-for-land-based compensation, but indeed they require a just rehabilitation policy under which the displaced remained entitled to ways of their life and to relocated in the better place or as earlier.

Gaps between 'needs and 'action, creates environment for the activist movements to flourish. This instrumentalist approach, however, does not address the problem of incommensurability thus posed, the worst-off people may never be fully compensated for the destruction of the quality of life.

Aside from this the 'blighting' ROLC and HRC remain seldom taken in to account by developmentalist. Blighting costs occur, as everyone knows from the moment a development site stands notified. No matter how long it takes to develop.

The land-for-land based compensation polices provide meagre relief and rehabilitation for those whose lands were submerged. However, as activists (and not just in India) have demonstrated, this policy postures systemically under/non-compensates those whose livelihood stands derived from non-land-based occupations and vocations (such as village priest, local hairdresser, midwives, hakims, and the dai's among a whole range of related service, occupations). Further such policies who scant regard for cultural practices in relocated citizen peoples at distant sites in south Gujarat had to traverse a long distances to pray at a mosque or to bury their dead because the rehab. Policies simply overlooked these basic needs. Truth to till, the developers professing such policies remain unable to conceptualize these costs of development, even at the peril of the incitement of 'communalist' developmentalist policy and pursuits.

It would therefore be in the context to give a figurative outline of the persons and families who have been forced to leave their habitat.

Following is an account of number of families and people displaced from their homes as a result of various dams, projects undertaken by the govt. and various causes of displacement.

S.L.	*No. of Families*	*Dam/Project*	*Source*
1.	16,000 families	Pong Dam in the Bias Valley	*Surya India, Feb.* 1990
2.	18,500 families	Ukai Dam, Gujarat	*Surya India, Feb.* 1990
3.	162 villages would be submerged	Bargi Dam in Madhya Pradesh (one of the big 30 Dams to be constructed in Narmada Valley)	*Frontline, July 30,* 1993
4.	1,00,000 people to be displaced	Madhya Pradesh, 30 big, 135 medium and 3000 minor dams in Narmada Valley	*Frontline, July 30,* 1993
5.	90,000 people to be evicted	Sarda Sarovar, Gujarat	*Illustrated Weekly of India, Jan. 5-6,* 1991
6.	1,900 families to be evicted in Maharashtra	Sardar, Sarovar, Maharashtra side	*Ibid.*

Contd...

S.L.	*No. of Families*	*Dam/Project*	*Source*
7.	2,00,000 families to be evicted	Both sides of Sardar Sarovar	*Ibid.*
8.	70,000 families to be evicted	Bisalpur Dam, Deoli, Tonk Distt. Rajasthan	*Times of India* Sept. 7, 1994
9.	37 Villages to be evicted	Kishan Dam at Tons River, U.P. and H.P. Border (construction to begin in June 1996)	*Times of India* March. 3, 1995
10.	1,10,000 people evicted	Damodar Valley Project	*Times of India* July. 17, 1994
11.	6,00,000 people displaced	As assortment of industries including the Heavy Electricals Corporation, Ranchi and the Bokaro Thermal Power and Steel Plants.	*Ibid.*
12.	1,70,000	Coal mining in Bihar	*Ibid.*
13.	12,00,000	A clutch of associated industries and coal mining in Bihar.	*Ibid.*
14.	1,00,000	Firing range (Agni and Prithvi Misiles) Baliapal and Bhogarai blocks in Balasore district of Orissa where National Test Range Project was launched in 1987.	*Times of India* Dec. 13, 1989
15.	27 villages to be evacuated	Angul-Talcher Coal fields operations	*Times of India* Sept. 26, 1994
16.	2,50,000 people to be evicted	Netrahat Firing Range (Artillery) in Chhotanagpur area Bihar, mostly tribals	*Times of India* Jan. 17, 1994
17.	Scores of families left village	Food crisis in Longphum, South Tripura.	*Times of India* Nov. 19, 1994
18.	20,000 people affected at the verge of eviction	Subsidence of mining area in East Singhbum	*Times of India* Nov. 7 1994
19.	1,85,00,000 persons displaced	Various projects all over India between 1951 and 1991.	*Times of India* July. 17, 1994

The Problems

The foregoing chart shows, figures of displaced persons of only and not their agony as a displacement. It is strange that the elite and the political power talk of development and at the ground reality people are faced with starvation. These are few sites pertains to displacement and their rehabilitation.

Coalmines in Talcher (Orissa)

The massive coalfield operation and the consequent rapid industrialization in Angul-Talcher area in Orissa has created problems of livelihood and residence for thousands of people. What is more disturbing is that hundreds of areas of land, are being acquired every year for mining. The authorities plan to evacuate 27 villages completely. A tug of war has developed between the village and the Mahanadi Coalfields Ltd.; on the issue of compensation, rehabilitation and jobs in the coalmines.

The Jagannath and Ananta open cast mines have advanced right to the doorsteps of the villagers' houses. There is no house in the villages which has not been damaged by the regular blastings.

The threat of displacement is hanging like a Damocles' sword on all of them. In Jembu Behan village alone, 246 acres of land has been acquired, no compensation paid and authorities have asked them to leave bag and baggage. Director of the Central Cooperative Bank, Chatnya Sahoo, alleged that the MCL had asked all the villages to leave the area by the end of 1994., But no alternative site had been provided to them. According to District Collector of Angul, Prasant nayak, three sites had been selected by the state for rehabilitation, but villagers refuse to move. There is discrimination in aid programmers. In one part of Angul district, Kanhia, Rs. 50,000 is paid over and above the compensation, no such amount is paid in Talcher in the same district.

Netrahat Firing Range

Netrahat plateau in Chota Nagpur tribal belt, a forested tribal belt area which extends across the Gumla and Palamau districts of Bihar,[5] has been used continuously for field firing practices by the Indian army since 1956. Stretching over 1471 sq. km. of traditional tribal land, the proposed Netrahat Field Firing Range will permit the 23 Artillery Brigade to perfect its battle skills. It will annihilate 245 villages and deprive 2,24,940 people of their homes and land. Of this number, 78 per cent belong to such tribes as the Oraon, Munda, Kisan, Khewar Birija and Asur. It is a catastrophe even by the standards of the Indian republic. It is the largest single displacement of a tribal population contemplated since independence.

Besides the question of rehabilitation, the project would spell a sentence of death for the Asur and Birjia who are on the verge of extinction. When they are no more, we would have lost the oldest stream of the Indian population. The Asur were the subcontinent's first iron smelters envied for their skills by the metal questing Aryans who drove them from the Gangetic plains into the Chota Nagpur highlands in 800 B.C. It is irony that birth of a male child in one of the islands in Andaman and Nicobar becomes a national news worthy of telecast on national hookup, but the imminet danger of extinction of the oldest tribe a India does not provoke emotion or concern.

The state has sacrificed the tribals at the alter of a so-called development programme which does not in any way benefit them; indeed, contributes to their immigration.

To assess the human cost of the nation's development programme in Bihar alone, one has only to place the displacement figures against the development projects since 1951. The Damodar Valley Project disposed 1,10,000 people; an assortment of industries, including the Heavy Electricals Corporation, Ranchi and the Bokaro thermal power and steel plants, dishoused 6,00,000 persons. A further 17,00,000 people have been displaced, by coal mining and a clutch of associated projects have turned 12,00,000 persons into refugees in their own country.

As in Bastar, Dahanu, Hirakund, Koraput, Bhakra, Malkangiri, and other project sites, the displaced become wood cutters, bonded labourers brick kin workers, or migrate to the city, where some become domestic servants, and others turn to crimes. Propelled from a hunter-gatherer context into a monetary economy, whose working they do not understand, they are brutally exploited. it is estimated that of the 1,85,00,000 people displaced by various projects between 1951; only 52,50,000 people have been resettled after a fashion, the rest have been abandoned to their fate.

These mass evictions have had disastrous demographic consequences. The tribals, who constituted 60 per cent of Chota Nagpur, population in 1951, have now been reduced to a mere 30 per cent.

The tribals are brow beaten into signing away their rights by an insensitive bureaucracy which keeps them in the dark about legal and administrative procedures, so that they cannot even understand the injustices visited upon them by forces outside their control.

Sardar Sarovar and Problems

The final report of the Ram Chandra Singh Deo Committee of Madhya Pradesh MLAs demanded that the Madhya Pradesh government should stop the construction of the Sardar Sarovar Dam. Rehabilitation, the report argued, was a human problem of gigantic dimensions, and noted that oustees were living in hardship and their future bleak.

A September 1994 study, Rehabilitation of Madhya Pradesh Project Affected Families in Gujrat, carried out by the Narmada Conrol Authority (NCA), described the subhuman conditions oustees resettled in Gujaratwere living in. At the Kukra site, most of those rehabilitated had not been given their land entitlement; others were given fragmented pieces of little value. Inadequate drainage, waterlogging, hostility and assault by local villagers, abysmal fuel, fodder and drinking water supplies: these conditions were endemic.

Impoverishment is arguably the least dangerous consequence of these conditions. During the 1994 monsoon Gujaratnewspapers reported that a cholera epidemic raged through the resettlement sites, after their poorly designed tin sheds were flooded. Crops and household materials were lost, and hundreds of tribals were hospitalized at Baroda and Vaghodia. Since no health care facilities are available nearby, this imposed a heavy financial burden on these impoverished families. Many died given that these conditions prevail when only 700 of 33,504 Madhya Pradesh families have as yet been resettled, the urgency is clear.

The Narmada Water Dispute Tribunal originally had ordered that the rehabilitation be completed at least a year prior to submergence. It needs an independent monitoring mechanism. Of the 3,100 families to have been resettled in Gujaratfrom Madhya Pradesh in 1992-93, land has actually been found for 1190 only. In 1993-94 of the Project Affected people (PAP) families to be shifted to Gujrat, only 986 were moved. Another problem of serious consequence has cropped up. Around 2,000 migrants from Madhya Pradesh to Gujrat, as a result of Sardar Sarovar evacuation, would not be eligible for getting benefit of reservation in view of the decision of the Supreme Court. The reason is that the caste or tribe of these people is not enumerated in the list meant for reservation benefit in Gujrat. This has created further problems leading to political implications. On the one hand political leaders are strongly advising not to leave their villages, on the other, they would be drowned if not evacuated as their villages fall under the submergence zone.

The Sardar Sarovar dam will submerge the habitants of 245 village, Most of these are tribals. The dam is being built in Gujrat, However, the artificial reservoir created would affect large population in the neighbouring states of Madhya Pradesh and Maharashtra.

The rehabilitation and resettlement progress has not been satisfactory by any standard. A senior member of the World Bank appraisal team, Conable, in his report dated August 29, 1989, stated that a regards rehabilitation progress between 1985 and 1989, there has been a very serious deterioration. He noted that in Madhya Pradesh 150 out of 193 villages had become openly against the dam. It was the December, 1989 report that gave details of non-implementation of 'minimum action'. The Madhya Pradesh government was required, for nstance, to provide a detailed plan, with data on land; infrastructure, time table for the first 17 villagers to resettle in M.P., the written confirmation of arrangements satisfactory for resettlement of the 17 villages for M.P. to be resettled in Gujrat, a detailed plan for rehabilitation work in 1990-91.

However, the government had not even completed the bench-mark survey of the first 17 villages by 1991. Instead of collaborating with the dam affected people, the government used force when faced with non-cooperation of the tribals opposing the dam. On its part, the Government of Maharashtra sat by and did nothing. It could not identify any land for the 1,900 families of Maharashtra oustees of Sardar Sarovar Project (SSP). Despite the outward declarations of satisfactory progress on the rehabilitation front, the World Bank wrote to the three concerned states, Gujarat, Maharashtra and Madhya Pradesh and gave a deadline of May 15, 1990 to improve rehabilitation. It then took another unprecedented step: it delayed the appraisal report to 1992. This is proof, if any are required, that the rehabilitation measures had not satisfied even the elementary conditions set by the Bank. In March, 1990 Conable, one of the World Bank high officials expressed concern. He said, "we hope the SSP does not affect the quality of life in the neighborhood of the Narmada. But it is for the borrowing government to establish its priorities". He also expressed his views on the rehabilitation issue saying, "We do not govern your country (India). We only provide financial assistance". It is thus apparent that rehabilitation progress of the displaced persons was an utter failure - a disgrace to enforcement agencies for human rights.

One of the major sticking points so far has been the manner in which the resettlement of the oustees has been conduced. The Jayant Patil Committee, which was set up to review the project, found that this has been far from adequate. The land allotted to them has largely been of poor quality, under dispute and severally lacking in civic amenities. This has naturally led to many of the oustees attempting to return to their original homes which are now in the submergence zone. If this is the condition of the oustees, who at present constitute only tow per cent of the total of 33,000 families who are to be rehabilitated, then the task of resettling all of them in a manner acceptable to rehabilitated, then the task of resettling all of them in a manner acceptable to them seems virtually impossible. At the conception stage it was agreed upon that apart from certain other conditions, rehabilitation shall be made as the construction progressed. The fact that this has not been done adequately is in direct contravention to the stipulations of the Narmada Tribunal Award.

Tihari Dam project is one of the dream projects in the series. Since is coverage area was confined to chilly area only and it was found out precisely, there was no difficulty in rehabilitating the people of ousted towns. So far as known to the author, proper measures have been undertaken by the government to put the inhabitants of the coverage area in new places almost in the same position as they were earlier. Unfortunately it does not happen in many situations.

The rehabilitation of persons displaced by the big dams prove to be the most thorny problem so far. The displacements are there to stay and permanently. The process of rehabilitation has always raised a volley of questions, not only from the displaced persons but from all conscious people also; the discrepancies are bound to be there. People who have an easy reach to the bureaucracy and politicians, get whatever is due to them and even that which is not due to them. But the poor, who are disorganized are left to fend for themselves. The rehabilitation of persons, uprooted from the command areas of dams has never been complete and it has created more problems than it has solved. The evacuees are generally transferred either to barren lands or infertile or waste land. Sensitivity to the real needs of the uprooted on whom a new lifestyle in a different socio-political milieu is being imposed is copiously lacking. The result often is an identity crisis and cultural shock. It must be realized that freedom and liberty cannot thrive on empty stomachs, and bare bodies. Traditional civil and political rights, important as they are, have no meaning unless they are accompanied by social and economic rights.

Right to education, be it under the UN Charter or a part of Article 221 of the Constitution of India as expanded by the Supreme Court, is non-existent for lakhs children of displaced persons. It is the moral and legal duty of the government to establish schools for the children up to 14 years of age and only then the question of children going to school arises. In the case of displaced persons, the primary concern for them is to find and alternative source of survival. The children have been left uncared for in all the respects including education and nutrition. It is sad to say that these children have been deprived of their basic right to of life. The are destined to lead a life of want and misery. It is, therefore, most vital for the advancement and fulfillment of human rights promise that the policy makers and resettlement authorities must provide proper schools for the education of displaced persons so that they should not be damned for the remaining period of their lives.

Legal Position

The Fundamental Right to Property as guaranteed under Articles 19(1,f) and 31 is no more. Instead, it has been provided under Article 300A that no person shall be deprived to his property save by authority of law. There might have been controversy about the fate of the property right after the 44th Amendment. There are areas, however, where some of the decisions of the High Courts and the Supreme Court which point out towards a definite direction. In *Rakesh Prasad Tiwari v. Union of India,* the Andhra Pradesh High Court has held that if the property is acquired for public purpose and vests in the government which claims it, such claim is illegal as long as the necessary compensations are not paid. Denying the citizen his property would be amounting to violation of Article 300A of the Constitution. State cannot claim the privilege of denying its citizens their valuable property rights. Inaction on the government in not paying the compensation even after nine years infringement of right guaranteed under Article 300A.

The other provisions in that direction, are the judicially expanded scope of right to life under Article 21 of the Constitution of India, including within it right to education, right to livelihood, right to shelter, right to pollution-free habitat and right to a dignified life. Article 40 of the Constitution of India provides that the state shall promote with special care the educational and economic interests of the weaker sections of the people, and, in particular, of the Scheduled Castes and Scheduled Tribes, and shall protect them from social injustice and all forms of exploitation. Article 39(b) and (c) of the Constitution provides that the state shall take special care in laying down its policies, that benefits of natural resources of the country reaches to all and there is no concentration of wealth into few hands. Needless to say that these provisions of the Constitution of India embody the spirit of various clauses of the UN Declaration and the International Convention on Human Rights, particularly Article 25 and Article 11 (2).

Telco Experience of Displacement in Lucknwo Distt. of U.P.

The industrial development in the state was a classic case what was declared but was not genuine. Despite often repetitive objective of the spatial dispersal of industrial units the tendency of packing-up in the pre-existing nodes was strong. This process strengthed the uneven spatial pattern of industry. The spatial monopolistic process was highly sentimental to micro-environmental health in urban centers. In such places the risk of environmental pollution and health hazards escalated high.

TELCO had located its factory on the Dewa road in chinhat block of district lucknow TELCO was started in 1991 but the process of land acquisition was started in 1988. The villagers of proposed sites of plant had been agitating to drop the proposal of land acquisition by TECLO on the ground that they are poor farmers depending for their livelihood on the cultivations of their land.

The project has acquired 11, 472 acres land for plant, township and vehicular movements. The two auxiliary units which are based and TELCO hold also acquired the 587 acres land this has affected 15 villages directly or indirectly and displace 1627 families from their workplace and community. The survey undertaken by the researcher revealed when their lands would actually be acquired and how the compensation due to them actually disbursed. Many of the displaced people got much loss compensation for their evacuated houses rather than prevailing market value, while it is welcoming to note that the TELCO is reaching the neighboring villages through various peripheral development programmes.

As I have noted in the case of all above sites including TELCO. Three stands of ideas are articulated at three different levels - micro, meso and macro - in the case of all the hi - tech driven large project. Thus, issues that the displacees are concerned with are related to livelihood security, appropriate and adequate compensation of displacees are concerned with are livelihood security, appropriate and adequate compensation if displaced, and the preservation of their identify and culture within their traditional habitats. The meso - level articulations are made by numerous NGO,s that champion the cause of displacees. A part from the immediate welfare of the victims, they are also concerned with issues of sustainable development and, hence, their interest in environmental and ecological problems. They attempt to sensitize the displacees about the long term consequences of the policy of rapid industrialization. Pursued by govt. through private corporation finally, those who articulate the macro issues are concerned with the political economy of development, neocolonialism/imperialism.

The tension between the concept of private property held by the state and. Communal property internalized by the tribals, the illegitimacy of the very notion of profit, and the like. It is not very easy to mesh into one unified whole the ideas and articulation of the three levels and than state them into programme of action.

Suggestation

During land acquisition process if planners will follow the framework given below, then not only the goal of sustainable development will fulfill as well as the rights of oustees, can preserve and maintain. In our integrative framework we suggest that instead of EIA (Environmental Impact Assessment), project promoters should look at impacts of land acquisition proposals on the flow of ecosystem services. By adopting a "No net loss" of ecosystem service flows as a principle, promoters can simultaneously internalize both social well being and business well-being concerns into their land acquisition proposals. This implies that business will minimize loss of ecosystem service flows and also make good any less through compensatory interventions. Initially, this may should like a tall order for the promoters, but in vies of bet current understanding on the subject, it also makes sound business sense (WRI, 2008).

The extended integrative frame work in presented in how chart given below:

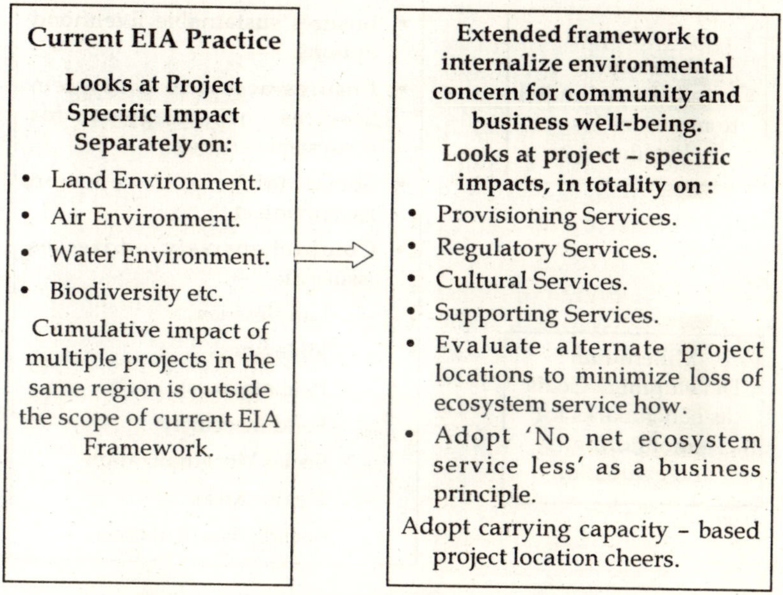

Figure 1: Environmental Sustainability Framework

Internalizing Social Well-Being Concerns in to Land Acquisition

The scope of SIA in India is typically limited to minimizing the impacts on livelihoods. This proposes a broader framework that aims at maximizing social well-being of affected communities (Figure 2). It is proposed that social well-being concern in land acquisition propose are extended to provide sustainable livelihood options and comprehensively cover all affected stakeholders namely landless, jobless, homeless, elderly, and the destitute. The contribution of each infrastructure project to the social well-being of the local communities should be monitored and evaluated by taking. Millennium Development Goals (MDGs) as benchmarks, It is envisaged that the new framework, when aligned with project proposals in the true spirit, will reduce conflict between the project promotions and communities.

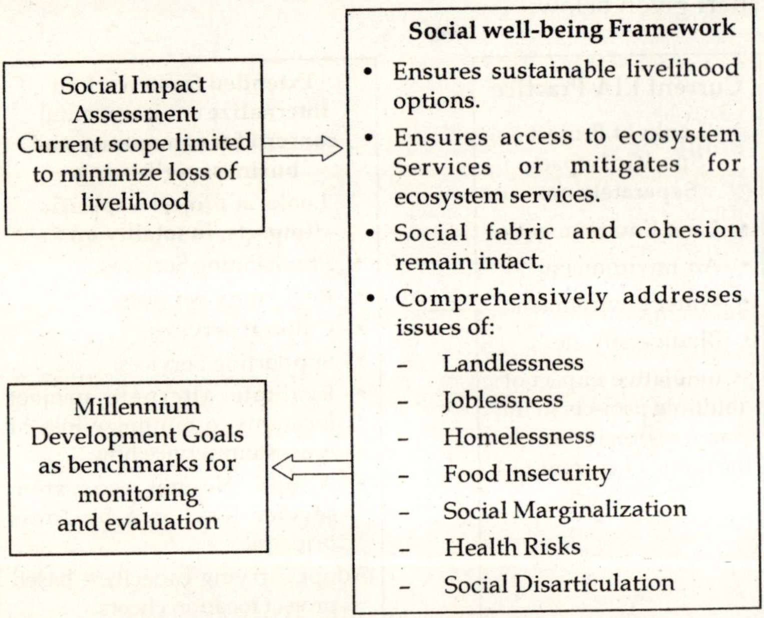

Figure 2 : Social well-being Framework

Source: The world Resources Institute (WRI, 2008).

The existing compensation and R & R packages are reported as being fraught with ambiguity. In the absence of clearly defined rights of the project-affected population, the communities, one the ten short changed by the project proponents. We propose the adoption of the following model by projects. to gain social consent for land acquisition and project viability (Figure 3).

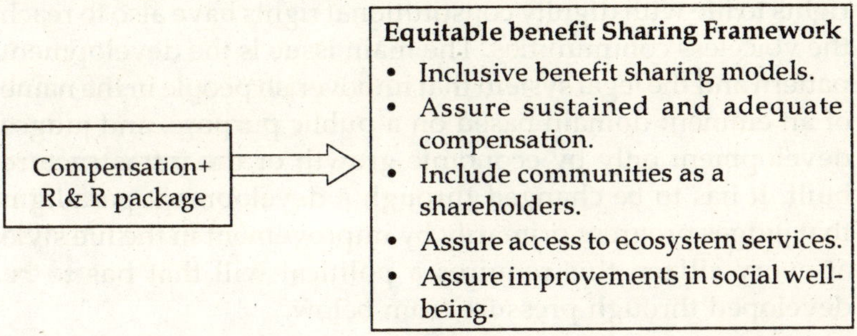

Figure 3

Concluding Remark

Compared with the policy commitment towards the need to minimize the incidence as well as the adverse impacts of their form of development and the displacement and to give priority to the "least displacing option" mode of development' the draft bill of National Rehabilitation Policy that leaved out in the cold the promise of the earlier version of policy, otherwise evolved in terms, of partnership between state policy makers and the civil society.

No burden is fully cast on the various new authorities thus proposed to actually follow the mission of minimum displacement. How further may policy makers practice fidelity to this virtue in the enormous devastation of the human rights of life and livelihood of the SEZ-affected people, given the fact that even in times of erstwhile state action the minimal assurance of providing each displaced family with one job (employment opportunity) was breached more than honoured?

What is needed instead is a detailed legislation for each 'major, development project under which the costs of development and identified together with the specific measures aimed at the amelioration of HRC and ROLC for each project. What we need so much is not any overall or overarching law, but specific project law-type norms and standards that bring to legislative and informed public security each and every development project.

Thus main issue in the discussion on development- induced displacement is not compensation or rehabilitation, but the rights to life with dignity constitutional rights have also to reach the voiceless communities. The main issue is the development pattern and the legal system that impoverish people in the name of an eminent domain based on a public purpose, and judges development only by economic growth or the infrastructure built. It has to be changed through a development paradigm that judges progress primarily by improvement in the life style at every citizen this requires a political will that has to be developed through pressure from below.

References

Baxi, Upendra, (1969), State of Gujarat vs Shantilal: A Requisem for Just Compensation? *Jaipur Law Journal*, 9, 29-27 (Vol. & Issue).

Mathur, Hari Mohan and David Marsden (eds), (1998), Development Projects and Impoverishment Risks: Resettlement of Project Affected Public in India New Delhi: Oxford University Press.

Black, Maggie, (2002), The No-Nonsense Guide to International Development. Oxford/London: New Internationalist Publications Ltd.

Cernea, Michael M. (1995), 'Understanding and Preventing Impoverishment from Displacement: Reflections on the state of Knowledge presented at the International Conference on Development - induced Displacement and Impoverishment held at the University of Oxford, 3-7 January.

Turton, David, (2002),'Forced Displacement and the Nation-State' in Jenny Robinson (ed) development and Displacement. Oxford University Press, pp. 19-21.

Seabrook, Jeremy, (1993), Victims of Development: Resistance and Alternatives. London/New York.

Mathur, Hari Mohan, (1999), The Impoverishing Potential of Development Projects: Resettlement Requires Risk Analysis, Oxford: Oxford University Press.

Multiple Action Research Groups (MARG), (1986), Sardar Sarovar Austees in M.P., What do they Know? New Delhi.

Baxi, Upendra, (2007),Human Rights in a Post Human World: Critical Essays, New Delhi, Oxford University Press.

World Commission on Dams (WCD) (2007), Dams and Development: A New Framework for Integrated Decision - Making, London : Earth can.

9

Human Rights, Women and Panchayati Raj Institutions in India

BIR PAL SINGH

Objectives of the Study

The study proposes the following objectives.

1. To find out the socio-economic and educational levels of elected women representatives.
2. To investigate the level of knowledge and understanding of various development schemes especially those related to their own development.
3. To unravel the problems and difficulties including those related to discrimination and injustices done against them while participating and functioning at the Gram Panchayat level.
4. To place suggestions towards the strengthening and protection of human rights as regards their participation and functioning at the Gram Panchayat level.

Method of Study

The selection of Gram Panchayats has been done on the basis of the purposive sampling and both the primary and secondary sources of data collection have been applied. The present study is related to the Gram Panchayat of Mendori which comes under the Janpad Panchayat of Phanda in district Bhopal, Madhya Pradesh (India). The field work for the present study was carried out in the month of August, 2008.

I

Human society is known as the systematic ordering of social relations in a definite pattern of social structure. The development of human society depends on the shoulders of both men and women. Both have their role in the developmental process of any country. And thus today the study of gender has special importance to understand the dual nature of human society where males have always privilege at every step of development or benefits. The planers of country have recognized the role of women in the progress of the country. Therefore, the empowerment of women has been the primary concern of every government. Without considering the role of women in every sphere of human life, the society can not further progress in the democratic way. The Planning Commission and UNDP have minutely observed the meagre conditions of women in the social and political levels. In India, women are not able to lead what the planning commission calls: Fuller, Richer and more varied life and what UNDP calls long healthy and creative life. If the wisdom of grassroots organizations, especially the courage and clarity of women is to become policy, it will not be through the art of intellectual persuasion but by the arrangements made within a political system for their voice to have power. Bringing women into power is thus a matter of equity, of correcting an unjust and unrepresentative system. (Sinha, 2004: 11).

The International and National Organizations have already recognized the rights of every human being in its various Covenant and Conventions. The security and protection of each and every right of human beings, which make them 'human', is the duty of every Nation. The International Covenant and Conventions have categorically mentioned equal rights of men and women in all spheres of human activities. The resolution adopted by the general assembly in 1952 regarding the convention on the political rights of women states that women shall be entitled to hold public office and to exercise all public functions establishes by national law, on equal teems with men, without any discrimination. It was clearly indicated at the World Conference on Agrarian Reforms & Rural Development, held in Rome in 1979, that participation by rural people in the institutions that govern their lives is a basic Human Right.

Women being the producer of human society have same right as their men folk. Although the status of women had never been satisfactory so far the rights and respectful living of them is considered. The agitation and protest march led by radical scholars including women themselves have created a world view towards the human rights of women as a living being of the same society where men forcefully occupy all the right which women also deserve. The United Nations declared 1975 as the 'International Women's Year' and 1980 as the 'Year for development of Women'. The decade 1975-1985 was declared as the 'Women's Development Decade' by the member nations. Since then the demand for women's rights started gaining momentum and it is still continue. Generally there are three main areas where women all over the world, face the problem of discrimination. These are social, economic and political. Human Rights are an egalitarian way of allocating membership in a collectivity to all physical persons. Everyone has the human rights. They are not merely a set of values expressed in religious or secular culture but also a set of rights that law, government, and all other social institutions are organized to defend. The dependency of women on their men folk and bureaucratic set ups of the country have also been responsible for the participation of women at the levels of Panchayats. Pal (2004:9) has vividly quoted the words of B.N. Yugandhar (former secretary to the Ministry of Rural Development) regarding the tardy role of bureaucracy: ' — *the bureaucrat is a well trained horse ans has to be ridden well at every level. If the "horse" is not performing well or is not responsible and is impersonal, no doubt, people will get alarmed. But they will be angry not at the horse but at the rider. And the rider has to give the horse a proper signal what we find instead is that the riders are complaining bitterly against the horse."* The study conducted by Behera & Nanda (1997:158-159) among the Bhuiyan women, a Scheduled Tribe reveals that:

> *The discrimination is mainly rooted in the social dependence of women on their menfolk. Factors such as high rate illiteracy, respect for tradition, lack of any ambition, absence of infrastructure for development, non-availability of any opportunity for technical training suited for women, conception of marriage as their ultimate goal, etc. are responsible for this utter dependence of women on their menfolk.*

In the Vedic era of traditional Indian Society women had have equal status with men whether these are related to education, religion, politics, property, inheritance or any other. The degradation of statuses of women started in the later Vedic period during which patriarchy rooted in the every sphere of human life. The gender based discrimination started to take roots during this period and resulted in various social evils directly hitting the soul of women in the form of *sati pratha* (burning the women in the funeral pyre of the husband), dowry, widow marriage, *parda pratha*(veil system),and child marriage, etc. The philosophy of '*Yatra Naryastu Pujyante, Ramante Tatra Devta*' (wherever women are worshiped, deity resides) was forgotten by the male dominating society.

The aforesaid paragraph highlights the conditions and perception of people towards the women in the society. In order to bring women par with their men, at every level of decision making, the representation of women in Local Self Government has been the mile stone in the history of the independent India. The equality of righteous living in all matters of human activities have been guaranteed by the articles 14,15, 16(2), 39(a), 39(d), 39(e) and article 42 of the highest law of land i. e. Constitution of India. The introduction of the Panchayati Raj system and the thrust on municipal governance with a one-third representation of women supports the Government claim that it is committed to transferring power to the people. The policy of reservation for Scheduled Castes, Scheduled Tribes and Women, is held up as evidence of its long-term commitment to adequate representation for socially, economically and educationally backward sections of Indian society. The entry of women at the political sphere of the country perhaps makes India as the first country that successfully included women in Local Self Government. Taking inspiration from world organization, India also celebrated the year 2001 as the Year of Women Empowerment. Thus women have been given roles in decision-makings of their society through the political participation.

II

The Panchayat system is not a new phenomenon in Indian society. It is a very old concept. The difference between the present structure and old structure of Panchayat is only the procedure adopted for the selection of members of Panchayats. In Ancient times, the selection of members of Panchayat at the village level was done in informal ways where seasoned and experienced persons specially males were selected on the common consensus of the all villagers. The present structure of the Panchayat system is known as the formal system of Local Government entirely based on the election of members of Panchayat. The basic aim of Panchayat system was/is all round development of the rural people. The progress of country could be real only when the planners of the country would realize the development of the village as well as the villagers.

Going back to history, it is notable that the first ever reference in a document of constitutional significance to Village Panchayats as Local Self- Government institutions was made in the report of the Royal Commission on Decentralization in 1909. Though, the tradition of *Panch Parmeshwar* has been in existence since time immemorial in India. The report of Commission resulted into the Minto-Morley Reforms of 1909, which led to the enlargement of the elective process in the Local Self-Government structure of India. (Bajpai & Verma 1995: 2). India lives in its villages, with these words; the father of Nation Mahatma Gandhi advocated the importance of villages in the development process of the country. He had well documented concept of Village Swaraj in his paper 'Harijan' dated 26 July 1942:

> *My idea of Village Swaraj is that it is a complete republic; independent of its neighbours for its vital wants and yet interdependent for many others in which dependence is a necessity. Thus, every village's first concern will be to grow its own food, crops and cotton for cloths. It should have a reserve for its cattle, recreation and playgrounds for its adult and children. Then if there is more land available, it will grow useful money crops. The village will maintain a village theatre, school and public hall. It will have its own water works ensuring clean supply. Education will be compulsory upto the final basic course. As far as possible every activity will be conducted on cooperative basis. There will be a compulsory service of village guards, who will be selected by rotation from register maintained by the village. The Government of the village will be conducted by the Panchayats of 5 persons elected annually by the adult villagers, male and female both possessing minimum prescribed qualifications. These will have all the authorities and jurisdiction required. This Panchayat will be legislature, judiciary and executive combined, to operate for its year of office. Any village can become such a republic today without interference.*

In view of the above statement, Article 40 of the Constitution deals about the formation of Panchayats with adequate powers and functions in each State of the country. The Constitutional power of Panchayats could not change the tardy progress of villages, as many of the State had not implemented the Article 40 in their State policy as a major development of the villages. Further the failure of Community Development Programme (launched in the year 1952) forced the planners of the country to adopt a uniform scheme of the rural development in which villagers themselves have participation, roles and right of decisions related to all round development of rural society. Various committees have observed the intricacies of Panchayat system in India. The first major step was taken in the year 1957 when Mehta Committee under the Chairmanship of Balwant Rai Mehta looked into the affairs related to the failure of Community Development Programme in the country. The Mehta Committee concluded that lack of People's participation was the major failure in the proper implementation of Community Development Programme. The Committee recommended the establishment of Panchayat Raj Institutions having three tier structures beginning from village level to intermediate level and finally to district level. The committee also took the serious note regarding the inclusion of women members in Panchayats. It suggested the inclusion of two women members in order to carry on the specific programmes for women and children. Another major committee was constituted by the Janta Party Government and headed by Ashok Mehta in the year 1977, which submitted its findings in 1978. The Committee recommended a two-tier system with Mandal Panchayats at the base and Zila Parishad at the top.

After passing the 73rd and 74th constitutional amendments and getting the consent of President of India, the Panchyat System became the legal affairs and applicable all over the country from 24th April 1994. After this many states had adopted their own Panchayat Acts. The greatest achievement of New Panchayati Raj Institutions was the representation of people weaker sections of Indian society especially Scheduled Castes, Scheduled Tribess and Women. The one-third seats are reserved for women in local government. The Constitution (73rd amendment act, 1992, article 243 D (3) reads:

> *Not less than one- third (including the number of seats reserved for men belonging to the Scheduled Castes and Scheduled Tribes) of the total number of seats to be filled up by direct election in every Panchayat shall be reserved for women and such seats may be allotted by rotation to different constituencies in a Panchyat.*

The inclusion of women in Panchayati Raj Institutions accelerated to look the cause of women in the country when National Commission on Women was setup by an Act of Parliament in 1990. Ghosh and Pramanik (1999:222) have quoted the excerpt of the declaration of 1992, an International Seminar at Seol on the participation of women in politics. – Convinced that any fair, representative and efficient society, women should be active participants at the policy making level in all forums that contribute to the political process and that they should be active executors of policy one made. Krishnamurti (1999:152) concludes that society as a whole and men in particular will benefit if they are intelligent enough to share the responsibilities of good local self-government with the women of this land.

Empowerment of women also calls for strict and rigid implementation of all the laws and programmes that have a bearing in their lives. Mere passing of laws and launching of welfare schemes have little meaning for rural women. Those in authority should have the will to enforce al women development programmes and protective laws, which it done in right earnest can go a long way in empowering women. (Mohanty. Pattnaik, and Mohanty (1996:341).

III

The nomenclature of different tiers of Panchayati Raj Institutions differs from State to State. Thus all the issues related to rural development of people fall under the purview of Madhya Pradesh Panchyati Raj Avam Gram Swaraj Adhiniyam, 1993. This Act provides the three tier Panchayat structure with a Gram Panchayat at the village or group of villages level, a Janpad Panchayat at the block level. The basic operating Panchayat System is the Gram Panchayat and success of really results into decentralization process of Panchayati Raj Institutions. The elected head of the Gram Panchayat is known as Sarapanch in the state of Madhya Pradesh. The other members who support the Sarapanch in smooth functioning of Panchayat activities are known as Panches. The elected Panches selects a Up Sarpanch (Deputy Sarapanch) among themselves.

The intermediate level is known as Janapad Panchayat. It consists of members elected from the constituencies and the MLAs from the area. To look the matters of village development, a Janpad Panchayat can constitute five standing committees i.e. general administration, education, agriculture, communication and water, and co-operation and industries committee to plan and implement projects related to their representative areas of concern. The top most layer of the Panchayat Raj Institution is known as Zilla Panchayat in Madhya Pradesh. It consists of members elected from panchayats and municipalities, chairperson of the District

Cooperative bank, all members of Legislative Assembly and members of Rajya Sabha whose names appear in the voter's list of the Gram Panchayat within a given district.

Growth with social justice has been prime concern of both Center and State Governments. A society can not progress until and unless all the pillars i.e. every human groups beyond their caste, race and religious boundary get the representation in the development process of its citizens. Indian society has been known for the complex structure of caste system all over the world. Traditionally the dominance of upper caste people in each and every path of human activities debarred the lower caste people to get the benefits of development programmes. The New Panchayati Raj System is one of the major innovative ideas of modern India with a motive to provide roles to the different sections of caste based Indian society in the development and decision making activities of their own society at the each level of Panchayats. The major concern is related to the representation of women members in Panchayats.

IV

The Gram Panchayat Mendori is 10 kilometer away from Bhopal, the capital city of State of Madhya Pradesh. The Gram Panchayat has no building of its own. Any meeting related to discussion about the development plans and other related issues of people under the purview of Gram Panchayat takes place in the building of Rajiv Gandhi Shiksha Bhawan known as Swaraj Bhawan. The Gram Panchayat Mendori consists of 20 members including the head of the Gram Panchayat known as Sarpanch (President). Out of 19 Panches, the women representatives are 5 in number. There is no woman Panch who belongs to general category. Thus out of 5 women Panches. 1 belongs to Other Backward Class, 2 Scheduled Tribes and remaining 2 to Scheduled Castes. A probe into the educational status of the women Panches reveals that none of them educated well except 1 Panch who studied up to fifth class. Though out of 5 women Panches 3 know how to put signature. They can be treated as semi literate according to the researcher because they are not able to write or read anything except their thumb impression or signature.

The economic status of women Panches is not that much strong except 3 who have some land as *patta* (lease). When asked by the researcher about the possession of land as provided by the Government, the women Panches replied that land is not cultivable and thus mere possessing of land will not facilitate any economic gain to them and their family members. The major occupation of the women Panches except one is to work outside as labourers besides households' activities. Basically all the women Panches belong to lower stratum of societal structure. They have no other alternative for the survival except to work outside as their men are not in a position to earn much. All women Panches are in the age group of 45-55. So far the knowledge of the women Panches is concerned about the schemes, plans, activities and functioning of the Gram Panchayat except one woman Panch of village Mendora none have any idea. Out of 5 women Panches, one woman Panch has never attended any Panchayat meeting after being elected. When researcher enquired to concern woman Panch regarding her unwillingness in attending the Panchayat meeting and not taking any interest in development process of villagers. She aptly remarked that *ham panchayat mein ka karab. Sara paisa to Sarpanch aur Sachiv milkar kha jate hai. Gaon ke liye kuchh bhi nahi karte hai. Yadi kuchh hota hai to unke apne admi pate hai.*(emphasis mine). 'Why should I go to Panchayat? All the money is taken by the Sarpanch and Sachiv (Secretary of Gram Panchayat) in the name of development. The benefits of welfare schemes go in the hands of people who are near and dear to Sarpanch.' The remark of this particular woman Panch was also stated by the other women Panches. Who say that we belong to Scheduled Castes and Scheduled Tribes and therefore Sarpanch never pay any attention towards us.

The women Panches who belong to Scheduled Tribes have the some idea about the meeting of the Gram Panchayat and Gram Sabha. One woman Panch replied to researcher that there is a provision to hold the meeting of Gram Sabha four times in a year and Gram Panchayat meeting every month. But rarely

Gram Sabha meetings take place according to the provision except on the days of 15 August and 26 January. The meeting of Gram Panchayat does not take place in every month. She further said that Sarpanch never informs us about the meetings and also about the running schemes related to the development of villagers and more especially to women. But this woman Panch attends the meeting of Panchayats whenever it comes to her knowledge. She accepted that she is the member of Educational Committee and she has also some information about the other Committee like Security Committee, Vigilance Committee and Health Committee. The Educational Committee consists of 5 members including one woman which she is the member. But she has not given any task to perform as a member of Educational Committee till date.

The women Panches who belong to Scheduled Castes have no idea about any functioning of Gram Panchayat. They are not aware about any scheme of Panchayat and have occasional participation in the meetings of Gram Panchayats and Gram Sabha. Like other women Panches, their reply was also the same that they get nothing from the Panchayat in monetary terms. They work as labourers to earn their livelihood. If they pay the attention to the development of village how they will survive.

The women Panches face discrimination in Gram Panchayat which is the clear violation of their human rights. Being elected representatives of Gram Panchayat, their participation never takes place at the level of decision and development process of the villages and its people. They are even not aware about the schemes and plans dealing with the sensitive issues of women and children. Though they have some awareness about the Employment Guarantee Scheme provided that someone first tell the name of this scheme as the researcher did. They themselves do not tell or may be not aware about the scheme. The kind of treatment they receive in the meetings of Panchayats is totally against the dignity of women Panches and also the violation their human rights as they do not receive any respect from the officials and male representatives of the Gram Panchayat as well as from the gatherings while participating in the meetings of Panchayat. There is no arrangement of proper sitting for these women Panches in the meetings. They generally sit on the ground amongst the gathering just totally assimilating themselves with the crowd or gathering. When asked by the researcher, the women Panches said that though they are interested to sit together with the officials and members of the Gram Panchayat but they are being directed by their men folk not to sit in front of the village elders. They will loose respect in their family as well as in the village if they do so. They have no voice in Panchayat meeting except the one woman Panch of village Mendora who told the researcher that she always asks to Sarpanch about the welfare schemes and related issues but her words have no role in male dominating society.

Thus it is clear from the above versions of women Panches that they have their representation at the level of Gram Panchayat but they have no participatory roles to perform in the development and decision making processes. Legally they have right to know each and every matter of Gram Panchayat but their rights are not taken into consideration. The women Panches of this particular Gram Panchayat are certain extent different from the other women Panches of their counterparts in the sense that male members of their families also not attend the meetings of Gram Panchayat on behalf of them. It has also been found that due to illiteracy, lack of confidence, awareness or experience and a general isolation from public life being women, they are often unable to handle issues at the level of Panchayat. The prevalent customs and norms of their own village society most of the time make their independence and political participation difficult. Rarely any woman representative (Panch) raises her voice on issues which is directly related to development of her ward in the village. It seems that mere introducing the policy of women reservation in Panchayats will not bring any positive change in socio-economic and political empowerment of the women. There is a collective need to organize the training and awareness programme for women representatives to know about the rights, duties and functions as representatives of Gram Panchayat. What the legal remedies they have if the violation of their human rights occurs? There is need to launch the proper sensitization programme on regular basis just to highlight the roles and rights of women representatives and the welfare schemes related to development of women themselves.

References

Bajpai, A. & Verma, M. S. (1995), *Panchayati Raj in India: A New Thrust.* Vol.1, Delhi, Sahitya Prakashan.

Behera, D.K. & Nanda, N. (1997), *Gender Inequalities in a Tribal Context: Some Reflections from Orissa* in Pfeffer, G. & Behera, D.K. (eds.) *Contemporary Society: Tribal Studies.* Vol. 1. New Delhi, Concept Publishing Company.

Ghosh, R. & Pramanik, A. K. (1999), *Women's Participation in Panchayats: Some Steps in* Ghosh, R. & Pramanik, A. K. *Panchayat System in India: Historical, Constitutional and Financial Analysis.* New Delhi, Kanishka Publishers, Distributors.

Krishnamurti, L. (1996), *Empowerment of Women in Rural Development* in Palenithurai, G. (ed.) *New Panchayat Raj System: Status and Prospects.* New Delhi, Kanishka Publishers, Distributors.

Mohanty, S., Pattnaik, J. K. and Mohanty, N. (1996), *Elected Women Representatives to the Village Panchayat: A Critical Appraisal* in Samel, P.K.(ed.) *Tribal Development: Options.* Nanital: Gyanodaya Prkashan.

Pal, M. (Dr.) (2004), From 'Raj' Governance to Swaraj Governance: Progress, Performance and Perspective. *Kurukshetra,* August.

Sinha, A. (2004), Women in Local Self Governance. *Kurukshetra,* August.

10

Terrorism and Human Rights

V. P. Singh

The violence and the fear perpetuated by terrorism have been a prevalent distressing feature of the modern society. The acts of violence has been occurring with alarming frequency, representing serious attacks against the crucial rights of man, not only it posed great threat to the rights of the individual, it has also affected the democratic governments and institution too. Numerous notorious incidents of terrorism around the world in recent years have confirmed that terrorism remains an on going and serious threat to the protection of human rights and to regional and international peace and security.

However, the adoption of Vienna Declaration 1993, demonstrates that there are few if any, human rights issues today, which are not of international concern. It is in this context that the statement in Paragraph 4 of the Declaration that 'the promotion and protection of all human rights is a legitimate concern of the international community gain its significance'. (Buerganthal, 2002 : 16). The similar idea also finds expression in another, equally important, principle proclaimed in the said Declaration. Paragraph 5 of that instrument declares: 'All human rights are universal, indivisible, and interdependent and interrelated. The international community must treat human rights globally in a fair and equal manner, on the same footing, and with the same emphasis. While the significance of national and regional particularities and various historical, cultural and religious backgrounds must be born in mind, it is the duty of the states, regardless of their political, economic and cultural systems, to promote and protect all human rights and fundamental freedoms'. (*Ibid*).

The recognition of the universal character of human rights and the concomitant rejection of cultural relativism, which has traditionally sought to justify violations of human rights by reference to some special religious or cultural imperatives, laid the foundation for global effort to improve the human rights situation of all human beings.

The direct relation between terrorism and violation of human rights was recognized by the World Conference on Human Rights (Vienna, 1993) of the Vienna Declaration and its Programme of Action which stipulated that:

> "the acts, methods and practices of terrorism in all its forms and manifestations as well as linking in some countries to drug trafficking are activities aimed at the destruction of human rights, fundamental freedoms and democracy, threatening territorial integrity, security of states and destabilizing legitimately constituted Government" (Vienna, 1993).

The growing consciousness of international community of the negative effects of terrorism in all its forms on the full enjoyment of the human rights, fundamental freedoms, on the establishment of Rule of Law and democratic freedoms as enshrined in the UN Charter and the International Covenants on Human Rights. All states are required to suppress all or any form of terrorist activities within their borders as terrorism represented globalization of fear and contempt for the role of international law.

It was for the first time in the UN history that 168 member states participated in the discussion of a single agenda item on international terrorism, which started on 1st October, 2001. This demonstrates the seriousness of the International Community that regarded acts of terrorism as assaults on civilization itself. The dangerous trend towards an expansion of the scope of the terrorism had turned it into real and apparent threat to mankind.

It is interesting to note that the concept of terrorism and human rights have some features in common; both entered the political discourse roughly at the time of the French Revolution. Edmund Burke's sensitive denunciation of the Jacobin reign of terror in his "Reflection of the French Revolution" and his opponent Thomas Paine's equally impassioned contention "The right of Man", helped to bring these ideas into English political dictionary. Terrorism and human rights are strongly debated concepts from the beginning; as a result there of they became indispensable part of modern moral and political vocabulary. (Wilkson, 2007).

The similarities between the concept of terrorism and human rights does not go further and ends there; unless one argue that there is an inherent human right to blow up or shoot your fellow human beings or to hold them hostages or to terrorise them by any other means but then the terrorism is fundamental threat to human rights. After all, what could be a more fundamental human right than the right to life itself.(Ibid).

In considering the human rights dimensions of terrorism, it is not only the number of victims that should be taken into account but also its impact on the victims, the society and the state. Killing innocent people, destroying their property and creating an atmosphere of fear and terror in the minds of the people violates the human rights of these innocent victims.

Generally, it is regarded that the states are the guarantors, protectors and violators of human rights; the term terrorism is generally understood as an unlawful, co-coordinated, politically motivated violence against 'innocents' or 'civilians' with the effect of terrorising the population and this unlawful co-coordinated, politically motivated violence is generally practiced by non-state actors. The state too in certain cases practices terrorism but its act usually fits into the well established framework of human rights and humanitarian law.

Terrorist acts are always considered to be a crime, but usually not, strictly speaking, a human rights violation, notwithstanding how heinous they may be. But, it is a true fact that terrorism has serious and damaging effects on human rights, beyond the loss of life, injury and torture that are immediate products of terrorist attacks; there exist the web of other rights that too are also violated. Terrorism, generally affects the economy of state, either through discouraging trade and investment or shifting state resources to counter- terrorism measures, and as a consequence thereof, economic and social rights such as health care and education are violated. Civil and Political rights, such as privacy and security of correspondence and home, may be abridged. The exercise of freedom of speech may be inhibited or repressed in an atmosphere of crisis, and intolerance of groups associated with the enemy may flourish, sometimes reaching the level of violent reprisal. (HRW, 2002).

Another facet to the relationship between human rights and terrorism is the motivational factor which tends the person to practice terrorism. The state violation of human rights can degrade social norms more generally, terrorists time to time attempt to justify their acts as a lawful means to accomplish or achieve protection and benefits provided by human rights standards for themselves or for others in their communities. In other words, terrorists demand the authority of the rule of law to legitimize human rights protections or benefits and argue that their acts are a legitimate means to achieve redress of these demands. And, in many cases, measures of state repression can also promote militancy in the public, swelling ranks of terrorist recruits. (DIILS, 2007).

It is a true fact that terrorist acts violates human rights, it is equally true that state response in countering the menace of terrorism have a degrading effect, though sometimes less visible. The impact of any given terrorist act is usually limited in time, but restrictive state responses may have long duration, and affects many more than the attacks that prompted the response.

The impact of restrictive measures may include the arbitrary deprivation of life or liberty, curtailment of due process guarantees, privacy incursions, limits on speech, and restrictions on the rights of aliens, among others.

Many nations which are already saddled with the worst human rights records in the region, they in the name of counter -terrorism policy opened new doors to further curb down the freedom of expression and privacy and other human rights. The state authorities in the name of combating terrorism, misused their powers for their own personal benefits or purposes, and thus violated the rights of others, as they are exempted or are exempted from damages for inflicting harm during counter- terrorism operation and are authorised to harm the lives, health and property of terrorists.

Many nations have enacted laws that restrict and violate human rights, in the name of the war on Terror. One need not have to go any where to find questionable counter- terrorism. India, one of the world's largest democracies, had two specific anti-terrorist laws one Terrorist and Disruptive Activities (Prevention Act, 1987 (TADA) and the second one was Prevention of Terrorism Act, 2001 (POTA). These two laws were known for its harsh and draconian features and which were also in contravention with the well established tenets of Criminal Justice System founded on rule of law. These two draconian laws from the statute book of the largest democracy straightway were in confrontation with the basic human rights some of which are enshrined in Part III of the Constitution of India.

The obnoxious provisions of TADA and POTA had been adversely criticized. TADA and POTA were found to have been involved more often in states not affected by terrorism. Innocent people were detained, harassed due to extensive abuse of these two anti-terrorist laws. Only few of the accused were convicted under the due process of law. Both these anti-terrorism laws were used as a tool to fight trade unions and to detain Muslims, Sikhs, Dalits, and Political opponents. The Supreme Court of India, observing the misuse of the anti-terrorism laws stated that when the law visits a person with serious penal consequences extra care and precaution must be taken to ensure that those whom the legislature did not intend to be covered by the express language of the statue are not to be roped in by stretching the language of the law.

A draconian anti-terrorism law had has been enacted in Britain without any proper parliamentary scrutiny. The Anti-Terrorism, Crime and Security Act which had same aim as United States Patriot Act permits indefinite detention without trial - internment by another name - on non - Britons whom the Home Secretary 'reasonably' believes are terrorists or have links with an international terrorist group or are 'a risk' to national security. 'Terrorism' is defined in the Act covering 'the use or threat of action' designed to influence the government or to advance a 'political', religious or ideological cause'. Such action includes the threat of committing ' serious damage to property'. (Koshy , 2003 : 93).

To impose indefinite detention, the British government had to suspend its obligations under the European Convention on Human Rights and the United Nation's International Covenant on Civil and Political Rights. The 'derogation order' tabled by the Home Secretary meant the emergency was such that there was 'a threat to the life of the nation'. The order was made even though the security services reported that they did not have any evidence of specific threat to Britain. The Sunday Observer of London wrote on March 10, 2002: 'we do not lack legal powers to tackle terrorism - for from it. The new power is simply about imprisoning people where there is no quality evidence that they have committed any crime'. (*Ibid*).

United Nations senior officials realized the facts that the Security Council Resolution 1373 of September 28 was being misused by some member states to justify repression of domestic dissent. Bacre Waly Ndiaye, the Chief Human Rights officer at United Nations Secretariat told the Council's new Counter-Terrorism committee-'There is evidence that some countries are now introducing measures that may erode human rights safeguards.' In some countries Ndiaye told the committee at its December 13,2001, meeting 'non-violent activities have been considered as terrorism and excessive measures have been taken to suppress or restrict individual rights including the presumption of innocence, the right to a fair trial, freedom from torture, privacy rights, freedom of expression and assembly and right to seek asylum.

The impossibility of trying to restrain terrorism while not jeopardizing human rights, to some extent cannot be denied but then in a country that craves strength, order and stability, and believes that only laws provide them, while it remembers anxiously, paranoically, the past, we cannot afford to give in to any kind to hysteria when the very liberty is at stake.

In Rex V Halliday Lord Atkinson observed as follows:

> "However precious the personal liberty of the subject may be, there is some thing for which it may be, to some extent, sacrificed by legal enactment, namely, national success in war, or escape from national plunder or enslavement."

However, it must be kept in mind that, the greater the power, the more dangerous abuse. Burke has expressed his just fear more than two and two and a half centuries ago in his letter to the Hon'ble Chief Justice Fox (8 October 1777),

> "People crushed by law have no hopes but from power. If laws are their enemies, they will be enemies to Laws; and those, who have much hope and nothing to lose, will always be dangerous, more or less." (Swaroop, 1993 : 9).

So approach has to be cautious and only those roped in who could be termed terrorists as a matter of fact. The harassment and sacrifice of the liberty of the innocents in the name of prevention of terrorist activities is inadmissible.

Justice Mathew in Prabhu Dayal Deorath etc. The District Magistrate, Kamrup and others[1], while delivering the majority judgment laid emphasis on the preservation of personal liberty and expressed his views that:

> "We say and we think it is necessary to repeat, that gravity of the evil to the community resulting from the antisocial activities can never furnish an adequate reason for evading the personal liberty of a citizen, accept in accordance with the procedure established by the constitution and the laws. The history of personal liberty is largely the history of insistence on observance of procedure. Observance of procedure has been bastion against wanton assaults on personal liberty over the years under our Constitution, the only guarantee of personal liberty for a person is that he shall not be deprived of it except in accordance with the procedure established by law."

Often doubt is raised about the possible conflict between respect of human rights and combating terrorism. There is really no such conflict. International humanitarian law is a part of human rights law applicable even in armed conflict. There is a growing convergence between the two since the object of both is the same and that is to respect human dignity and abjure needless violence. The fundamental concepts of laws of war are based on the balance between military necessity and humanity which includes proportionality of the force used. Military necessity does not admit of cruelty or wounding in fight except or of torture to extract confessions. Geneva Conventions are for humane treatment even of the prisoner of wars. How a party to a conflict is to behave in relation to people at its mercy is governed by humanitarian laws. If humane considerations prevail even in armed conflict with an enemy, the treatment of persons dealt with in low intensity conflict can not be harsher because they are often not the enemies of the nations. The whole regimen of Hague laws and Geneva laws covers the field and there is growing convergence between there. (Verma, 2007: 107).

Infact, Human rights advocates argue that role of human rights protection is an inseparable part to fight against menace of terrorism. This suggests that respecting human rights may indeed help us to incur security. The incorporation of human rights laws in all anti-terrorism programmes and policies of national governments as well as international bodies."(Mehta, 2007: 127).

The advancement of freedom and human dignity through effective democracy is the long-term solution for winning the War on Terrorism. Effective democracies honour and uphold basic human rights, including freedom of religion, conscience, speech, assembly, association, and press. They are responsive to their citizens, submitting to the will of the people. Effective democracies also limit the reach of government, protecting the institution of civil society. Such democracies exercise effective sovereignty and maintain order with in their own borders; address causes of conflict peacefully, protect independent and impartial systems of justice, punish crime, embrace the rule of law, and resist corruption. In such democracies freedom is indivisible. And they are the long-term antidote to the ideology of terrorism today. (*Ibid*, 684)

Defending human rights is a prerequisite to every aspect of any effective counter-terrorism strategy. It is a bond that brings the different components together. That means the human rights of all—of the victims of the terrorism, of those suspected of terrorism, of those affected by the consequences of the terrorism. No person who supports human rights can support terrorism which is a grave violation of human rights. Human rights are the basic necessity without which the advancement of the humans will stagnate, it is not the luxury not a topic for Sunday mall shopping that can be kept aside when confronted with much more important issues, combating terrorism and other problems are important issues but not as important as promoting human rights. No doubt, terrorism is gravest problem, but we cannot afford to take any action in haste when the human rights are at stake. Human rights democracy and rule of law are the most solid foundations for stability of peace. There is no conflict between respect for human rights and combating terrorism. Ms. Mary Robison, the United Nations High Commissioner for Human Rights, to emphasize that government action must be guided by human rights principles, which strike a balance between the enjoyment of freedoms and the legitimate concerns for national security.

References

Thomas, Buerganthal, "International Human Rights in an Historical Perspective", Janusz Symonides (ed.) *Human Rights Concepts and Standards,* p. 16.

Ibid.

The Viena Declaration and Programme of Action, World Conference on Human Rights, Vienna, 14-25 June 1993, at *http://www.unhchr.ch/huridocda/*. Accessed on 25 November 2005.

Paul Wilkson, "Terrorism and Human Rights", at *www.standrews.ac.uk/intrel/research/cstpv/journals/articles/commonwealthministersreferencebook2007.pdf.* Accessed on 7 June 2004..

Ibid.

6. Human Rights Watch, "We are not enemy: Hate Crimes against Arabs, Muslims, and Those Perceived to be Arabs or Muslims, After September 11". In a Short Human Rights Watch Report, Vol. 14, No. 6, Nov. 2002, at *http://www.hrw.org/reports/2002/usahate/usa1102.pdf.* Accessed on 4 July 2006.

Defence Institute of International Legal Studies: Human Rights and Terrorism, at *http://www.dsca.mil/Diils/251%20Human%20Rights%20and%20Terrorism%20.pdf.* Accessed on 24 January 2007.

Ninan Koshy, *The War on Terror,* (2003), p. 93.

Ibid.

R. Swaroop, *Cases and Material on TADA,* (1993), p. 9.

J. S.Verma, *The New Universe of Human Rights,* (2004) p. 107.

Maj. Gen. R. S. Mehta (ed.), *International Encyclopaedia of Terrorism Laws,* (2007), p. 127.

Ibid, 684.

11

UNO's Human Rights Declaration: Historical Context and Sociological Perspective in a Developing Country Like India

D. P. Saxena

The history of human rights is very ancient. Initially in order to protect human rights this concept exercised a control over the aristocratic use of power by the bureaucracy. Hence this concept in ancient tunes was confined with in the state, having no international appeal. The Magna Charta of the 13th century was a sort of compromise between king and his elitist courtiers. Its main object was to protect and ensure special rights to these elitist courtiers in the state.

Later on revolutionary leaders extensively enlarged the scope of human rights and after dethroning the king sentenced him to death and through a bill of rights 1686 determined some basic liberties meant for the common citizens of the state.

After a century in 1776 American Revolutionaries also after getting rid of British domination in their Declaration of liberty, included such like liberty and search for human happiness necessary for human rights.

After sometimes the French revolution also dethroned their king and after putting him to death made a declaration that

"Man is born free and lives in freedom having a right to equality." They also announced that the aim of any political alliance should be for confirmation and protection of human rights of liberty, property, security and no exploitation in respect of common citizens of the country.

The above events clearly confirm that the concept of human Rights emerged out of revolutionary thinking. In San Francisco Assembly after world war Human Rights and liberties found their due place in the declaration adopted by UNO.

The British Magna Charta and Bill of Rights, the French declaration of the rights of the man (1789) and American declaration of Independence (1776) and the Indian Constitution (1949) show their concern for equality, justice, liberty and fraternity. After world war I treaty of Versailles (1919) created permanent mechanisms for international violation of human rights but the second world war (1939-45) witnessed not only the tremendous loss of private property but considerable degradation of human rights. The suppression of racial and ethnic groups and minorities hammered the conscience of the world. The sad experience of the 2nd world warded to create a belief that international protection of human rights is a precondition for global peace and progress. The UNO emerged out of the ashes of the II world war and attempted to put stress on promotion and fostering of human rights and basic freedom. The Second World War witnessed the untold miseries and violation of human rights as a result of the negative uses of modernity which turned into genocide. Further the Nazi Germany with the help of official machinery and bureaucracy setup the gas chambers in which thousands of Jews were thrown and they were reduced to ashes. The event has certainly shaken the world. The untold miseries of the people have the way for the world body United Nations Organization and Article 1 of the U.N. charter lists the protection of human rights as one of the objectives of United Nations.

Hence the universal declaration of human rights on December 10th 1948 by the General Assembly of the united Nations was historical date. human rights are innate in individual and hence that violates them in its laws and interpretation breaches one of the very prerequisites of civil co-existence. The Charter of the United Nations does not define the contents of human rights. It is perhaps left to the organizations themselves- "The concept of human rights is wide and much inclusive of the concerns about oppression, exploitation, atrocity and torture. Freedom from torture and inhuman and cruel treatment of punishment is held as fundamental rights of human being in the universal declaration of human rights which consists of 30 Articles. A human rights concern has become a political idiom of normative expression today. The basic philosophy is to restore a life of dignity, respect and social justice.

The following are some of the basic principles behind the world wide declarations of human rights.

(a) All men are born free and equal in view of human rights and dignity. With these reasons and intellect they should reciprocally behave with the feeling of fraternity.

(b) Any man of whatever caste, colour, sex, language, community, religion and political or of any other thinking or of any nation or social origin has, without any sort of discrimination, full rights over the exercise of declared liberties and rights.

(c) Every man has a right to live, freedom and his security.

(d) None can be made slave and slavery in any form is prohibited, Man in Custody cannot be sold or purchased like a slave.

(e) None can be tortured nor any cruel, inhuman or below dignity punishment can be given.

(f) Every man has a right to obtain recognition before the law.

(g) Every man is equal before law and enjoys legal protection without any discriminations.

(h) There is emphasis on the universalization of rights on the basis of equality amongst all.

(i) All have been vested with the civil, political, economic, social and cultural rights.

(j) States responsibility be fixed for ensuring human rights to all.

(k) Establishment of an International process for fixing standard norms of human rights and analyzing them properly.

After accepting the ideal of Human Rights in the charter of U.N.O., a draft was prepared for the worldwide declaration of human Rights through Human Rights Commission. After some amendment it was collectively accepted on the 10th December 1948 and this auspicious date was declared as Human Rights Day. There are 30 Articles in U.N. resolution adopted on the 10th of December 1948 granting recognition to human rights. The importance was given to civil and potential rights more than the social, economic and cultural human rights. The details of 30 Articles of U.N. Charter pertaining of civil and potential rights are as follows:

1. In Article 1 & 2 of UNO's Charter there is a description of liberty to all without any discrimination of caste, religion, class, sex, language, political and other views and caste status. All were granted full human rights and liberties.
2. In Article 3 to 15 there are life, liberty, individual protection and equality before law. All such attempts/steps effective cruel torture are strictly prohibited and emphasis as on human dignity and rights.
3. In Article 16 all the adult males and females without any consideration of caste, nationality or religion can exercise their rights to many of their own choice and establish their families.
4. In Article 17 there is right to property ownership to every individual.
5. In Article 18 & 19 there are liberty to practice religion and to express therein view and opinion to every citizen.
6. In article 20 & 21 all individuals have the right to assemble at any place peacefully, organize their community and participation in the task for making

their own government and enter into public services of their own county.

7. In Articles from 22 to 26 there are descriptions of economic and social rights of the citizen. In this way under these articles right to work, right to choose his own occupation, equal salary for the same work. Right to enjoy rest and holidays, unemployment, ill-health inability, old age, protection against many sudden incident/accident and face primary education etc.
8. In Article 27 every citizen has a right to take part freely in his community's cultural activities. Every one has right to enjoy art and benefits of scene. Further every one has the right to protect his mural and material testes.
9. In article 28 every citizen has a right to obtain social and International system so that he can enjoy all rights and liberties as publicly announced at the international level about human rights.
10. In Article 29 every one has a right to exercise his liberties and rights without hindering others to enjoy these rights and liberties.
11. In article 30 the interpretation of any announcement shall not be made in a way harming the already written rights to individuals or class.

In India President passed human rights protection bill 1993 which finally started working from 28th December 1998. The universal declaration of human rights indicates two sorts of rights the traditional civil and political rights (article 2-21) and the new social and economic rights (article 22 to 28) the constitution of India incorporates the first set of rights (article 12 to 25 of the constitution) and the second set of rights under the Directive Principles (articles 36 to 51).

The essence of complete conduct of human rights is that every man must live with human dignity. The rule of law and equality before law are well accepted legal norms. Society today is being governed in two contending forces one force is rule of laws and the other forces arbitrary, whimsy behavior of the bureaucracy functioning under the cover of impunity.

Violations of human rights have become the legitimate concern of the 191 member nations of the world. The human rights movements require to be more strengthened by the Academia, Judges, lawyers and the social activities in Asia, Africa because the countries of these continents have inbuilt social, economic, cultural and historical diversities.

The condition in the third world countries, especially in Asia, Africa and Latin America are prima facie different from those in Europe and America. These are-predominantly agrarian and combating with the challenges of poverty, illiteracy, ignorance malnutrition, health hazards, sub human condition and indigenous communal and ethnic feuds. Poverty and IIliteracy undermines human dignity and without human dignity the question of human rights is futile. It is therefore argued that the effective Judicial System in these countries can play significant role in promoting consciousness conducive to solve these problems and promote a social mileu which will strengthen human rights concern.

The universal declaration of human rights has a much wide spectrum and includes a number of areas concerning violations of liberty dignity and justice ranging from welfare measures to women, children, forced labor, slavery, labor relation, public and their protection, eradication of hunger, malnutrition racial ethnic issues, torture, atrocities, prevention, prison reforms, foreign victims and numerous such other cases which encroach upon liberty, equality, dignity and social justice.

Functions and Powers of Human Rights Commision

The commission shall perform all or any the following functions.

(a) Inquiry into suo motu or on a petition presented to it by a victim or any person on his behalf into complaint of.

(i) Violation of human rights or abatement there of for.

(ii) Negligence in the prevention of such violation by a public servent

(b) Intervene in any proceeding involving any allegation of violation of human rights pending before a court with the approval of such court.

(c) Visit under intimation to the state govt. any jail or any other institution under the control of the state govt. where persons are detained or lodged for purpose of treatment, reformation and protection to study the living conditions of the inmates and make recommendation there-on.

(d) Review the factors, including act of Terrorism that inhibit the enjoyment of human rights and recommend appropriate remedial measures.

(e) Review the safeguards provided by or under the constitution or any law for the time being inforce for the protection of human rights and recommend measures for their effective implementation.

(f) Study treaties and other international instruments on human rights and make recommendations for their effective implementation.

(g) Undertake and promote research in the field of human rights.

(h) Spread human rights literacy among various sections of society and prompt awareness of the safeguards available for the protection of these rights through publications the media, the seminars and other available means.

(i) Encourage the efforts of non-government organizations and institutions working in the field of human rights.

(j) Such other functions it may consider necessary for the promotion of human rights.

Powers Relating To Inquiries

(1) The commission shall, while inquiring into complaints under this Act. Have all the powers of a civil court tying a suit under the code of Civil Court procedure 1908 (5 of 1908) and in particular in respect of the following matters namely.

(a) Summoning and enforcing the attendance of witnesses and examining them on oath.

(b) Discovery and production of any document.

(c) Recording evidence on affidavits.

(d) Requisitioning any public record or copy there of from any court or office.

(e) Issuing commissions for the examination of witnesses or documents.

(f) Any other matter which may be prescribed.

2. The commission shall have power to require any person, subject to any privilege which may be claimed by that person under any law for the time being in force to furnish information on such points or matters, in the opinion of the commission, may be useful for, or relevant to, the subject-matter of the inquiry and any person so required shall be deemed to be legally bound to furnish such information within the meaning of the section 176 and section 177 of the Indian Penal Code (45 of 1860).

3. The commission or any other officer not below the rank of a Gazetted officer, specially authorized in this behalf by the commission may enter any building or place where the commission has reason to believe that any document relating to the subject matter of the inquiry may be found and may seize any such document or take extracts or copies there from subject to the provision of section 100 of the code of criminal procedure 1973 (2 of 1974) in so far as it may be applicable.

4. The commission shall be deemed to be a civil court and when any offence as is described in section 175, section 178, section 179, section 180 or section 228 of Indian Penal code (45 of 1860) is committed in the view or presence of the commission may after recording the facts constituting the offence and the statement of the accused as provided for the code of criminal procedure, 1973 (2 of 1974) forward the case to a magistrate having jurisdiction to try the same and the magistrate to whom any such case is forwarded shall proceed to hear the complaint against the accused as if the case has been forwarded to him under section 346 of the code of Criminal Procedure.

5. Every proceeding before the commission shall be deemed to be a judicial proceeding within the meaning of the section 193 and 228 and for the propose of section 196, of the Indian

penal code (45 to 1866) and the commission shall be deemed to be civil court for all the purpose of section 195 and chapter xxiv of the code of criminal procedure 1973 to 1974.

Sociological Prespectives

"Many of the countries particularly of Asia which are partners and signatory to the Universal Declaration, feel that using Human Rights as instruments for the political and ideological hegemony there is also a sense of dissatisfaction about the purely Western interference of human rights which focus on delicate matters of culture and identities, In this control the western slogan of human rights is not taken favourably by the Asian countries. Such focus came into sharp contradictions and controversies in U.N. Conference on human Rights held in Vienna in July 1993 "Universality of Human Rights is a western imposition on countries which have different moral conditions and social traditions and hence it amounts to moral and cultural imperialism. The countries like Singapore and Malaysia had the arguments that the culture matrix within which relation between the individual and the state are embedded are fundamentally different in Asia from the west.

The consensus building approach of Asia is collectivist while there is an overtone of individualistic ethos in the west Further the western societies with expansionist and establishmentarian ambitions are hankering after rights and rights alone. Sidelining the major concerns for human duties. The Indian philosophical, ideological and classical literature pleads for the prior devotion to duty and duty consciousness. The rights are according to Indian philosophic tradition and classical jurisprudence, the outcome of human duties.

"The economic and social circumstances of Asian Countries are not similar for example Japan, South Korea, Signapore, Hong Kong are some of the most prosperous countries while there are poverty stricken countries like Bangladesh, Philippines, Sri Lanka, Bhutan, Nepal, Pakistan and to some extent India. From sociological perspective one can view poverty illiteracy, ignorance and lack of scientific outlook as a great cause of the denial of the spirit of human duties and the human rights. It attenuates human dignity and without awareness about human sense of duty, there can be no human rights Proper social order and political stability are the necessary pre-requisite for economic growth. These cannot be a social justice and human dignity".

The current blast and bombardment by the militant mercenaries and hard core terrorists give not only an alarming signal to the violation of human rights but a challenge to the advocates and experiments of human rights.

Indian is facing artificial problem: One of cross-border terrorism and another of indigenous extremism in terms of Naxalism. The consequences of both are death, distraction, devastation and chaos, education, health, food, shelter and the protection of their cultural identities, freedom from bonded slavery and forced labor in the regions of Madhya Pradesh, Orrisa and Jharkhand require special awareness regarding their and responsibilities. The Human rights education programming in such areas will be a commendable service to humanity. Further the regional ethnicity, communal problems in such problems of caste conflicts in such movements emerging from time to time in the gangetic belt of India as also in the hill regions especially in North East require serious political and administrative attention. The encroachment upon life and liberty of the people, the innocent masses, and peasantry agrarian labor women and children have to be eliminated. The criminalization of politics and the entry of politicization into the parliament and state legislatives with history of criminal's records must be stopped. Thanks to Indian Judiciary especially in High Court and the supreme court of India that have taken steady and serious note of the corrupt bureaucracy and the criminal politicians to the prevailing practice of nepotism.

It would be unfair to observe that judicial system in India puts constraints in the process of development. As a matter of fact it is Indian judiciary and activism that have worked as custodian of not only constitution but also of democracy. The National Human Rights commission in Indian has rendered marvelous services to promote the case of justice, liberty and dignity of the citizens in the country. The emerging social consciousness and the citizens and the public interest writs petitions in the High courts and the Supreme Court are prima facie evidence that people have sound faith in the Indian Judiciary.

Conclusion

The commission and committees alone cannot fulfill the cherished goals unless a congenial and conducive social climate is created. This presupposes and outlook of persistence of attitudes, perseverance of will and forbearances of mind among the people to restore and protect the sense of human dignity, social reciprocation, cooperation and co-existence and righteousness in the conduct. So the nurseries and catastrophe of the history whether of the previous world wars or the struggle against previous regimes may not be repeated.

Reference

Govt. of India, Protection of Human Right Act 1992 Eastern Book Company, Lucknow (pp. 1, 8, & 9).

Kapoor, A.C. (2002), Human Rights Refreshers Training Pamphlet, Indian Council of Human Rights, North Zone Office Civil Lines, Kanpur.

Kapoor, A.C., "Human Rights Awareness for Kanpur City." Indian Council of Human Rights, North Zone Office Civil Lines, Kanpur.

Melhotra, Anil Kumar (2002), "Symposium on Human Rights", (Workshop on Legal & Educational Awareness Context Organized by Indian Council of Human Rights, North Zone Core Office Civil Lines, Kanpur 30th Oct. June 2002.

Pandey, R. R. (2003), Souvenir on Human Rights – Current Prestective (National Seminar organized by C.R.D. Army Mahila P.G. College (GKP) University Gorakpur. 14-15 Febuary.

Pandey, P. N. (2005), "Human Rights Concerns: Persrectives & Context in Developing Societies", A Working Paper in National Seminar on Human Rights, The Indian Scene Organized by DAV PG College Affiliated to C.S.J.M. University Kanpur December 12.

Singh, Anoop (2005), Edited Souvenir on Human Rights : The Indian Scene (National Seminar organized by DAV (P.G.) College, affiliated to C.S.J.M. University, Kanpur, 12, 2005.

12

Global Ageing: A Triumph and a Challenge to Protect Rights

Yogendra Kumar Srivastava

Population aging is first and foremost a success story for public health policies as well as economic and social development.
– Grow Harlem Brundtland : *Director General , WHO 1999*

Population ageing is one of humanity's greatest triumphs. Worldwide, the proportion of people age 60 and over is growing faster than any other age group. Between 1970 and 2025, a growth in older persons of some 694 million or 223 per cent is expected. In 2025, there will be a total of about 1.2 billion people over the age of 60 by 2050 there will be 2 billion with 80 per cent of them living in developing countries. Population ageing raises many fundamental questions for policy makers. How do we help people remain independent and active as they age? How can we strengthen health promotion and prevention policies, especially those directed to older people? As people are living longer, how can the quality of life in old age are improved? Will large numbers of older people bankrupt our health care and social security systems? How do we best balance the role of the family and the state when it comes to caring for people who need assistance; as they grow older? How do we acknowledge and support the major role that people play as they age in caring for others?

This article is designed to address these questions and other concerns about population ageing. It targets government decision making at all levels, the non- governmental sector and the private sector, all of whom are responsible for the formulation of policies and programmes on ageing. We are to achieve the goal that healthy older persons remain a resource to their families, communities and economies, as stated in the WHO Brasilla Declaration on Ageing and Health in 1996.

Population ageing refers to a decline in the proportion of children and young people and an increase in the proportion of people age 60 and over. Decreasing fertility rates and increasing longevity will ensure the continued "greying" of the world's population, despite setbacks in life expectancy in some African countries (due to AIDS) and is some newly independent states (due to increased death caused by cardiovascular disease and violence). Sharp decrease in fertility rates are being observed throughout the world. It is estimated that by 2025, 120 countries will have reached total fertility rates below replacement level (average fertility rate of 2.1 children per woman), a substantial increase compared to 1975, when just 22 countries had a total fertility rate below or equal to the replacement level. The current figure is 70 countries. Until now, population ageing has been mostly associated with the more developed regions of the world. For example, currently nine of the ten countries with more than ten million inhabitants and the largest proportion of older people are in Europe (See Table 1).

Little change in the ranking is expected by 2025 when people age 60 and over will make up about one third of population in countries like Japan, Germany and Italy, closely followed by other European countries. (See Table 1).

What is less known is the speed and significance of population ageing in less developed regions? Already, older people - around 70 per cent live in developing countries (See Table 2). In all countries, especially in developed ones the older population itself is also ageing, People of over the age of 80 currently number some 69 million, the majority of whom live

Table 1
Countries with more than 10 Million Inhabitants (in 2002) with the Highest Proportion of Persons above Age 60

	2002		*2025*
Italy	24.5%	Japan	35.1%
Japan	24.3%	Italy	34.0%
Germany	24.0%	Germany	33.2%
Greece	23.9%	Greece	31.6%
Belgium	22.3%	Spain	31.4%
Spain	22.1%	Belgium	31.2%
Portugal	21.1%	United Kingdom	29.4%
United Kingdom	20.8%	Netherlands	29.5%
Ukraine	20.7%	France	28.7%
France	20.5%	Canada	27.9%

Source: UN, 2001

in more developed region. Although people over the age of 80 make up about one per cent of the world's population and three per cent of the population in developed regions. This age group is the fastest growing segment of the older population.

Table 2
Absolute Number of Persons (in million) above 60 Years of Age in Countries with a Total Population Approaching or above 100 Million Inhabitants (in 2002)

	2002		*2025*
China	134.2	China	287.5
India	81.0	India	168.5
United State of America	46.9	United states of America	86.1
Japan	31.0	Japan	43.5
Russian Fedration	26.2	Indonesia	35.0
Indonesia	17.1	Brazil	33.4
Brazil	14.1	Russian Federation	32.7
Pakistan	8.6	Pakistan	18.3
Mexico	7.3	Bangladesh	17.7
Bangladesh	7.2	Mexico	17.6
Nigeria	5.7	Nigeria	11.4

Source: UN, 2001.

Old-age dependency ratios are changing quickly throughout the world. In Japan for example, there are current 39 people over age 60 for every 100 in the age group 15-60. In 2025 this number will increase to 66. The old age dependency ratio (i.e. the total population age 60 and over divided by the population age 15 to 60) (Table 3) is primarily used by economists and actuaries who forecast the financial implications of pension policies. However, it is also useful for those concerned with management and planning of caring services.

Table 3
Old Age Dependency Ratio for Selected Countries /Regions

	2002		*2025*
Japan	0.39	Japan	0.66
North America	0.26	North America	0.44
European Union	0.36	European Union	0.56

Rapid Population Ageing in Developing Countries: In 2002, almost 400 million people aged 60 and over lived in the developing world. By 2025, this will have increased to developing world by 2025; this will have increased to approximately 840 million representing 70 per cent of all older people worldwide. In terms of regions, over half of the world's older people live in Asia. Asia's share of the world's oldest people will continue to increase the most while Europe's share as a proportion of the global older population will increase the most over the next two decades. Compared to the developed world, socio- economic development in developing countries has often not kept pace with the rapid speed of population ageing. For example, white it took 115 years for the proportion of older people in France to double from 7 to 14 per cent; it will take china only 27 years to achieve the same increase. In most of the developed world, Population ageing was a gradual process following steady socio-economic growth over several decades and generations. In developing countries, the process in being compressed into two or three decades. Thus, while developed countries grew affluent before they become old, developing countries are getting old before as substantial increase in wealth occurs. Rapid ageing in developing countries is accompanied by dramatic changes in family structures and roles, as well as in labour patterns and migration. Urbanization, the migration of young people to cities in search of jobs, smaller families and more women entering the formal workforce mean that fewer people are available to care for older people when they need assistance.

Indian Scenario

In India, persons above 60 years of aged are considered as Senior citizens. Advances in medical sciences and health techniques have led to reduction of mortalities, the people now understand the value of good nutrition and the life expectancy has increased. This has led to increased number of elderly in the country. Sadly, however, the plight of many is not good.

Statistical Scenario

Year	*2001*	*2013*	*2025*	*2050*
Elderly persons in India (in millions)	77	100	177	324

In India, persons above 60 years of aged are considered as senior citizens. Advances in medical sciences and health techniques have led to reduction of mortalities, the people now understand the value of good nutrition and the life expectancy has increased. This has led to increased number of elderly in the country.

As per statistics available by NGOs working for the elderly, those aged 60 and above constitutes 6% of India's population and number nearly 43 millions (1981 census data). 90% of the older persons are from the unorganized sector, with no social security at the age of 60. 30% of the elderly live below the poverty line and another 33% just marginally over it. 80% live in rural areas, 73% are illiterate and can only be engaged in physical labour. 55% of women over 60 are widows, many of them with no support whatsoever. There are nearly 2, 00,000 centenarians in India. The percentage may be a worrying issue. But even more problematic is the fact that 80% of India's population lives in the villages. This naturally means that most of the elderly too reside here.

The Right of the Ageing

The question of old age rights was for the first time raised in the General Assembly in 1948 by Argentina when it submitted a Draft Declaration of Old Age Rights. This Draft Declaration was transmitted to the social commission and the Commission on Human Rights through Economic and Social Council for study and report on the subject but it remained on the agenda of those two commissions for several years without any definite result.

However the General Assembly again took the "Question of the elderly and aged" for discussion in 1969 at the request of Malta. The matter was discussed in General Assembly at its several sessions and finally on 16 December 1977 the General Assembly decided to hold a World Assembly on Ageing Elderly. Later on its title was changed to World Assembly on Ageing.

The World Assembly on Ageing was held at Vienna from 26 July to 6 August 1982. it prepared and adopted the Vienna International Plan of Action on Ageing which was endorsed by the General Assembly on 3 December 1982. It was resolved at the World Assembly the fundamental and inalienable rights contained in the Universal Declaration of Human Rights applied fully to ageing; that the quality of life is as much importance as the longevity: that the aged should be enabled to enjoy a life of fulfillment, health, security and contentment and that they should be treated integral part of the society.

A provision was incorporated in the International Plan of Action on Ageing for a periodic review and appraisal of its implementation, to be made by the Commission for Social Development. The General Assembly in its Resolution of 3 December 1982 requested the Economic and Social Council to ask the Commission for Social Development to review the implementation of the Plan of Action every four year. The first review was conducted in 1985. The second in 1989 and the third in 1993. The findings of the commission for the Social Development indicated that through considerable awareness concerning the problem of ageing of population had been created in many part of World bout no concrete measures were adopted for implementing the plan of action.

The General Assembly on 30 November 1987 decided to observe the tenth anniversary of the 1982 World Assembly on Ageing in order to increase global awareness towards the problem of ageing. An action programme on ageing for 1992 and beyond was prepared by the Secretary General and endorsed by the General Assembly on 14 December 1990. It envisaged a dual approach, (a) developing a practical strategy on ageing for the Decade 1992-2001 whose core element would be the election of targets on ageing; and (b) a series of promotional activities focused on 1992, the tenth anniversary of the adoption of the International plan of Action on Ageing; regular observance of 1 October as a International Day for Elderly designated by the General Assembly on its Resolution 45/106 of 14 December 1990 , and the establishment and regular updating of a global calendar of events on ageing.

United Nations Principles for Older Person: The General Assembly on 16 December 1991 adopted the United Nations Principles for Older Persons based on the International Plan of Action on Ageing. These principals are to be incorporated by the Governments in their national programmes. This principle may be described as follows:

(a) *Principles of Independence:* Following principles should be observed in order to enable the older persons to maintain their independence:

(i) Older persons should have access to adequate food, water, shelter, clothing, and health care through the provision of income, family and community support.

(ii) Older persons should have the opportunity to work or to have access to other income- generating opportunities.

(iii) Older persons should be able to participate in determining when and at what pace withdrawal from the labour force takes place.

(iv) Older persons should have access to appropriate educational and training programmes.

(v) Older persons should able to live in environments that are safe and adoptable to personal preference and changing capacities.

(vi) Older persons should be able to reside at home as long as possible.

(b) *Principles of Participation:* Following principles should be observed to enable the participation of older persons:

(i) Older persons should remain integrated in society, participate actively in the formulation and implementation of policies that directly affect their well-being and share their knowledge and skills with younger generations.

(ii) Older persons should be able to seek and develop opportunities for service to community and to serve and volunteers in positions appropriate to their interest and capabilities.

(iii) Older persons should be able to form movements or associations of older persons.

(c) *Principles of Cares:* Following principles provide for the family and community care:

(i) Older persons should benefit from family and community care and protection in accordance with each society's system of cultural values.

(ii) Older persons should have access to health care to help them maintain or regain the optimum level of physical, mental and emotional well being and to prevent or delay the onset of illness.

(iii) Older persons should have access to social and legal services to enhance their autonomy, protection and care.

(iv) Older persons should be able to utilize appropriate level of institutional care providing protection, rehabilitation and social and mental stimulation in a humane and secure environment.

(v) Older persons should be able to enjoy human rights and fundamental freedoms when residing in any shelter, care or treatment facility, including full respect for their dignity, beliefs, needs and privacy and for the right to make decisions about their care and the quality of their lives.

(d) Principles of Self- fulfillment:

(i) Older persons should be able to pursue opportunities for the full development of their potential.

(ii) Older persons should have access to the education, cultural, spiritual and recreational resources of society.

(e) Principles of Dignity:

(i) Older persons should be able to live in dignity and security and be free of exploitation and physical or mental abuse.

(ii) Older persons should be treated fairly regardless of age, gender, racial or ethnic background, disability of other status and be valued independently of their economic contribution.

Key Policy Proposals

The ageing of the population is a global phenomenon that demands international, national, regional and local action. In an increasingly interconnected world, failure to deal with the demographic imperative and rapid changes in disease patterns in a rational way in any part of the world will have socio-economic and political consequences every where. The policy frame–work require action on three basic pillars:

Health: When the right factors (both environmental and behavioral) for chronic disease and functional decline are kept low while the protective factors are kept high, people will enjoy both a longer quantity and quality of life; they will remain healthy and able to manage their own lives as they grow older; fewer older adults will need costly medical treatment and care services. For those who do need care, they should have access to the entire range of health and social services that address the needs and rights of women and men as they age.

Participation: When labour market, employment, education, health in socio-economic, cultural and spiritual activities, according to their basic human right, capacities, needs and preferences, people will continue to make a productive contribution to society in both paid and unpaid activities as they age.

Security: When policy and programmes address the social, financial and physical security needs and rights of people as they age. Older people are ensured of protection, dignity and care in the event that they are no longer able to support and protect themselves. Families and communities are supported in efforts to care for their older members.

Despite the magnificent progress made by man, age continues to defy any control. Old age is a natural biological phenomenon that cannot be reversed. The elderly do not really want money, as much as they crave for love and affection. This is the time when a person who has devoted his entire life for his family and made contribution to the society expects to be respected. It is important that the feeling of being no longer of any use does not creep it. Several old age homes have come up in recent years that not only provide dignity to the elderly but also ensure the care they deserve. However, it is equally pertinent that family members made the elderly feel special.

The emergence of nuclear families has made the elderly quite vulnerable in many cases. The fear of abandonment's high in many. The aged are considered a liability. The shift of the youth to the urban areas and the increasingly competitive life has left little for the elderly. Indian society known for years to worship parents, now feels they are better off some where else. Experts say it is necessary to first assess the needs the elderly, which may vary from person to person. Those taking care need to have information at hand on doctors, insurance etc. The elderly also need to be shown a lot of respect though they may not be able to perform many duties. There is a need for compassion to be shown to them.

Attaining the goal of active ageing will require action in a variety of sectors in addition to health and social services, including education, employment and labour, finance, social security, housing, transportation, justice and rural and urban development. While it is clear that the health sector does not have direct responsibility for policies in all of these other sectors, they belong in the broadest sense within the scope of public health because they support the goals if improved health through intersectoral action. This kind of an approach stresses the importance of the numerous different public health sectors as a catalyst for action. Further more, all policies need to support intergenerational solidarity and include specific targets to reduce inequities between women and men and among different subgroups within the older population. Particular attention needs to be paid to older people who are poor and marginalized and who live in rural areas. An active ageing approach seeks to eliminate age discrimination and recognize the diversity of older population. Older people and their caregivers need to be actively involved in the planning, implementation and evaluation of policies programmes and knowledge development activities related to active ageing. To advance the movement for active ageing, all stakeholders will need to clarify and popularize the term active ageing through dialogue, discussion and debate in the political arena, the education sector, public flora and media such as radio and television programming. Action on all three pillars of active ageing needs to be supported by knowledge development activities including evaluation, research and surveillance and the dissemination of research findings. The results of research need to be share in clear language and accessible and practical formats with policy makers, non- governmental organization representing older people, the private sector and the public at large.

References

www.helpage.org

Action on Elder Abuse (AEA) (1995) Bulletin (11) May-June. London.

Cutler D (2001), "Declining Disability Among the Elderly." Health Affairs Vol. 20 (6) : 11-27

International Labour office (ILO) (2000), "Income Security and Social Protection in a Changing World". World Labour Report. Geneva: ILO.

Kalachea A and Kickbush I (1997), "A Globla Strategy for Healthy Ageing", World Health. (4) July-August, 4-5

OECD (1998), Maintaining Prosperity in an Ageing Society, Paris: Organization for Economic Cooperation and Development.

Wilkinson RG (1996), Unhealthy Societies: The Affliction of Inequality. London: Routledge.

Wolf DA (2001), "Population Change: Friend or foe of the Chronic Care System", *Health Affairs,* Vol. 20 (6), 28-42

WHO (1998), Growing Older. Staying Well. Ageing and Physical Activity in Everyday life. Prepared by Heikkinen RL. Geneva: World Health Organization.

13

Human Rights Violation and Women Empowerment: With Special Reference to North East India

Sanjoy Roy

The idea of human rights is as old as our civilisation, although the concept may be a modern one having so many colours with in it. Universal ethical values, which form the foundation of human rights, are contained in all the great religious books of the world (Yadav, 2002:6). However, human rights as tools for protecting the worth and dignity of human beings is a fairly recent phenomenon. Human rights are those rights which are purely inherent in our nature and without it we can not live as human beings. Basically the human rights and fundamental freedoms allow us to fully develop and also use our human qualities, our intelligence, our talent, our consciousness, our confidence and to satisfy our social, economic, cultural, spiritual and related needs in day to day life.

In the modern age, the concept of human rights has assumed universal proportion, accepted virtually by all states and societies regardless of historical, cultural, ideological, economic or other differences. Now the universalization of human rights is a political fact. The Universal Declaration of

Human Rights adopted by UN General Assembly in 1948 has virtually accepted by all the members of states, even those which had abstained when the Declaration was approved. They now formally accepted in the Final Act of the Conference on Secretary and Co-operation. A third world's status have accepted the comprehensive agreements, the International Covenant on Civil and Political Rights as well as the International Covenant on Economic, Social and Cultural Rights, with more states joining every year.

Human Rights derive their justification from certain principles that mankind now considers as self-evident. These basic principles have gained universal acceptance against the historic background of millennia of strife and wars, mankind's experiences relating to different systems of governance, different kinds of social structures and differing legal systems, the havoc wrought by wars, deprivations, terrorism, lawlessness and indignities of various kinds. The first principle on which human rights are founded is the principle of inherent dignity and worth of every individual, and the need to secure to each person an equal and inalienable right to live in freedom, to enjoy equality, to be treated equally and to live in peace. But, though universally accepted, human rights are yet to be realised in the daily lives of a majority of ordinary men and women. Human beings are found in chains everywhere, denied basic human rights because they are tied down by inequitable system of governance, by traditions, cultures and beliefs based on unjust or inequitable distinctions between men and women, men and men or grown up children. Also providing human rights to women would lead to empowerment.

The recognition of women's human rights has come late because certain human rights and human entitlements have received recognition as basic rights of human kind relatively recently. From the days of Magna Carta, the right of an individual to be protected against the might of the state was well accepted. Those rights are to be known as Civil and Political Rights. Then Social, Economic and Cultural Rights took a longer tome to be accepted as basic human rights by different countries. However, the Universal Declaration of Human

Rights, 1948 has unequivocally included all these rights as basic rights of human beings. Everyone is entitled to all rights set forth in the Declaration without distinction of any kind such as sex, race, colour, language, religion, political or other opinion, national or social origin, property, birth or other status. A strong reiteration of women's human rights was made at the 1993 World Conference on Human Rights. It was said there "The human rights of the women and of the girl child are inalienable, integral and indivisible part of the Universal Human Rights. The full and equal participation of women in political, civil, economic and cultural life at the national, regional and international level and eradication of all forms of discrimination on grounds of sex are the priority objectives of the international community".

In the Fourth World Conference on Women in Beijing in September 1995, the then UN Secretary General made a statement that the violence against women had assumed a universal proportion that must be universally condemned and this condition growing continuously. Since the inception of the UN, the issue of women rights has been concerning. But the global dimension of female targeted violence was not explicitly acknowledged by the international community until December 1993, when UN General Assembly adopted the Declaration on the Elimination of Violence against women. Most of the governments until now tended to violence against women largely as a private matter between individuals, and not as a pervasive human rights problem requiring state intervention. So, truly the Declaration on the Elimination of Violence against Women was the first international human rights instruments to exclusively and explicitly address the women issue related to violence. The Declaration provides that a definition of gender-based abuse, calling it "any act of gender-based violence that results in or is likely in, physical, sexual or psychological harm or suffering to women, including threats of such acts, coercion or arbitrary deprivation of liberty, whether occurring in public or in private life". The definition is amplified in the Article 2 of the Declaration which identifies three areas in which violence usually and commonly takes place (1) Physical Sexual and Psychological violence that commonly occur in the family, including battering, sexual abuse of female children, dowry related violence, marital rape, female genital mutilation and other harmful traditional practices, (2) Physical, Sexual and Psychological violence that occurs within the general community, including rape, sexual abuse, sexual harassment and other intimidation in education and elsewhere, trafficking in women and force of prostitution and (3) Physical, Sexual and Psychological violence perpetrated by the state wherever it occurs.

According to Amnesty International, thousands of women held in custody are routinely raped in police detention centres worldwide. The report of the Special Reporters underlines the necessity for state to prosecute those accused of abusing women while in detentions and to hold them accountable for their action. But question is are they getting justice or are those guilty persons or accused kept behind the bar? The answer is simple, 'No'. And this phenomenon is all over the world whether it is developed or developing countries.

Most developed country like USA, women are being beaten, raped or made victim other physical and sexual assault every year. They suffer humiliation and brutalities especially when the men folk of their families are put behind the bar. Even in India, according to official records around 1000 women get raped every year who generally belong to Scheduled Caste and Scheduled Tribal inhabited areas. In several areas of Bihar, UP, frequently reports are published about women's molestation resorted to by the powerful and influential landholders in retaliation for refusal of the depressed classes on the use of bullocks and the like by the landholders. But unfortunately all these cases are not investigated by the police personnel and very few are reported and get justice.

Here I have tried to inculcate about the human rights violation against women and their empowerment. My focus is on the broader area of attitude i.e. if we want to minimise rather to control the human rights violation against women, they need to be socially, economically, politically empowered and for that matter government machinery (should be strong), welfare agencies, NGOs, judiciary, legislation and social worker have a pivotal role to play.

Concept of Empowerment

The term 'empowerment' is a broader concept and it has been defined by different social scientists in their own perspectives in a different connotation. The prefix *'em'* is attached to the noun *'power'* to create a verb. In Webster's New World Dictionary (1982), the prefix *'em'* is used as verb which means '*to make*', '*to make into or like*', '*cause to be*'. Thus 'to empower' is to make or cause power.

The Social Work Dictionary (Barker, 1991) defines the term empowerment as the process of helping a group or community to achieve political influence or relevant legal authority.

The *Oxford English Dictionary* defines empowerment as: (1) to invest, legally or formally to power, to license. (2) to bestow power upon, make powerful.

Empowerment relates to POWER and it is the process of changing the balance of power in favour of the relatively weak and the powerless. It enables the weaker sections to exercise power of exerting influence over the process of decision making at various levels.

Rappaport (1987,122) defines the term empowerment as a process, a mechanism by which people, organizations and communities gain mastery over their affairs and involve themselves in the democratic process of their community and employing institutions.

Robert Adams (1990, 42-43) defines empowerment as a process by which individuals, groups and communities become able to take control of their circumstances and achieve their goals, thereby being able to work towards maximizing the quality of their lives.

M. Karl (1995,14) conceptualized the term empowerment as a process of awareness and capacity building leading to greater participation to greater decision making and control and to transform action.

Pillai (1995, 60) states that empowerment as an active, multidimensional process which should enable individuals or a group of individuals to realise their full identity and powers in all spheres of life. It also consists of greater access to knowledge and resources, greater autonomy in decision making to enable them to have greater ability to plan their lives or have greater control over the circumstances that influence their lives, and free from restraints imposed on them by custom, belief and practice.

According to Lorraine and Robert (1999), empowerment is a process of increasing personal, interpersonal or political power so that individuals, families and communities can take action to improve their situations.

Gangrade (2001, 1) defines empowerment as decentralization of authority and power and aims at getting participation of deprived sections of people in decision making process.

So empowerment suggests individuals, groups or communities' determination over their own life and it conveys both a psychological sense of control or influence and a concern with actual social, physical, political and legal rights. It also emancipates the process of enabling sections of people deprived of their rights to have a legal platform. True empowerment comes when people feel empowered from all the above and develop a positive attitude towards their own self esteem and self confidence.

What is Women Empowerment?

Women empowerment as a concept was first introduced at the International Women's Conference at Nairobi in 1985 where it had defined as redistribution of social power and control of resources in favour of women. Mass illiteracy, unemployment, ill health and their limited access to economic assets mark the situation of women in India. So, women's empowerment in India initially aims at enhancing their social functioning by qualitative and quantitative changes particularly in the field of education, health, employment etc.

Women empowerment also refers to the process by which women acquire due recognition on par with men, to participate in the development process of the society through the political institutions like Panchayati Raj Institution as a partner with human dignity.

So empowerment of women is not a one way process rather it is a two way process in which we empower and get empowered in turn.

Empowerment of women indicates to improve their living conditions. It also attempts at enabling people to understand their existing realities, the factor shaping the current situation and ultimately, taking steps to affect improvements. Though the process and level of empowerment, women must be enable to develop multidimensional skills and capacities so that they may participate more effectively at different socio-political arena.

In this regards UNICEF (1993) had given a framework of women empowerment as:

Welfare: It addresses only the basic needs of women. Various programmes and schemes have been launched for the improvement of their conditions.

Access: It involves equality of access of resources and opportunities

Conscientization: Here women are made aware and conscious of gender inequalities as well as structural and institutional discrimination inherent in the whole system.

Participation: Women get empowered by organizing themselves and working collectively to gain and increase participation and representation in decision making par with men.

Control: The ultimate empowerment and level of equality, where women are able to make decisions over the various aspects of their lives and play an active role I the development process and their contributions are fully recognised and rewarded.

Women empowerment will be real and effective only when women are endowed income and property so that they may stand on their own feet and make an identity with dignity in the society. Prof.Amartya Sen, taking a much wider view of development talks of development as the process of expansion of entitlement i.e. giving freedom. Economic independence is the fundamental premise behind empowerment while women's participation in the development process provides them employment opportunities and the opportunities to get out of the clutches of poverty, malnutrition, illiteracy and other social milieu.

So the dimensions of women empowerment basically indicate of:

1. Individual Empowerment
2. Social Empowerment
3. Economic Empowerment
4. Physical Empowerment
5. Psychological Empowerment
6. Political Empowerment
7. Legal Rights Empowerment

Now Lets See How Human Rights Lead to Women's Empowerment

Most important right now recognised for women from all other rights which are very vital for their empowerment is economic rights which are important because it gives self-respect to women. These rights includes the right to work, the right to just and favourable condition of work, the right to equal pay for equal work and right to rest and leisure including limitation of working hours and periodic holidays with pay and lastly right to get maternity benefit. Economic empowerment is crucial to women's empowerment and right to work outside the home and the right not to be sexually harassed at work place, the right to be treated justly and to receive adequate remuneration are all embodied in this set of rights. The social rights mentioned in the Declaration in *Article* 25 and which say that everyone has a right to a standard of living adequate for the health and well being of himself or herself, and his or her family, including food, clothing, housing, medical care and necessary social services and the right to security in the event of unemployment, sickness, disability, or lack of livelihood in circumstances beyond one's control. Also the second part of the *Article* 25 states that motherhood and childhood are entitled to special care and assistance. *Article* 26 also proclaimed that everyone has the right to have education. Education shall be free at least in the elementary stage. *Article* 27 states that everyone has the right to participate freely in the cultural life of the community, to enjoy the arts and share scientific advancement and its benefits.

Obstacles in Enjoying Human Rights of Women

The women and grown up girl child have to faces lots of obstacles in the society all over the world even in India for their tradition, value system and beliefs. These obstacles are social, economic, cultural or political etc. and it makes very difficult to enjoy the rights or to have these rights enforced through the judicial system. The *Human Development Report* in 2000 published by United Nations Development Programme points out that around 90 million children are out of school at the primary level and most of them are girl child. Now in India around 40 million girl child are not having basic education. In Gender Index, India also ranked very low. So there is a glaring inequality between boys and girls especially who receive education, the disparities becoming greater at the higher education and training level which affect women's economic and education right and to be self-reliant at a greater aspect. Even in legislative and in parliament very few women are representing because of enough social support and most of the local bodies i.e. panchayats and municipalities, women's role are as a rubber stamp. Still now women have little say in law making or law enforcement. This also explains why they still face discrimination in family laws. For an example, very few States Legislatures have amended the Hindu Succession Act to give to women a share in the joint family property by birth though now this law has amended in 2005 where women have right in parental property. On the Muslim law of inheritance and succession gives women only half of the share that men get on inheritance. Even Dowry prohibition act is not strongly affected in rural areas of India and there are so many cases of dowry death comes our notice in newspaper or in television. Also dowry related crimes, murder have been increasing day by day.

This table shows that dowry deaths are increasing in every year in most of the states of India and it has become a common phenomenon in news paper now a day.

Recently Women and Child Development Ministry says in Lok Sabha that in last two years i.e. 2007 & 2008, the total case of dowry death is around 15000 and more 1000 cases came into being in police.

Dowry Death in Some of the States

State	*2006*	*2007*
Assam	4504	4332
Bihar	1188	2755
Kerala	25	22
M.P	746	745
Rajasthan	1394	2547
U.P	1798	2205
West Bengal	445	549

Source: Jugasankha, Silchar, 27-12-08

Although the *Indian Penal Code* (IPC) has been amended to expressly provide for dowry murders and cruelty to women, as also rapes by those who are in a position of authority over women, or gang rapes, crimes in these areas have continued to rise and the current report of the Crime records Bureau seems to suggest that crimes against women will increase at a rate higher than the rate of growth of population. There is some evidence that convicts get punished but it is very rare, mostly get out of bell because of their money and muscle power. So, it becomes very important to analyse the factors which deny the rights of women, their basic human rights and how these rights could be enforced and sustained in the context of modern times. Another relative reason is the discrimination against women. Discrimination especially in the areas of economic, political and social opportunities, inequality in family life including health care, marriage and in reproductive decision-making and gender based violence ranging from violence in the community by the state and by the armed conflict. Such discrimination has also resulted in the denial of women's basic human rights. Social discrimination against women has affects her human rights from birth, or even before birth. Female foetuses are aborted as unwanted child under social and family pressure. So this incidence disables her social and family status. Every woman has a right to lead her life with full of dignity and without humiliations from the hands of her own family or other members. She has a right to live free from violence at the hands of her husband, parents or in-laws etc. She must be empowered to seek succour against such violence. She also has a right to be freed of helplessness which comes from economic dependence and psychological subjugation. Unless a woman's right to lead a life with dignity, her right to education, health care, her right to have a control over reproduction and her own body, her right to access information and knowledge, her right to participate in the economic and political processes, get recognition and respect, a woman can not be empowered to lead a fulfilling life or to contribute to the process of the nation.

Even the *International Convention on the Elimination of all Forms of Discrimination against Women* has stated that discrimination against women "violets the principles of equality of rights and respect for human dignity, is an obstacle to the participation of women on equal terms with men in the political, social, economic and cultural life of their countries, hampers the growth of the prosperity of society and the family and makes more difficult the full development of the potentialities of women in the service of their countries and of humanity". The Convention also states that in situations of poverty women has the least access to food, health, education, training and opportunities for employment. *Article 5* of the Convention says that state parties must take measures to modify the social and cultural patterns of conduct of men and women, with a view to achieving elimination of prejudices and customary and all other practices which are based on the idea of inferiority or superiority of either sex. The measures must be ensured that family education includes a proper understanding of maternity as a social function and the recognition of the common responsibility of men and women in the upbringing of children. *Article 10* states the equal right to education; *Article 11* seeks elimination of discrimination in employment, *Article 12* in the field of health care and *Article 13* in the area of economic and social life. Their empowerment depends of all the above.

If we really go into the deep in reality of those incidences, it becomes very clear to us that still our society has not been able to provide equality, equity share in all spheres of life and they are considered as commodity. There is a need to change our attitude towards the benefit of the women.

Some Incidence of Human Rights Violence against Women in Other Countries during World Wars

Over the years, human rights have been shaped by three critical factors; the role of the state, the universalisation of ideas and concepts, and world events like the World Wars. The two Wars and their holocaust forced the development of a universal human rights language, to provide a healing and protective touch to the badly damaged humanity. This was also a phase when colonial regimes were collapsing giving rise to new states mainly in Asia and Africa, which were regaining their right to self-rule. Post World War II; there was a new relationship between so called 'developed' and 'developing' nations. The concept of development was now being based on the principle of equity. It aimed at ensuring and enlarging human choices and leading to equality of opportunities for all people in society so that they participated in and benefited from the development process. The formation of the United Nations and the Universal Declaration of Human Rights (UDHR) in 1948 pronouncing "All human beings are born free and equal in dignity and rights, set the tone for the future". All these international processes facilitated the emergence of the human rights perspective as a powerful political theory, which brought greater clarity to the role of the state and its obligations towards its citizens irrespective of sex, caste, religion etc.

Human rights violation could be identified from sexuality, rape or terrorism which attacks on women. Here some stories about systematic attacks on women which has compelled the international community to think.

In the *20th century,* the frequency of the use of sexual violence in armed conflict is staggering. German WWI troops raped women of each village conquered to prove their dominance; in 1937, Japanese troops raped a staggering 20,000 women a day for three days in what became known as "The rape of Nanking"; the Japanese imprisoned up to 200,000

Korean, Chinese, and Filipino "comfort women" in rape camps; and Russian troops raped an estimated two million German women as they vanquished Nazi Germany. Thousands of Korean women, 15 to 22 years old, were abducted between 1937 and 1943 to serve in Japanese army brothels, often very near battle lines. Some women have told of being forced to have intercourse with as many as 30 soldiers a day. Women in China, the Philippines, Taiwan, and Indonesia suffered a similar fate. In the years after the war, this part of history was ignored, if not covered up. In the late 1980's, women academics in Korea began releasing research and hosting academic conferences on Japanese atrocities against women during the colonial era. Public interest increased sharply when a Filipina, a former comfort woman, went public with her experiences in 1990 in Manila. When Korean women speak about their lives since forced sex slavery, they use the word '*han*'. *Han* can be translated as "profound psychological suffering". It has the sense of a prolonged, oppressive hurting, a chronic wound that will not heal and that the victim feels every waking moment. The political nature of these attacks on women is either marginalised in favour of the 'main' story, or is not even recognised as having political connotations because women, by and large, are of insignificant social and political value. (The Statesman, 16-03-2009).

Human Rights Violation in North-East India

Human rights violation of women has been a world wide phenomenon and almost all the countries of the world, irrespective of their advanced or backward socio-economic conditions, have not been free from this crime. In almost every country, women are the victims of social crimes such as domestic violence, rape, sexual harassment, women battering etc. Even we can see that they suffer humiliation and brutalities especially when the men folk of their families are put behind the bars. An easy method of violating women's human rights has been outraging their modesty including sexual assaults. Because this acts, severe mental and physical torture is inflicted on the woman prisoners. Moreover, whenever an army rule has been imposed, widespread violation of women rights has been resorted to. In India, since independence vast areas had, almost the year round and sometimes for years together, been under the quasi-military rule. By a simple procedure of a proclamation through a gazette notification, the Government can declare any area in any state as a 'Disturbed Area', although no objective criteria provide definition to the occurrences justifying such a declaration. In a disturbed areas, the army is given a virtual 'carte blanche' to conduct search and destroy operation to enter private premises and search them, to arrest individuals without arrest warrant and even to shoot and kill. As a result, harrowing accounts of violation of human rights of women in those areas can be reported. Such reports have been came to public so many times and one thing it could be observed that whenever in the North-Eastern states (it includes total seven states but at present it is eight states) President Rule or Disturbed Areas Act has been declared, violations of women's rights has been rampant.

North-East India bas been named as its terrorism activities, bomb blast, kidnapping, rape, murder etc. which are common phenomenon and issues which could be heard everyday since from the last decades. North-East comprises the states of Assam, Arunachal Pradesh, Manipur, Meghalaya, Mizoram, Nagaland, Tripura and now Sikkim. They are connected to the rest of the Indian parts only through a narrow corridor called the 'Chicken's Neck'. Also some adjoining International countries have its boundaries such as Bangladesh, Bhutan, Nepal and Myanmar converge over a few kilometres.

There was a report on the violation of human rights by the security forces in the seven sates of the North-East. The two member team says 'Generation of Military Supervision' have takes a heavy toll on the people's lives, livelihood, attitude and in fact the very concept of '*Normalcy of Life*'. It also says that in Manipur and Nagaland which had declared of a virtual army rule, it is as thought the peoples can not imagine a life that is not under the barrel of the gun. A report that an army operation against the insurgency was carried out in the deep and dense jungle in the Jaintia hills of *Meghalaya*. There were to signs of working in the jungle by the women. The groups of militants attacked on them and raped and their body were thrown away. But the public can not speak out seeing that army were close on them in the name of Army Operation. (*The Hindu*, 22 May, 1997).

Torture is regularly reported in *Manipur*. Youths are suspected to be the members or sympathisers of the insurgency. Those youths are arrested and they tortured with 'third degree' methods by the military to extract information on the activities of their groups. They are not only physically but psychologically tortured. On the other hand, Human Rights defenders have been deeply concerned on prolonged imposition of the Armed Forces (Special Power) Act 1958 and resulting violation of Fundamental Human Rights in Manipur continuously. During the meeting in Mumbai, Ashoka Fellows Colin Cronsalves and Bablo Loitongbam came up with the idea of conducting a 'People's Enquiry'. After returning to Manipur, Bablo Loitongbam through his organization, Human Rights Alert (HRA) convened a round-table of the legal fraternity, the human rights community and NGOs on 20th August, 2000 at Imphal. The round-table unanimously agreed to constitute an 'Independent People's Enquiry Commission' and to invite Justice H. Suresh, Former Judge of Bombay High Court to lead the Committee with the A.C.Sharma as the convenor was also constituted to work out the details of the commission.

Another very significant issue of human rights violation was the case of the TH. Manorama Devi, she was raped by the Assam Rifles and was murdered by the Army personnel after two days of her arrest. After that twelve Manipuri naked women stormed the Army headquarter in Imphal, holding sign that read 'Indian Army Rape Us'. Manorama's murder was far from being an exceptional case in Manipur where rape, abuse and murder are everyday realities. In their brave protest, Manipuri women shamed Indian Army by parading the very naked female body that brought humiliation and death to their sisters with their raw anger and amazing mobilization, these women refuse to get knocked down by the rape by the 'rape culture'. This human rights violation in Manipur are in fact, sanctioned by the state in the form of Armed Force (Special

Power) Act 1958, which gives enormous power to security forces. AFSPA has been operative in Manipur for over five decades and has given unaccounted power to security forces to search, arrest, detain or kill anyone on the basis of suspicious in the name of 'maintaining public order'. This abuse of power by security forces have resulted tremendous human rights violation especially with women in the region.

In *Assam*, on the 22nd May night, 1997, a group of men from 16 Rajput Regiment went to Ambari Sorubhera village in search of militants. The villagers were gathered in the field nearby meanwhile the jawans raped Santhali (17 year old girl) and Rangeela (15 year girl) in front of the villagers. Next day those army again came to the village and raped Rumuni (16 year girl), a student of class nine and Thingigi, a student of class ten standard, while they were on the way to school. A case was registered at the Tamulpur police station but no investigation was carried away so far. In this way, violations of human rights of women and girls have been taking place.

Another case i.e. 'Operation Rhino' was started on the night of 14th September, 1991. On the that day, around 45 thousands jawans of Indian Army aided by about a lakh of paramilitary force personals belonging to CRPF, BSF, Assam Rifles and state Police, went into action. The armed forces were operating under the permission of the acts namely, the Assam Disturbed areas Act, 1955 and the Armed Forces (Special powers) Act, 1958. Operation Rhino was started in Assam and AFSA was applied to all the seven North-Eastern States. During the operation army were arresting innocent people from various places at random. There were cases of indiscriminate raids, death, suicide, gang rape, torture in army camps, open fire, illegal detention of lawyers, newspaper and editors, looting private property. This was one of the biggest human rights violations in Assam rather in India.

Apart from this violation of women' rights takes place in other forms also such as torture on house wives, dowry deaths, unpaid work and unequal pay (especially in the brick industry in Assam, women are mostly working along with men who usually coming from Bihar and stay here, but they are not paid for which they deserve) etc.

Recently an incidence took place in Beltala, near Gwahati, (Assam) a tribal girl named Lakshmi Oraon was forced by local people and took out her clothes (sari) and she was running nakedly through the road to save herself where people were just observer only. The tribal people were fighting for ST reservation against state government and local people were opposing it. This horrifying picture indicates not only the violation of human rights of women, but also a violation of our moral value, ethics and culture.

Now it is pertinent to realise that the empowerment of women need to be prioritised and should be worked inside those stories so that they can get justice through promoting social, economic, political empowerment. Their human rights could be secured only when they will be empowered enough with in their self and self-realisation develops having mass mobilisation in the society against the human rights violators. Here I have discussed how human rights could be secured.

Securing Human Rights for Women

Now the vital question is how are these human rights to be secured? Our Constitution framers cast the burden of securing civil and political rights of men and women on the judiciary by making these rights justifiable. The judiciary has discharged its responsibilities in the area of realisation of human rights with care and concern. It has also interpreted its mandate broadly with the help of International Conventions to secure to the people the Fundamental Rights in Part III of the Constitution as also some of the economic and social rights by reading these rights into Part III. In 1997, on the enactment of the Protection of human Rights act, the National Human Rights Commission has been set up to promote and secure human rights, though programmes and policies need to be initiated by the states under the directions of directives of the Court or the National Human Rights Commission to secure for women and their rights. Then the National Commission for Women has also be entrusted with the task of women's empowerment through programmes and actions designed to promote their human rights. Let's discuss an interesting aspect of story. Last sixty years after independence, the burden of securing to women's human rights was fully on the shoulders of the judiciary. During this period there were several judgements upholding and enforcing women's fundamental or human rights time to time. We know, the Constitution protects women against discrimination by providing in *Article 14* for equality before the law and equal protection of the laws. *Article 15* of the Constitution prohibits discrimination by the State against any citizen on the ground inter alia of sex. It also included special prohibitions for being made in favour of women and children. Even some of the Directive Principles of State policy in our Constitution contains provisions for the justice of women. *Article 39* provides that men and women equally have the right to an adequate means of livelihood, that there must be equal pay for equal work for both men and women and that the health and strength of workers both men and women, and the tender age of children should not be abused. *Article 42* states on human conditions of work place and maternity leave. Some examples rather cases, have quoted where women have used the constitutional provisions to challenge in a discriminatory service conditions. In C.B.Muthamma Versus Union of India (AIR 1979 SC 1868) service conditions in Foreign Service requiring female employees to obtain government permission before marriage and denying married women a right to be employed, were struck down by the Supreme Court as discriminatory. A rule of the Orissa State Judicial service Rules, 1963 disqualifying women from being appointed as District Judges on marriage was held by the Orissa High Court as violating Article 15 (Radha Charan Versus State of Orissa, 1969).

In the well known case of Air India International Versus Nargesh Mirza, (1981) 4 SCC 335} the Supreme Court examined discriminatory service conditions of Air India. These provided that an Airhostess could not get married for the first four years of service and that she had to resign on becoming pregnant. There was also further service condition that she could serve only till she attained the age of 35 extendable to 45 at the discretion of Air India. The court did not interfere with the condition that an Airhostess could not get married before completing four years service stating that since Airhostess were recruited around the age of 19, the condition that they could not get married till 23 need not be interfered with . But the other service conditions were held unreasonable and, therefore, violation of Article 14. Unfortunately, the court did not feel that the conditions were discriminatory against women on the ground of sex. The court held that the distinction between the Airhostesses and males performing similar duties was not discrimination on the ground of sex but a classification based on sex! A classification based on sex which prescribes unfavourable service conditions for women has to be covered by Article 14 and 15.

The courts, on the whole, however, have been sympathetic towards women and their right to employment. In Visakha Versus State of Rajasthan [(1997) 6 SCC 241] sexual harassment has been held as a violation of a women's right to equal treatment in the work place. The same view has been reiterated in Apparel Exports Promotion Council Versus A.K.Chopra, [(1999) 1 SCC 759]. Internationally, there has been considerable litigation relating to unfavourable service conditions for women including discrimination in respect of pay. In order to check such discriminatory pay scales, especially differentiation alleged to be based on differences in job specification, the Courts have evolved the concept of comparable worth of work. If the comparable worth of two jobs is similar, then the job which is done by women can not have a lower pay scale. The same criteria has been broadly accepted by the Supreme Court in Mackinnon Mackenzie Versus Audrey D'Costa [(1987) 2 SCC 469] when it said that in deciding whether the work is of a similar nature, a broad view should be taken of the nature of the jobs.

Now we have to search about the measures for the human rights enforcement.

Measures for the Enforcement of Human Rights

Human rights embodied in the Indian Constitution are justifiable. All these rights now have the support of a large number of international conventions and human rights covenants dealing with human rights. Even the courts have used these international covenants to widen the scope of the human rights in the constitution. As a result, it is possible to judicially enforce a large number of human rights of women embodied in international covenants also. But the constitutional-cum-international mandate needs to be accompanied by correct social perceptions, support services and a basic change in family and societal values. A proper enforcement of these rights thus requires, educating people in these human rights so that these rights are respected and observed in practice. A soothing culture of human rights has to be developed in our country. National Human Right Commission has a greater role to play in dealing cases and need to recommend and take compensatory measures. People also need to aware about the commission and it is now for the people to take help of these available institutions in order to inculcate human rights values in the home, in the community, in the society and in the public. Also all the three pillars of the government i.e. legislature, executive and judiciary must now respect and promote this culture of human rights specially for the women, the weaker section of the society.

Even the NGOs, welfare agencies and social workers have to play an important role to secure the rights of the women through advocacy, providing legal aids and legal education in the grass-root level to top.

As India has a great tradition and culture of respect women, we have a tradition of respect for motherhood and also we have a tradition of respect for those who work for others at personal sacrifice. This respect now encompasses respect for the human rights of others, particularly of those who have worked for others, so that people of this country can lead a life with self-respect and honour. Women are one of the main partners for the creation of destiny of our country par with men because they plays a pivotal role. So their human rights must be respected and they should not be treated as inferior or subordinate human beings. Their contribution to the family and society should be appreciated not just paying lip service to their goodness, but by respecting their inborn human rights and values, only then we can think of a forward-looking and peace nation which could be able to deal their own problems with self-confident and full confident.

Role of the Structural Social Worker

To deal with structural discrimination and focusing on structural social work, one way could be to emulate the principle of substantive equality as a way forward. This would mean that social workers seek to promote temporary special measures for the women. These measures would have to be framed and design to target women facing multiple barriers and problems to advancement and achievements of their human rights. Here social worker must begin with a clear application of the concept of intersectional and locating various structures that oppress women's rights.

Specific prohibitions of the CEDAW reflect the need for temporary special measures to address the effects of intersectional discrimination and recognise the multiple barriers to equality that marginalised groups of women face. Say for example, in requiring state parties to take, all appropriate measures to eliminate discrimination against women in the areas of economic and social life, Article 13 provides that women have a 'right to bank loans, mortgages and other forms of financial credit'. Indeed, several micro-credit loan initiatives targeting women around the world demonstrate that because poor and rural women whose poverty and rural residence constitute barriers to their advancement -often lack credit histories and other pre-requisites to getting bank loans, gender specific measures are needed to assist them. On the other hand the Article 14 of the Convention states that state parties to implement measures to improve the general situation of rural women, in sites such as housing and health care. Then the social workers need to work towards developing and building force among women groups for collective mobilisation at the local levels, both in rural and urban. This collective mobilisation would integrate the understanding of substantive equality and intersectional discrimination. Social workers need to take some directions to develop strategies and to address intersectional discrimination and substantive equality through:

1. *Building Collective Consciousness:* An effecting way of building collective consciousness is by begging a dialogue among women which will allow them to arrive at an understanding of their oppression. Such dialogue could be initiated through workshops, social meeting in which women will be guided to reflect on them. Besides this, an affective methodology could be inculcated, such as writing, reading and enacting their own life stories based on daily life experiences which would encourage ventilation as well as the ability to articulate confidently in numeral formal and informal sessions. Then development and effective use of alternate media to portray the real life situations of their sufferings, larger discussions on intersectional discrimination, as well as some of the success stories need to be consistently highlighted for the development of such collective consciousness.
2. *Collective Mobilisation:* To develop an effective strategy, to develop leadership and create spaces for the women's voices is the collective experiences. When they will come together, they will make a social group and it will help them to articulate, clarify and understand oppression and violation of human rights in a more nuanced manner. Within this process, while they have been able to develop this consciousness, the immediate need is to build upon these experiences, connect them to others to build solidarity, replicate these and develop further leadership more specifically at the bottoms, both in the urban and rural context. Collective decision-making helps them to have a safe space where they are able to discuss and express their concerns easily. It has also been seen that this kind of Mahila Samakhya programme has enabled them such collective mobilisation, often far reaching goals.
3. *Capacity Building:* Capacity building is essential for women and it can be enabled by the social workers

through empowering them. Social worker can initiate income generating programmes for the suppressed women and for them whose rights have been violated and for this 'advocacy' could be an effective technique developing their inner-self and make them self-reliant.

4. *Dealing with Issues:* Social worker could, with the help of NGOs, welfare agencies or civil societies, take those issues to the people to give them justice. This could be a good platform for the women who could share their expectations.
5. *Providing Legal Aids and Secure Rehabilitation:* Social worker can provide legal aids to the victims who need support and for this social worker need to work with advocate, with laws, court etc. Social worker has to fight with the strong system where it is not easy to do that but they can try through social action mobilising mass support from all corners of the society. Also social worker can secure those effected and needy women providing proper rehabilitation in different governmental or non-governmental organizations and institutions.

For a peaceful and developed society (in terms of social, economic, cultural, political, ethical, spiritual, legal etc.) we need to create a society where both men and women should have equal rights and freedom and dignity to live. On the other hand, an egalitarian society could be possible only, when the human rights of women are not violated any more and this should be the vision of our government.

References

Gangrade, K. D. (2001), "Power to the Powerless-A Silent Revolution", *Community Development Journal*, Vol. 36, No. 1, January, 2001, Oxford University Press, p-72-74.

India, 2007, *A Reference Annual*, Publication Division, Ministry of Information and Broadcasting, Government of India.

Karl, Marilee (1995), '*Women and Empowerment, Participation and Decision Making*', London, Zed Books.

Kashyap, Subhash, C. (2003), *'Blueprint of Political Reform'* Shipra Publications, Delhi.

Nadkarni.Vimla, V. (2008), "Human Rights Perspective in Social Work: Illustrations from Health Social Work", *The Indian Journal of Social Work*, April, 2008, Vol. 69, p. 139-157.

Pillai, J. B. (1995), *'Women and Empowerment'*, New Delhi, Gyan Publishing House.

Rappaport, J. (1984), *"Studies in Empowerment: Introduction to the Issue"*, Prevention in Human Service, 3, p. 1-7.

Roy, Sanjoy, (2007), *'Vision of Gender Relations in the 21st Century: Myth and Reality'*, Facets of Empowerment-Policies, Programmes and Perspective, New Royal Book, Lucknow, p-114-121.

Yadav, S. (2002), *"Human Rights and the Medieval Indian States Systems: In perspectives on Human Rights*: Essays of Prof. Radhakrishnan, New Delhi, Radha Publication, p. 5-16.

Yojana (2008), *A Development Monthly*, "Women's Empowerment" Ministry of Information and Broadcasting, GOI, New Delhi, Vol. 52, October, p. 35-37.

14

Social Work Practice and Human Rights

KIRTI VIKRAM SINGH

Introduction

Broadly speaking human rights may be regarded as those fundamentals and inalienable rights, which are essential for life as human being. Human rights are the rights which are possessed by every human being, irrespective of his on her nationality, race, religion, sex, etc., simply because he or she is a human being. Human rights are thus those rights, which are inherent in our nature and without which we cannot live as human beings. Human rights and fundamental freedoms allow us to fully develop and use our human qualities, our intelligence, our talents, and our conscience and to satisfy our physical, spiritual and other needs, They are based on mankinds increasing demand for a life in which the inherent dignity and worth of each human being will receive respect and protection. "Human rights are sometimes called fundamental rights or basic rights or natural rights. As fundamental or basic rights they are the rights that cannot, rather must not, be taken away by any legislature or any act of the government and which are often set out in a Constitution. As natural rights they are seen as belonging to men and women by their very nature. They may also be described as 'common rights' for they are rights which all men and women in the world would share, just as the common law in England, for example, was the body of rules and customs which unlike local customs, governed the whole country. (Kapoor, S. K. 2004).

Human Rights encompass a wide variety of political, economic and social areas. Human Rights define needs but also present a set of rights for each individual, no matter where that individual resides.

United Nations and Human Rights

In 1948, the United Nations General Assembly issued the 'Declaration of Human Rights' which has unique importance, as this Declaration marks the victory of individual in national as well as in the international affairs. The preamble of the Declaration states. "The General Assembly proclaims this Universal Declaration of Human Rights as a common standard of achievement for all people and all nations to the end that every organ of the society, keeping this declaration constantly in mind, shall strive by teaching and education to promote respects for these rights and freedoms and by progressive measures, national and international, to secure their universal and effective recognition and observance both among the peoples of member States themselves and among the people of territories under their jurisdiction."

Human Rights may be Classified into Following Four Categories

(1) General (Articles 1 and 2)

(2) Civil and Political (Articles 3 to 21)

(3) Economic, Social and Cultural Rights (Articles 22 to 27) and

(4) Concluding (Article 28 to 30)

(i) *General* – Article 1 of the Universal Declaration provide that all human beings are born free and equal in dignity and rights. They are endowed with reason and conscience and should act towards one another in a spirit of brotherhood. Article 1 thus proclaims the interest freedom and equality in dignity and rights of all human beings.

According to Article 2, everyone is entitled to all the rights and freedoms set forth in this declaration, without distinction of any kind, such as, race, colour, sex, language, religion, political or other opinion, national or social origin, property, birth or other status.

Furthermore no distinction shall be made on the basis of the political, jurisdictional or international status of the country or territory to which a person belongs, whether it be independent, trust, non-self governing or under any other limitation of sovereignity.

As noted above, a remarkable thing about the Universal Declaration is that it is neither addressed to nations nor member States of the U.N. but to every individual. This is evident from Articles 1 and 2 Article 29 also deserves mention in this respect.

(ii) Civil and Political Rights – The civil and political rights enumerated under and Declaration include the following:

(1) Rights to life, liberty and security of person.

(2) Prohibition of slavery and slavery trade.

(3) Prohibition of torture, cruel, inhuman or degrading treatment or punishment.

(4) Rights to be recognized as a person before law.

(5) Equality before the law and equal protection of law against any discrimination in violation of the Declaration.

(6) Right to effective remedy by the competent national tribunals,

(7) Prohibition of arbitrary arrest, detention or exile.

(8) Right to a fully equality to a fair and public hearing by an independent and impartial tribunal.

(9) Right to be presumed innocent until proved guilty according to law in public trial.

(10) Freedom from ex-post facto laws,

(11) Freedom from arbitrary interference with privacy, family, home, correspondence or attack honour or reputation and right to protection by law against such interference.

(12) Right to freedom of movement and residence within the borders of State.

(13) Right to leave any country, including his own, and to return to his country.

(14) Right to seek and enjoy in other countries asylum from prosecution in respect of political crimes.

(15) Right to nationality.

(16) Freedom from arbitrary deprival of nationality and right to change nationality.

(17) Right to many and to found a family and equal rights as to marriage, during marriage and as its dissolution.

(18) Right to own property and freedom from arbitrary deprival of property.

(19) Right to freedom of thought, conscience and religion.

(20) Right to freedom of opinion and expression,

(21) Right to freedom of peaceful assembly and association,

(22) Right to take part in the government of his country, and

(23) Right of equal access to public service in his country.

(iii) Economic, Social and Cultural Rights – Economic, social and Cultural Rights are enumerated in Articles 22 to 27. They are :

(1) Right to social security and the right to realization of the economic, social and cultural rights

indispensable for his dignity and the free development of his personality,

(2) Right to work, free choice of employment, just and favorable conditions of work and protection against unemployment,

(3) Right to equal pay for equal work,

(4) Right to just and favourable remuneration,

(5) Right to form and to join trade Unions,

(6) Right to rest and leisure,

(7) Right of living adequate for the health and well-being of himself and his family.

(8) Right of all children to enjoy same social protection,

(9) Right to education,

(10) Right to parents to choose the kind of education for their children,

(11) Right to participate in cultural life of the community, and

(12) Right to protection of moral and material interests resulting from any scientific literary or artistic production of which he is the author.

(iv) Concluding or Miscellaneous Articles - Articles 28 to 30 may be referred as concluding ar miscellaneous Article because they do not fit in any of the above three categories. For example, Article 28 provides that everyone is entitled to a social and international order in which the rights and freedoms set forth in this Declaration can be fully realized. Besides this Article 29(1) is an exception because this is the only provision in the whole Declaration which speaks of duties. Article 29(1) provides that everyone has duties to the community in which alone the free and full development of his personality is possible. However, Article 29(2) makes it clear that in the exercise of his rights and freedoms, everyone shall be subject only to such limitations as are determined by law solely for the purpose of securing due recognition and respect for the rights and freedoms of others and of meeting the just requirements of morality, public order and the general welfare in a democratic society. Article 29(3) further provides that these rights and freedoms may in no case be exercised contrary to the purposes and principles of the United Nations.

The last article of the Declaration, namely, Article 30, incorporates a rule of interpretation or a saving clause by providing that nothing in this Declaration may be interpreted as implying for any state, group or person any right to engage in any activity or to person any act aimed at the destruction of any of the rights and freedoms set forth herein. (Kapoor, S. K., 2004).

Social Work and Human Rights

Based on established concepts and definition of human rights, social workers can readily identify a connection between human rights and their profession. The social work profession concerns itself will helping people. Human Rights cover an entire range of political, economic and cultural needs required to form a humane society. By any measure, social work and human rights have much in common. While a social work, practice based on human rights, no panacea for discrimination, inequality, poverty and other social problems. Knowledge of human rights can help the profession better understand it's role as a helping profession.

The social work profession has an obligation to advocate for human rights, with the first step being recognition that human rights play important part of social work policies and practices. Unfortunately, a primary obstacle in integrating human rights into the professional is the adherence to social justice as the guiding principle of social work. While important to social work social justice by itself does not provide a concrete set of guidelines for social workers to follow. (Reichert Elisabeth, 2006). Social justice sounds nice but remains vague. The International Federation of Social Workers (IFSW), The Association of Schools of Social Work in India, has taken a major step in moving beyond social justice by highlighting it's adherence to human rights within it's code ethics.

Human Rights and Ethics

For the social work profession, a code of ethics seems indispensable. After all, social workers should follow some rules of conduct in relation to clients, co-workers, and others with whom they interact. A code of ethics provide these rules. Ethics presents recognized rules of conduct with respect to a particular class of human action or to a particular group. Ethics also helps in determining a proper course of action within a particular situation. A social worker operates in termas of certain basic assumptions.

1. Respect for human personality.
2. Dignity of each human being, be he a prince or a pamper.
3. Matching resources with needs.
4. Stimulating changes calculated to enhance democratic values.
5. Accomplishing changes through co-operation on both intellectual and emotional levels.
6. Serving as a 'change agent' from behind the scene, so that the individual as the group of the community may feel that changes were not imposed from outside but was autonomously sought by the individual, groups or community. (Mishra, P.D. 2003).

Connection Between Ethical Principles of Social Work and Human Rights

Ethical Principles	*Corresponding Human Rights*
Primary goal of social workers Help people in need and address social problems.	Right to standard of living adequate for health and well-being of family, including food, clothing, housing, medical care, and necessary social services for health and well-being of family (Art.25) Right to employment and living wage (Art.23) Right to education (Art.26)

Contd...

Ethical Principles	*Corresponding Human Rights*
Social Justice	Right to social security and economic, social and cultural rights (Art.22)
Social workers should challenge social injustice	Right to be treated without discrimination (Art.7) Other rights involving political and civil freedoms, including right to dignity (Arts.1-21)
Dignity and worth of person	Right to inherent dignity (preamble and Art. 1)
Social workers should treat each person in caring and respectful fashion, with special consideration to cultural and ethnic diversity	
Importance of human relationships	Right to free association (Art. 20) Right to marriage and create family (Art. 16)
Social workers should recognize central importance of meaningful relationships in everyone's life	Right to participate in cultural life of community (Art. 27) Everyone has duties to community (Art. 29)
Integrity	
Social workers should act honestly and responsibly and behave in trustworthy manner.	
Competence social workers need to develop and enhance professional expertise.	Every individual shall strive by teaching and education to promote respect for human rights and freedoms (preamble).

Human Rights and Vulnerable Group

In human right sense, certain population groups often encounter discriminatory treatment or need special attention to avoid potential exploitation. These population make up what can be referred to as vulnerable groups. (Reichert Elisabeth, 2006).

Women as a Vulnerable Group

In societies around the world, female status generally is viewed as inferior and sub-ordinate to male status. Gender inequality is pervasive in various segments of society. Women who constitute half of the population have been subjected to the tyranny and oppression of a patriarchal order for centuries and infact, most of them are suffering from the same fate even today. It is this aspect that needs to be closely examined because the future of society in terms of its direction and pace is dependent on this question. Therefore, it is essential to identify and understand these realities in the light of women's human rights, if we have to get rid of them.

Children as a Vulnerable Group

Children occupy a special role within human rights protection. In it's convention on the Rights of the Child, the United Nations states that the "Child, by reason of his physical and mental maturity, needs special safeguards and care, including appropriate legal protection, before as well as after birth."

Despite hectic planning, welfare programmes, legislation and administrative action, a large majority of children all over the world continue to remain in distress and turmoil. Most, if not all, countries have little difficulty rcognizing the vulnerability of children in respect to human rights and other abuses.

Persons with Disabilities as a Vulnerable Group

Another group which needs special protection within a human rights context is that of persons with disabilities, including mental illness. United Nations Declaration defines a person with a disability as 'Any person unable to ensure by himself or herself, wholly or partly, the necessities of a normal individual and/or social life, as a result of deficiency, either congenital as not, in his or her physical or mental capabilities."

The issue of disability seems to be enveloped by the clouds of misinformation and misconception, as a result discrimination against the physically and mentally disabled individuals still persists. The problem of disabled have confronted man since the inception of civilization. It is essentially a multi-faceted problem and requires the active co-operation and involvement of all sections of human society including the disabled persons themselves.

Persons with HIV-AIDS as a vulnerable group :

The AIDS/HIV is not confined to any one class, community, religion, age-group, sex or profession. According to World Health Organization, HIV is currently spreading in the world at the rate of one new infection every fifty seconds. In mid 1999, the highest number of HIV infected cases were found in African region, followed by the regions of Asia. The current prevalence of persons with HIV/AIDS has become a major concern all over the world. Persons with HIV-AIDS often encounter discrimination, especially because of the association with homophobia and prostitutes.

Aged Persons as a Vulnerable Group

Aging is generally associated with fatigue and decline in functional capacity of the organs of the body due to physiological transformation. No sign of aging is by itself regards as a disease even though all of them in their totality farm the syndrome called old age.

The status of aged varies in different societies and cultures. For most persons in the middle salaried class aging means forced retirement. For poor and working class aging may mean a state of dependence and object poverty. The vast majority of aged are not able to or permitted to work. Loss of work and earning results in an increasing number of aged becoming not only economically dependent, but this process also brings about psychological and personality changes in the aged which affect their status and role.

In 1999, the United Nations issued a document known as 'Principles for the Older Person'. The document emphasized that "priority attention" should be given to the 'situation of older persons.' (Reichert, Elisabeth, 2006).

Social Work Practice and Human Rights

The importance of human rights to social work is clear. Human rights principles represent admissible policy statements, but without actual integration of those principles into every day practices, human rights can only remain incidental to the social work profession. While an important starting point in the integration of human rights into practice involves adherence to social work ethics, a second stage is also necessary to more fully adopt human rights to social work practice. Only by truly incorporating human right principles into actual interventions and day-today practice techniques, human rights can occupy the desired place in the social work profession (Reichert, 2006).

In order to ensure successful intervention, selection of appropriate intervention strategy and tactics is very necessary.

Selecting Appropriate Intervention Strategy

One of the first agenda items for a successful interventions is the selection of appropriate strategies and tactics. An 'Strategy' is regarded as 'an orchestrated attempt to influence a person or a system in relation to same goal which an actor desires.' In general, the following strategies may be considered by the social workers for integrating human rights into policies and practices, so that they can serve as a resource for those who have problems, who have problems, who have limited or no control over the changes that need to be made in order to resolve their problems, and who request or are willing to take accept help.

Identifying and Recognizing Human Rights

The first step in any strategy related to human rights is identifying or understanding the meaning of human rights. It is simply not possible to apply human rights to social work practice, without a thorough understanding of specific human rights, using actual document.

After obtaining knowledge about the meanings of human rights, social workers should recognize why human rights are valuable to any society.

The Reconnaissance

The next step in applying human rights involves analysis. Here the worker and other interested individuals assess the general situation of the target group (generally vulnerable groups of the society) whose rights are violated. At this point the problem presented may not be the care problem. Generally, social workers do not have a clear-cut intake policy that defines eligibility requirements for the offering of the service. Therefore, there is usually our exploratory phase, during which the appropriateness of the problem for intake is considered.

The Diagnosis

In this phase, the problem will be specified and the 'link' will be developed between the facility and the target group. A social - worker can also play the role of a "change agent" for helping the target group.

The Planning

Next step involves studying the problem carefully in all its pertinent aspects, facts and opinions are brought together. Plans for successful intervention are made.

Taking action to Realize Human Right: The Implementation

The final stage in applying human rights to social work practice and policies for the purpose of benefiting the target group involves implementation. The first four steps enable the social workers to identify, recognize, and analyze human rights in different situations and to plan intervention. The fifth and final step in that of realizing human rights. In this final phase, intervention or action takes place in order to get the predetermined objective i.e. improvement in the status of vulnerable groups of the society.

Selecting Appropriate Intervention Tactics

The choice of tactics is critical decision point in a planned change. Tactics refer to the specific techniques and behavior employed in relation to the target system designed to maximize the possibility that the strategy will be successful and the proposed change shall be adopted. In order to realize human rights of the target group following three tactics can be used.

1. Information, Education and Communication (IEC)
2. Behavior Change Communication (BCC)
3. Collaboration, Competition and Disruption (CCD)

Information, Education and Communication (IEC) : IEC can be defined as a tactic which attempts to change or reinforce a set of behavior in the target beneficiaries regarding a specific problem in pre-determined time frame. It is a multi-disciplinary and client centered approach. When carefully carried out with intervention strategies, helps to realize Human rights of the vulnerable groups.

Behaviour Change Communication (BCC): It is well established that the mere provision of services as well as information does not necessarily result in the utilization of the same. Specialists in human rights acknowledge the programmes have to be designed keeping in mind the psychological as well as sociological barriers to change that often prove far more difficult to address than the physical ones. Any behavioural change to be sustainable must be internalized as a value, as some thing that is viable in the long term. BCC is a dynamic process, which involves an exchange or sharing of ideas, information, attitudes, beliefs, myths, misconceptions and practices.

BCC uses multiple channels to transmit and reinforce messages that address well defined target groups to change the current behaviour to the desired behavoiur. This can be done by providing people the skills and tools for better understanding about human rights and to create a supportive environment for adopting the desired behaviuor for better out comes. Thus, at the foremost, it will be necessary to identify concrete and realistic behavioural target among the community, ways to reach them and appropriate messages to the target group.

Collaboration : In this tactic the social workers collaborate with local authorities, other authorities or agencies and with the target beneficiaries in order to bring about improvements in the existing social policies. The basis assumption of this tactic is homogeneity of values and interests, through which substantive agreement on proposals is obtainable.

Competition : In this tactic social workers try to persuade, to negotiate and to bargain, with a willingness to realize the human rights of their target beneficiaries.

Disruption : This tactic signifies more militant approach and it may include strikes, boycotts, fasts, submitting petitions, publicity campaigns, sit-in etc.

Application of Human Rights to Practice

By employing these strategies and tactics Human Rights can be applied to practice., Reichert Elisabeth 2006 has mentioned the following interventions.

Intervention 1: Challenging Oppression

Within the social work profession, challenging oppression is a primary form of intervention. Oppression refers to an unjust use of authority or power over an individual or group. Oppression can take many forms: racial and ethnic discriminations, policies that favour the wealthy over the poor, gender inequality, belittling of gay and lesbians, and other unjust uses of power. In many cases, oppression promotes notions or rage, anger, or self-effacement within the individual or group. For example, repeated exposure to oppression may cause a person or group to internalize negative self-images projected by the external oppressor. If those in power continually state that poor people are inferior to others, the affected group may begin to internalize these images of inferiority. This internalized oppression may lead to rage and resignation from the broader society. Yet, repression of this rage can lead to self-destructive behaviour or destructive behavior toward other.

Social workers have a responsibility to challenge individual and social relations that create and maintain oppression. According to social work ethics, the responsibility to challenge oppression rests upon the social work profession.

Human rights principles also view oppression as unjust and in direct contradiction to those principles. According to the Universal Declaration of Human Right (1948), every individual has an equal right to human dignity (Article 1). Everyone is entitled to all the rights and freedoms within the Universal Declaration without distinction as to race, colour, sex, language, religion, political or other opinion, national or social origin, property, birth or other status (Article 2). Oppression creates an unequal and unjust set of circumstances, which social work profession should challenge.

Intervention 2: Empowerment

Another important intervention within the social work profession is that of empowerment. Like the intervention of challenging oppression, empowerment aims to reduce inequitable power structures. The basis of empowerment rests upon an examination of circumstances that contribute to differential treatment concerning ethnicity, age, class, national origin, religion and sexual orientation. The social worker then persons to unaerstand their experiences of oppression and form appropriate responses.

Assisting individuals and groups to empower themselves to overcome inequitable treatment forms a key part of the social work profession. Empowerment can raise the consciousness level of all parties about inequitable treatment. By assisting other to empower themselves and leading them to available resources, social workers are also promoting human rights, which center on equitable treatment for all.

Intervention 3: Strengths Perspective

Another important social work intervention known as the strengths perspective focuses on an individual's or group's strengths, even though other circumstances may indicate drug addiction, child abuse, or some other obstacle. Rather than highlighting deficiencies within an individual's or group's situation, the strengths perspective aims to assist people in using their own attributes in overcoming or coping with particular obstacles. The strengths perspective helps social workers avoid the trap of viewing an individual or group as inadequate or otherwise incapable of improving their situation.

The realization that an individual's or group's situation in life may, at least in part, be a result of structural injustices and lack of resources or fair treatment helps principles. By acknowledging the strengths of individuals an groups, social workers are better poised to connect human rights to a particular situation.

Intervention 4: Feminist Practice

Feminist practice focuses on a critique of power relations characterized primarily by gender domination and subordination. Feminist practice recognizes that gender issues often become shaped by notions of domination and subordination. However, this intervention provides a more constructive approach to gender issues by promoting collaboration and cooperation rather than competition between males and females. The collaborative approach goes beyond the critique of which gender has power but addresses disempowerment or oppression o anyone, whether on the basis of race, religion, sexual orientation, or other category. The goal of feminist practice as an intervention is to be inclusive to all and not simply focus on a gender war.

The connection with human rights principles, feminist practice emphasize the inherent value of everyone, with the right to be free from discrimination and oppression. Human dignity and human value are primary within feminist practice, which corresponds to human rights principles.

In ultimate analysis it is to be understood that social work profession and human rights are intertwined. By drawing upon human rights principles, social workers can play a major role in protecting children and other vulnerable populations, they can easily carry out international relief work and occupy the frontlines of disaster assistance, they can efficiently assist in delivery of social services to all population and can much more effectively challenge the acts of oppression.

References

Friedlander, Walter (1958), Concept and Methods of Social Work, Englewood Cliffs, N.J. Hall.

Fenwick Hden (2004), Civil Liberties and Human Rights, Canvendish Pub. Ltd., London.

Kapoor, S. K. (2004), International Law and Human Rights, Central Law Agency, Allahabad.

Kettner (1993), Social Work, Macro-Practice, Arizona State University, Longman.

Mishra, P.D. (2000.), Social Work, Philosophy and Methods, Inter India Pub.

Reichert Elisabeth (2006), Understanding Human Rights, Sage Pub., New Delhi.

Symonides (2003), Human Rights; International Protection, Monitoring, Enforcement, UNESCO Pub., London.

15

Struggle for Human Rights Towards Equitable Society
(A Study With Regard to a Group of District Bahraich U.P.)

Alok Chantia, Preeti Misra & Rohit Misra

Introduction

In Indian 'context, caste system and value system has given a new horizon to equitable society. The equitable society is encompassed with social justice which comes from equal opportunity to everyone and awareness of human rights that everyone is born free and equal. Thus pillar of equitable society is casteless society. But irony is that there are certain groups of people who do not know their caste, they are casteless but still they are devoid of basic facilities of life. One such group of people is Dhankut living in District Bahraich of Uttar Pradesh, who are neither SC/ST/OBC nor listed in any caste or sub caste. They are very far from all those facilities which are available to weaker sections of a society. Due to small population (2687) and living at single place (Dhankutty pura), Dhankut could not draw any attention of the government for their upliftment. Since their caste is not known, cross-cousin and parallel cousin marriages generated amongst them in order to maintain their identity and lineage. Dhankut are very poor and mostly illiterates hence they have taken up small works like thela pulling, betel selling .They can be seen in the streets of Dhankuttypura selling ground nuts, grams etc. Dhankut women are making and selling cow dung cakes by collecting cow dung from the vicinity. Their children are also working to earn the livelihood for the family. Due to poverty they cannot go to hospital and civil court etc. hence they depend upon quacks for treatment and upon traditional panchayat for the resolution of their disputes. Dhankut are fighting for their identity since 1973 and they have formed "Dhankut Sangharsh Samiti" for the purpose. A case is also pending in this regard in State Backward Commission since 2004. Dhankut have occupied some seats in Municipal Board too in their struggle towards equitable society.

The objective of present article is to analyse how a group of people who do not know their caste, struggle and survive in the society. As the hypothesis is that one should be aware of its caste to reap the benefits of equitable society, the present paper examines in detail whether Dhankut are living in equitable society and what struggles they have made for their survival and growth.

We all are born free and everyone has right to live with pride and dignity. Equitable society is merely concerned with the feeling of humanity which produces the positive inclination of equality either by self consciousness or by law. Equitable society grants rights relating to life liberty, equality and dignity of the individual which is also guaranteed by the Constitution or embodied in the International Covenants and enforceable by courts in India.

Equitable society ensures such rights which are basic to a human being's existence. Moreover these are those rights which each human being is entitled to; to allow him/her freedom to life- a dignified, secure life of his/her choice. In Hindu Philosophy, 'Dharma' is perhaps the closest word to equitable society. Actually it has many levels of meaning - law, norms of conduct, truth, ritual, justice, morality, destiny, religion and more. "Vasudhaiv Kutumbakam. (The world is our family) is the underlying philosophy[1]. The universal principle found in our scriptures-the Vedanta is that, the goal of human life is dual,

(1) the spiritual release of our individual soul from bondage and

(2) the welfare of society and of the world. This welfare is not interpreted in any narrow, racial or religious terms: it is defined as the welfare and happiness of the many. When the Vedic sages of ancient India prayed that-

"Sarve Bhavantu Sukhina, Sarve Santu Niramaya, Sarve Bhadrani Pashyantu, Ma Kashchid Dukh Bhag Bhawet"

They recognised the existence of equitable society granting rights to all human beings, irrespective of caste, colour creed, sex, country or region to have good quality of life free from disease, want, degradations, tensions and worries. Its appeal was universal because the sages did not talk of the prosperity, health and freedom of a particular sect or section of a society in any particular clime or country but of all mankind with out any reservation or consideration whatsoever. It is really unfortunate that we do not see the fulfillment of their dreams and visions on the international or even on the national level. We notice that a great part of the world including India is in the grip of utter poverty, degradation, illiteracy, backwardness, terrorism, intolerance, fundamentalism, disease and drudgery.

Indian Constitution guarantees to all its citizens liberty, equality and justice- social, economic and political, irrespective of caste, colour, creed or sex. Fundamental rights unambiguously recognize the basic human rights of all individuals and aim to remove all kinds of inequities from the lives of its people. The Directives Principles of State Policy known as socio-economic charter aims to provide socio economic justice to all its citizens.[2]

Methodology

Present study was carried out between May-June 2006. It is a primary data based work with the help of participant observation and schedule based interview. Dhankut are 2687 in number (791 male and 799 female) (2001 census), 1097

(582 boys and 515 girls) are children i.e. below the age of 18 years. Therefore out of 1590 adults Dhankuts only 300 respondents above the age of 18 years have been chosen on the basis of random sampling for the present study. Out of 300, 156 are illiterate, 100 are educated up to 5th standard 119 up to 8th, 10 up to 10th, 10 up to 12th whereas 3 are guarantees and only 2 are post graduates.Equitable society ensures awareness and availability of human rights and also provides mechanism to enforce the same.A number of questions were asked about the awareness, availability and enforcement of human rights to analyse whether Dhankut society is equitable society or not and what efforts they have made for their survival and growth. The analysis of data revealed following facts.

Result & Discussion

Awareness of Human Rights

The knowledge and awareness of human rights is essential and sine qua non for the formation of equitable society. Only those people who are educated about and aware of their human rights can demand that their government observe those rights granting basic sustenance to life. Knowledge of human rights is essential as a tool for the observance and the protection of human rights in a just and equitable society. It also creates a climate of public opinion in which gross violation of human rights are unacceptable.[3]

So far as Dhankut are concerned they are not very much aware of the term "human rights". But they feel that some kinds of rights are required to uplift their position in life. Table 1 reveals Dhankut's awareness about human rights. It shows that majority of respondents 274 (91.3%), 136(86.6%) males and 138 (96.5%) females say that they have not heard the term "Human Rights." Dhankut are illiterate and Human right is a newly launched concept during last decade only, that is why only those who are literate, are familiar with this term. Only 26(8.7%) respondents, 21 (13.4%) males and 05 (3.5) females say that they have heard about the term "Human right."

Table 1
Awareness of Human Rights among the Respondents

	Have you heard about Human Rights?					
	Yes		*No*		*Total*	
Sex Ratio	*Nos.*	*%*	*Nos.*	*%*	*Nos.*	*%*
Male	21	13.4	136	86.4	157	52.3
Female	05	3.5	138	96.5	143	47.7
Total	26	8.7	274	91.3	300	100.0

Table 2
Meaning of Human Rights

	Understanding of Human rights?							
	It is concerned with individual right		*Government Help*		*Dignified Life*		*Total*	
Sex Ratio	*Nos.*	*%*	*Nos.*	*%*	*Nos.*	*%*	*Nos.*	*%*
Male	04	19	03	14.3	14	66.7	21	80.8
Female	01	20	01	20.0	03	60.0	05	19.2
Total	05	19.2	04	15.4	17	65.4	26	100.0

Availability of Human Rights

There are four salient features of Human Rights which include citizen's rights, liberty, safety and dignity. These are nothing but natural rights necessary for the development of Human personality and equitable society.

Even after the 59 years of independence, a large chunk of our population still lives below the poverty line. They do not get two square meals a day, have no access to sufficient clothing to cover their bodies and have no roof over their heads when they sleep at night. They are compelled to lead a life of semi nakedness, malnutrition, disease and drudgery. People are still illiterate and hence cannot make efforts to improve their living condition. This is nothing but negation of equitable society and great violation of the human rights. So far as Dhankut are concerned they are very poor and hence cannot afford even the basic minimum requirements of their lives. Their socio cultural and economic life is reflected in the Tables from 3 to 15 which reveals that they are living in inequitable society in this globalised world.

Table 3
Satisfaction with Housing Facility

	Are you satisfied with your house							
	Sufficient		*Unsatisfactory*		*Compromising*		*Total*	
Sex Ratio	*Nos.*	*%*	*Nos.*	*%*	*Nos.*	*%*	*Nos.*	*%*
Male	68	43.3	85	54.1	4	2.6	157	52.3
Female	44	30.7	76	53.1	23	16.2	143	47.3
Total	112	37.4	161	53.6	27	9.0	300	100.0

Housing Facility

Adequate housing is universally viewed as one of the most basic human needs. National as well as international laws emphasize upon the significance of a secure place to live for human dignity, physical and mental health and overall quality of life.[4]

The United Nations Centre for Human Settlements estimates that throughout the world, over one billion people live in inadequate housing, with in excess of 100 million people living in conditions classified as homelessness.[5] Besides according to figures released by the World Health Organization time to time, billions of people in developing countries do not have access to drinking water nor do they have access to adequate sanitation[6].

In India position is no different, homelessness or inadequate housing is nothing but denial of right to live with dignity. In *Prabhakaran Nair v. State of Tamil Nadu*[7]. The Supreme Court admitted that there is acute shortage of housing in India. In *Shankar Banerjee v. Durgapur Projects Ltd.*[8] it was held that "to ask a person to live in sub human conditions by depriving him even of the benefit of two small rooms which is the minimum requirement for a family to live and compelling him to live in one single room with his wife and children and to share the bath, toilet and kitchen with another family is nothing but animal existence". An important facet of human right is to live like a human being. Due to lack of space and over crowding in the houses people do suffer from many diseases such as pneumonia and tuberculosis. Reduced death rate is another problem and natural consequence of over crowding due to want of privacy. Since Dhankut are living at single place Dhankuttypura, their living place has shrinked due to increase in their population over the years.

Total 3 reveals that maximum 161 (53.6%) respondents, 85 (54.1%) males and 76 (53.1%) females are not satisfied with living condition in present houses. Whereas 68(43.3%) males and 44 (30.7%) females or 112(37.4%) respondents are satisfied with their present abode. 27(9%) respondents feel that present houses are only a compromise. It is noticeable that though Dhankut have houses but it is not fit for their proper living.

Maximum houses of Dhankut are non-cemented or kachcha, few houses are cemented of those Dhankut, who have acquired a good economic position. Rest of the houses are small in size. A big house is divided into many small houses according to the presence of number of families. Maximum houses (617) are without the basic amenities like water, electricity and sanitary, lavatory facility. 91 houses have a common kitchen, small veranda and one or two rooms. Most of the kachcha houses are made of clay and cow dung. The floor is non-cemented and the roofs are made of tiles (khaparale) and sticks (narkul).

Availability of Water

Every great civilization florished at the bank of a river because availability of water is must for smooth survival, we cannot imagine life without water. River and pond are natural resources of water and these are used to bring water for the requirement of life. The expansion of urban areas increased the requirement of water which is fulfilled by tube wells, hand pumps and tap water supply but all these devices want money. Dhankut is living in urban area and water is equally must for them, but maximum Dhankut have no water supply in their houses. They take water from public water supply. Dhankut are poor, hence they can't afford the expenditure of water connection. The water supply available in their houses is not sufficient as is evident from the Table 4, which shows that 247 (82.4%) respondents,132 (84.1%) males and 15 (80.5%) females have no water supply. Only 53(17.6%) respondents including

25(15.9%) males and 28(19.5%) females have water supply in their houses.

Table 4
Condition of Water in House

	Do you have water supply in house?					
	Yes		*No*		*Total*	
Sex Ratio	*Nos.*	*%*	*Nos.*	*%*	*Nos.*	*%*
Male	25	15.9	132	84.1	157	52.3
Female	28	19.5	115	80.5	143	47.7
Total	53	17.6	247	82.4	300	100.0

Situation of Lavatory

Man is a social animal and alike other birds and animals he/she also discharges excreta. In the very beginning he used forest and open space and when he settled down in village he/she used open field which were utilized as natural compost. But after the increase of urban areas, no forest or open fields were left. So lavatory system came in vogue-a specific place within the house for discharge of excreta. Dhankut houses are small and they are living in urban area where lavatory system is must. But in reality majority of Dhankut are not having lavatory system in their houses.

Table 5
Situation of Lavatory in Family

	Do you have lavatory system in your house?					
	Yes		*No*		*Total*	
Sex Ratio	*Nos.*	*%*	*Nos.*	*%*	*Nos.*	*%*
Male	22	14.1	135	85.9	157	52.3
Female	19	13.3	124	86.7	143	47.7
Total	41	13.7	259	86.3	300	100.0

Table 5 shows that 259 (86.3%) respondents, 135(85.9%) males and 124(86.7%) females have no lavatory in their houses. Dhankut are poor and their houses are very small. Maximum Dhankut use public drainage and open field for their routine work. They know that lavatory is must but they are helpless to have this basic requirement. Only 41 (13.2%) respondents including 22 (14.1%) males and 19(13.3%) females have lavatory in their houses.

Facility/Availability of Electricity

During the evolution of man, when he acquired the status of Homo sapiens he used fat for light in the cave. After progressing day by day man used a combination of oil and cotton for lighting but after the invention of electricity the whole scenario changed. Now he can do many works in the night, he/she can have sound sleep in a hot night or icy cold night. It is all possible because of electricity. But man's economic condition is responsible for affording different facilities. Since Dhankut are poor they cannot afford electricity. A very few Dhankut houses have facilities of electricity.

Table 6
Situation of Electricity in the Family

	Do you have electricity in your house?					
	Yes		*No*		*Total*	
Sex Ratio	*Nos.*	*%*	*Nos.*	*%*	*Nos.*	*%*
Male	22	14.1	13.5	85.9	157	52.3
Female	22	15.3	121	84.7	143	47.7
Total	44	14.6	256	85.4	300	100.0

Table 6 shows that 256 (85.4%) respondents including 135 (85.9%) males and 121 (84.7%) females have no electricity facility. They use lantern for this purpose. Only 22 (14.1%) males and 22 (15.3%) females or overall 44 (14.6%) respondents have electricity. Dhankut want to avail all modern facilities but it is not so. They are very far from basic necessities even after living in urban areas.

Education Facility

Education is enlightenment and pillar to equitable society. It lends dignity to a man. Education seeks to build up the personality of the pupil by assisting his physical, intellectual, moral and emotional development. In *University of Delhi v. Ram*

Nath[9] it was held that man without education is equal to animal. The notions of individual freedom, liberty and dignity of a person, which are the basic tenets of equitable society, are meaningless to those who are illiterate and ignorant. Education means knowledge which leads to liberation from ignorance. Without education a man cannot make the best of himself and of the opportunities. Article 26(1) of the Universal Declaration of Human Rights states that everyone has right to education and that elementary education shall be free and compulsory. Clause (2) further provides that education shall be directed to the full development of the human personality and to the strengthening of respect for human rights. Right to education has also been recognised under Art. 13(1) of the International Covenant on Economic Social and Cultural Rights and under Article 41 of the Indian Constitution.

Article 21 A (Constitutional 86th Amendment Act 2002) and Art. 45 of Indian Constitution recognize the right to education in consonance with the commitment of international community as contained in different international covenants in order to promote weaker sections of the society and to protect them from the social injustice and all forms of exploitation. Thus we see that without education the equitable society cannot be secured to the people, therefore right to education should include human rights education and should be made compulsory from the elementary stage itself.

Majority of Dhankut are illiterates and few of them are graduates and post graduates. The position of education among Dhankut women is not very good. The details of educational standard of Dhankut is given below in Table 7 which shows that Dhankut represent an illiterate group. Majority of respondents 158(52.7%) are illiterate. Only 79(26.4%) have studied upto 5th, 38(12.7%) up to 8th 10(3.3%) up to 10th, 10(3.3%) up to 12th 3(1.0%) up to graduation and only 2(0.6%) have studied up to post graduation. Table also shows that female literacy is lower to male. 90 females are illiterates whereas only 68 males are illiterates. As we proceed towards higher education, it is more clear. It shows that Dhankut are not very much interested in female Dhankut's education.

Table 7
Educational Qualification of Respondents

	Educational Status															
	illiterate		*1-5th*		*6-8th*		*10th*		*12th*		*Graduate*		*P.G.*		*Total*	
Sex Ratio	*Nos*	*%*	*Nos*	*%*	*Nos*	*%*	*Nos.*	*%*	*Nos*	*%*	*Nos*	*%*	*Nos*	*%*	*Nos*	*%*
Male	68	43.5	47	29.9	22	14.0	09	5.7	07	4.4	03	1.9	01	0.6	157	523
Female	90	62.9	32	22.4	16	11.2	01	06	03	2.3	-	-	01	0.6	143	47.7
Total	158	52.7	79	26.4	38	12.7	10	3.3	10	3.3	03	1.0	02	0.6	300	100.0

Availability of Occupation and Income

"Poverty is inability to attain minimal standard of living and is not just absence of wealth alone but a mixture of disabilities and circumstances which breeds a culture of its own"[11] Dr. Ambedkar viewed equality of opportunity for all citizens as the most important right and very heart and soul of any Constitution. He regarded the Directive Principles of State Policy of Indian Constitution of great value as they lay down the ideal of economic democracy for ending the poverty, ignorance and inequality of opportunity and wipe out tears from every eye.[12]

Poverty is a system which includes a continuous fight for survival, unemployment, low wages, unskilled labour, absence of food supplies, insufficient possibilities of privacy and child labour.[13]

The perceptions of the poor are coloured by the complex of deprivations which make up their life and hamper their economic and social progress. So far as Dhankut are concerned they are poor and cannot afford a decent standard of living. Most of them are engaged in small time retain work of thela pulling, grain selling, palledari etc. women are engaged in collection of cow dung and making of cow dung cakes. Children too are supporting family income by selling peanuts, and groundnuts etc.

Availability of Occupation

Occupation enhances the status of an individual. With the change in occupation status and living standard of a community also changes. The group under study is involved in different occupations Here it is also important to note that their traditional work was cereal selling which was given up due to emergence of new market system. Dhankut is a non-agricultural group, living in urban area. Diversity of occupation among Dhankut is due to their illiteracy and poverty.

Table 8
Occupational Description of Respondents

	Particulars of Business/Occupations													
	Labour		*Service*		*Business*		*Agri-culture*		*Others*		*None*		*Total*	
Sex Ratio	*Nos*	*%*	*Nos*	*%*	*Nos*	*%*	*Nos*	*%*	*Nos*	*%*	*Nos*	*%*	*Nos*	*%*
Male	60	38.2	03	1.0	62	39.4	09	5.7	-	-	23	14.6	157	52.3
Female	08	5.5	-	-	-	-	-	-	16	11.2	119	83.3	143	47.7
Total	68	22.7	03	1.0	62	20.6	09	3.0	16	5.3	142	47.4	300	100.0

Table 8 Shows that Dhankut are engaged in different occupations. Maximum females 119 (83.3%) are not involved in any occupation/business. Participant observation revealed that 16 (11.2%) respondents are doing other works such as collection of cow dung and selling of wood etc. Whereas only 8 (5.5%) women are engaged as labourers. But males are doing different works 62 (39.4%) are engaged in different businesses as betel shop, fruit shop, cereal selling etc., 60 (38.2%) are doing labour work, 23 (14.6%) are doing nothing, 9 (5.7%) are engaged in agriculture. Dhankut is a non-agriculture community but during last decade some Dhankut have purchased agricultural land in Meerpur village for their livelihood. In the whole community only 3 (1.7%) are in government services. They are all in fourth class job.

Right to Marriage

Right to marriage is recognised under Article 21 of Indian Constitution as part of right to life and personal liberty and is judicially recognised too. Section 5(iv) of Hindu marriage Act, 1955 also guarantees close relation marriages in the name of custom and usage which is otherwise void. It is very unhealthy practice and leads to a number of genetical problems due to inbreeding and thus devoids the person of right to health which is again a fundamental right under Article 21 of Indian Constitution. In 60 years of independence the government is not able to do away with this unhealthy practice which continues in the name of usage and custom with the sanction of the government.

Among Dhankut, cross cousin and parallel cousin marriages are found to be existent. A girl may be married into that house, where her bua (father's sister) has got married. It is also a notable point that when a girl gets married into one lineage (it means a group of kinsmen to trace themselves back to male or female to a common ancestor) then the girl from this lineage is not accepted as Bahu (daughter-in-law).

Cross cousin marriage is of two types namely matrilineal cross cousin marriage in which son of father's sister (Bua) and daughter of mother's brother (Mama) is permitted. Whereas in matrilineal marriage it is vice versa. In case of Dhankut no restriction is placed on such kind of marriages nor any mutual consent is required. What is the opinion of Dhankut for such marriages is given in table below:

Table 9
Opinion About Cross-cousin Marriage Among Close Relatives

	Do you practice cross-cousin marriage?					
	Yes		*No*		*Total*	
Sex Ratio	*Nos.*	*%*	*Nos.*	*%*	*Nos.*	*%*
Male	-	-	157	100	157	52.3
Female	-	-	143	100	143	47.7
Total	-	-	300	100	300	100.0

Table 9 shows that all the respondents favour marriage between close relatives. All 300(100%) respondents say that they are practicing such type of marriage. Why they are practicing such kind of marriage is shown in Table 10.

Causes of Cross Cousin Marriage

Cross cousin marriage is influenced by the hypothesis of integrity that brother and sister attach with each other by the marriage of their daughters and sons. Dhankut is an endogamous group who practice cross cousin marriage Table 10 shows that 141 (47%) respondents, 71 (45.2%) males and 70 (49%) females say that they indulge in cross cousin marriage because of non-recognition of their caste by adjacent communities. Since their caste is not described in district gazetteer, people from other communities do not like to give their daughters and sons in Dhankut for marriage.135 respondents, 73(46.5%) males and 62(43.3%) females say they indulge in such kind of marriage to save their communities identity and existence.13 (4.3%) respondents, 6(3.8%) males and 7(4.9%) females prefer such marriage due to their culture. Whereas 11(3.7%) respondents, 7(4.5%) males and 4(2.8%) females go for such marriage due to lack of mobility, which is result of their poor economic status.

Table 10
Cause of Cross Cousin Marriage

Why do you practice such marriage?										
	Due to culture		*To save community existence/ identity*		*Lack of mobility*		*Non-recognition by other communities*		*Total*	
Sex Ratio	*Nos*	*%*	*Nos*	*%*	*Nos*	*%*	*Nos*	*%*	*Nos*	*%*
Male	6	3.8	73	46.5	7	4.5	71	45.2	157	52.3
Female	7	4.9	62	43.3	4	2.8	70	49.0	143	47.7
Total	13	4.3	135	45.0	11	3.7	141	47.0	300	100.0

Participant observation revealed that Dhankut is mainly concentrated in Dhankutty pura and their population is very small i.e. 2687. So they have no option as no girl or boy is available for marriage from outside Dhankutty pura.

Right to Health

Article 25 of the United Nations Declaration on Human Rights (UNDHR) asserts that every one should have a standard of living adequate for the health and well being of themselves and their families including among other things medical care. Other than the UNDHR there are several other declarations which have a bearing on the right to health. For instance, the Declaration of the Rights of the Child, proclaimed on 29 November 1959 states (in its Principle 4) that children shall enjoy the benefits of social security, and shall be entitled to grow in health. For this, the declaration stressed that special care should be given to the child and her mother, including adequate pre-natal and post-natal care. It further stated that the child shall have right to adequate nutrition, housing and medical facilities. The International Convention on Economic, Social and Cultural Rights (ICESCR),in its Article 12 recognizes everyone's right to the enjoyment of the highest attainable standard of physical and mental health.

Article 24 of the United Nations Convention on the Rights of the Child, 1989, ratified by the Government of India on 11th December 1992 provides that state shall recognise the right of the child to the enjoyment of highest attainable standard of health and to facilitate for the treatment of illness and rehabilitation of health. The state parties shall strive to ensure that no child is deprived of his/her right of access to such health care services. The Alma Ata Declaration 1978 to which India is a signatory, pledged "Health for all by 2000 AD". It declared health as a fundamental human right and defined it as a state of complete physical, mental and social well being (WHO-UNICEF 1978).

The main goal of a health system is to improve the health status of the population, which is measured by indicators such as mortality, morbidity, mental health, etc. Health acts as an indicator of the level of social, economic, cultural and environmental development of a society. So far as Dhankut are concerned the situation is not good, due to lack of education and poverty they are not aware of various health schemes which play an important role in monitoring good health.

Male and female Dhankut suffer from impotency and other reproductive problems due to cross cousin and parallel cousin marriages.Infertility is a major problem among Dhankut because of consanguineous marriages. In different studies definite effect of consanguinity on fertility has been noted (Mukherjee and Bhaskar, 1974)[14] and various other studies also reveal that mortality rate is high among offspring of consanguineous marriages (kumar et al. 1967; Murty and Jamil, 1972; Rao and Reddy, 1977 and Rao, 1978)[15]. Out of 715 families of Dhankut there are 120 issueless couples, which is the direct effect of consanguineous marriages. Dhankut are illiterate so they are unable to correlate morbidity and mortality with inbreeding but participant observation revealed high rate of mortality (Table 11) and morbidity (Table 12) among Dhankut.

Table 11
Rate of Mortality in the Offspring of Consanguineous Marriages

Age group of children	*Year* 2003 *Nos.*	%	2004 *Nos.*	%	2005 *Nos.*	%	*Total* *Nos.*	%
0-1 yrs	01	16.7	03	50.0	02	33.3	06	100.0
1-2 yrs	-	-	01	25.0	03	75.0	04	100.0
2-3 yrs	01	50.0	01	50.0	-	-	02	100.0
3-4 yrs	01	50.0	-	-	01	50.0	02	100.0
Total	03	21.4	05	35.7	06	42.9	14	100.0

Table 11 Shows that mortality rate is high among the offspring of Dhankut which is a small group of 2687 people in total, due to consanguineous marriage in 2003, 03 children died, in 2004, 05 and in 2005, 06 children died. Present table also reveals that in the age group of 0-1 yrs, 6 children died, in 1 to 2 yrs 4, in 2-3 yrs 2 and in 3-4 yrs of age group 2 children died. Thus we notice that during the last three years between 2003-05, 14 children died in Dhankuttypura of Baharaich.

Participant observation revealed that consanguineous marriages among Dhankut have generated recessive genes of albinism, epilepsy and feeblemindedness due to inbreeding.[16] Table 12 Shows that albinism is most frequent among marriage type of MBD among Dhankut Other health problems inflicting them is epilepsy and feeble mindedness. In the present research group 21 are having albinism, 2 are inflicted with epilepsy and 3 with feeble mindedness. Table also shows that rate of morbidity is higher in MBD type of marriages as compared to FSD type of marriages.

Table 12
Rate of Morbidity in the Offspring of Consanguineous Marriages

Nature of Morbidity	*Marriage type*	*Male*		*Female*		*Total*	
		Nos.	*%*	*Nos.*	*%*	*Nos.*	*%*
Albinism	MBD	08	38.1	13	61.9	21	100.0
Epilepsy	MBD	02	100.0	-	-	02	100.0
Feeble Mindedness	FSD	02	66.7	01	33.3	03	100.0
Total		12	46.2	14	53.8	26	100.0

MBD: Mother's brother daughter, FSD: Father's Sister Daughter.

Efforts Towards Equitable Society

"Implementation of the human rights" is a subject of great importance in any equitable society. In a developing society such as ours where around 50 per cent people are living below poverty live and around 70 per cent of the people are illiterate and large number of men and women are living a life of want and destitution, misery and suffering, this subject assumes much great importance. It is a huge task to ensure human rights to large sections of the society who are suffering from untold hardship and misery on account of massive deception and exploitation and who cannot live as ordinary human beings with basic human dignity.[17]

We all know that government is the saviour of right. In a welfare state it is the responsibility of the government to provide all facilities to its people for their upliftment. Generally human rights are guaranteed by the government, protected by the police and ensured by the court. Majority of Dhankut looks towards the government for the guarantee of human rights as is reflected in Table 13 12 (63.2%) respondents, 9 (64.3%) males and 3 (60%) females, say that human right, is guaranteed by the government as human right is concerned with community, 4 (21.1%) respondents, 3 (21.4%) males and 1 (20%) female say that human right is provided by court. 03 (15.7%) respondents, 2 (14.3%) males and 1 (20%) female are of the view that human right is ensured by police. Majority of respondents 12 (63.2%) know that human right can only be guaranteed by the government.

All human societies must co-ordinate and regulate the behaviour of their members by mechanisms of making and enforcing decisions. There are two ways in which societies organize and regulate themselves. One is called as political organization the patterned ways in which legitimate power or authority is used to co-ordinate and regulate the behaviour. The other is law consisting of the enforcement mechanisms of the decision made.

Table 13
Guarantee of Human Rights

	Who guarantees human right?							
	It is given by government		*By Court*		*By Police*		*Total*	
Sex Ratio	*Nos.*	*%*	*Nos.*	*%*	*Nos.*	*%*	*Nos.*	*%*
Male	09	64.3	03	21.4	02	14.3	14	73.7
Female	3	6	01	20.0	01	20.0	05	26.3
Total	12	63.2	04	21.1	03	15.7	19	100.0

So at every level an authority acts and solves the problems of people according to its capacity. In the tribal community, it is in the form of headship, which is equivalent to the government. It takes every decision in the welfare of the citizens. So political organization is mainly concerned with the concentration of power, which creates an environment of security.

Which type of political organization exists in an area, it depends upon the situation and tradition of that area. At the level of community, people want security of their lands and other immovable property from their own community men. They also want to solve their social and family disputes within the community. So they form a political organization in the form of Panchayat. It is a cultural form of court without any written literature. The elders of the community listen to the community problems and take decisions regarding social disputes.[18] Except in murder cases, which are judicial matter, almost everyone follows its decision.

In civil society hierarchy of courts is maintained to enforce the human rights, but in rural or simple society, people are not very much interested in a judicial system due to its complexity. They feel, it is a time taking and expensive process. But due to the effect of acculturation, knowledge about human rights and social justice, they are also attracted towards the judicial system for the solution of their dispute. In this regard their traditional political organization are loosing its identity. The people, who have faith in their traditional panchayat, go to the panchayat but when they see that the other party of the dispute is going to the judicial court for justice then ultimately they also go to the court. But the decisions of court are mainly based on evidence. The courts are not aware about their social and cultural environment. Since their decision is only based on rules, they are not beneficial for a traditional community.[19]

Panchayat As Guarantor of Human Rights

Dhankut, have evolved Panchayat system for the vindication of their rights and still believe in their traditional panchayat. Even though the civil court is at 500 yards away from their living place (Dhankutty Pura), they do not prefer going to the court. Due to poor economic condition, they go to the panchayat for the solution of their problems except in murder and other criminal matters, which are judicial matters. In the panchayat, they bring matrimonial and other social disputes. They have no land disputes due to the absence of agricultural land.

Panchayat is the very axis of Dhankut, around which revolves the lives of Dhankut. Panchayat is also a supporting factor of their lives, hence they cannot leave it. Even process of acculturation and urbanization could not affect its existence. What Dhankut think about the existence of Panchayat and why they do not prefer going to court is reflected in Table 14.

Table shows that 160 (53.3%) respondents, 70 (44.6%) males and 90 (62.9%) females say that it is an inexpensive system for solving disputes. 131 (43.6%) respondents, 82 (52.3%) males and 49 (34.3%) females think that it is easy to approach panchayat for dispute resolution as it is free from the technicalities and formalities of the court. 9 (3.1%)respondents, 5 (3.1%) males and 4 (2.8%) females say that it is unavoidable for the community. Participant observation revealed that Panchayat system still holds control in traditional communities. Majority of Dhankut prefer Panchayat system for solving disputes as they can not afford the expenses of court.

Table 14
Opinion about Panchayat

	What do you think about Panchayat							
	Easy access for dispute resolution		*Inexpensive way of solving dispute*		*Unavoidable for the community*		*Total*	
Sex Ratio	*Nos.*	*%*	*Nos.*	*%*	*Nos.*	*%*	*Nos.*	*%*
Male	82	52.3	70	44.6	05	3.1	157	52.3
Female	49	34.3	90	62.9	04	2.8	143	47.7
Total	131	43.6	160	53.3	09	3.1	300	100.0

A smooth life is a prime requirement of everyone and an individual make effort for it but everything is not within his/ her reach. In a democratic and welfare State, government is the guarantor of rights. Dhankut are living in scarcity and they want many rights for their smooth survival from the Government. Some of the rights aspired by them for an equitable society are depicted in Table 15.

Table 15
Required Rights in Life

	Which rights are necessary in your life?									
	Rights to basic facilities		*Recognition of their caste*		*Right to live with dignity/ prestige*		*Right to reservation*		*Total*	
Sex Ratio	*Nos.*	*%*	*Nos.*	*%*	*Nos.*	*%*	*Nos.*	*%*	*Nos.*	*%*
Male	37	23.6	25	15.9	63	40.1	32	20.4	157	52.3
Female	29	20.3	17	11.9	72	50.3	25	17.5	143	47.7
Total	66	22.0	42	14.0	135	45.0	57	19.0	30	100.0

Table shows that 135 (45%) respondents, 63 (40.1%) males and 72 (50.3%) females say that they want right to live with dignity and prestige. 37 (23.6%) males and 29 (20.3%) female or overall 66 (22%) respondents say that they want basic facilities in life i.e. right to food, water, shelter, electricity etc. 42 (14%) respondents, 25 (15.9%) males and 17 (11.9%) females say that they want their caste to be recognized by the Government. Since their caste is not recognized they are looked down upon by the members of adjacent communities and can not enjoy the right to dignity and prestige. 57 (19%) respondents, 32 (20.4%) males and 25 (17.5%) females demanded right to reservation in government jobs for their growth and development.

Conclusion

It is astonishing to note that even after the 60 years of independence there is a group which does not know as to which caste it belongs to. The monthly income of Dhankut is very meager, they live in congested houses ,in unhealthy environment, they have no water and electricity supply in their houses. Their women have to go, to open fields to answer the call of nature which is quite unhealthy and also put their safety at stake.

Dhankut is an isolated group; it has no caste identity of its own. They are not recognised by the adjacent communities of the district. Due to their poor economic position and lack of education they are looked down upon by the members of other communities.. Due to living at single place, poor economy and non recognition by other communities, they are practicing cross cousin and parallel cousin marriage in order to save their lineage. They do not know the genetic effect of inbreeding - a consequence of consanguineous marriage which has led to low infertility, high mortality and to a high rate of albinism in their group. Panchayat plays an important role in their lives. Due to financial crisis they don't go to the court for the solution of their disputes which is only 500 yards away from their living place. Everyone is bound to obey the order of the panchayat. Though Dhankut are aware of their rights and want to access them like the members of other communities, but poverty, non recognition of their caste and living at single place make an environment for human right violation and deprive them of all facilities which are available around them.

Though Dhankut do not know the exact meaning of equitable society, but they know that it is something guaranteed by the government. They want all basic facilities such as food, water, shelter, electricity, education besides recognition of their caste and reservation in jobs by the government. They want to lead a dignified life with right to equality of status with other communities.

Lastly, it is suggested that Dhankut should immediately be categorized either as Scheduled Caste, Scheduled Tribe or Other Backward Class, so as to provide them with socio-cultural identity of their own, which is very essential for the maintenance of equitable society and for the enjoyment of basic facilities of life. It is further suggested that with regard to Dhankut tenets of equitable society should be developed as the way of life and should not be limited to mere slogans. They should be made aware of human rights, its significance, availability and enforcement. The government must chalk out some specific policies and programmes to make Dhankut an equitable society and to enable them to live in dignity and respect so as to improve their moral and social values.

Notes and References

1. Hitopdesh 1.2.
2. Articles 39 (b) & (c) of Indian Constitution
3. Theodore Meron (1984) "Teaching Human Rights : An Overview" in Human Rights in International Law: Legal and Policy Issues, 1-24 at 2.
4. United Nations Publication on the Human Rights to Adequate Housing, Fact sheet, No. 21, p. 3.
5. *Ibid* at, pp. 3-4.
6. World Health Organisation, Decade Assessment Report.
7. AIR 1987 SC 2117.
8. AIR 1988 cal 136.
9. (1964) 2 SCR 703 at 710.
10. Jaswal P.S. and Jaswal N. "Right to Education and Human Rights" in Human Rights in India, Problems and Perspectives (ed) B.P. Singh Sehgal. (2001) p. 124-128.
11. NR Madhava Menon,"Legal Aid and Justice for the Poor" published in Law and Poverty-Critical Essays (ed) Upendra Baxi(1988), p.342
12. Constitutional Assembly Debates, Vol. III, p. 494

13. Peter Townshed quoted in "Poverty and Planning in India" (ed) Gangadhar Rakshit (1977) p.1

14. Mukherjee D.P. and Bhaskar (1974), "Studies on Inbreeding and its Effects on Some Endogamous Population of Chittor District, Andhra Pradesh.

15. Kumar S., Pai R.A. and Swaminathan N.S. (1967) Consanguineous Marriages and the Genetic Load Due to Lethal Genes in Kerala; Murty J.S. and Jamil T. (1972) Inbreeding Load in the New Born at Hyderabad; P.ao, A.P. and Reddy V. Rami (1977) Consanguineous Marriages and their Effects on Fertility and Off spring Mortality in a Rural Yadav Population of South Eastern Andhra Pradesh; Rao P.S.S. (1978) Inbreeding in Tamil Nadu and its Effects on Human Reproduction in Medical Genetics in India, Vol. 2 (Eds) I.C. Verma, Auroma Enterprises, Pondicherry.

16. Chantia, Alok (2001), Socio-cultural Profile of Dhankutta-An Endogamons Group of Bahraich District of U.P.,Unpublished Thesis.

17. Bhagwati,P.N., "Human Rights and Democratisation of Remedies", *Indian Bar Review,* Vol. 10(4) (1983), p. 584.

18. Anirudha Misra (1979) Constraints on Indian Political Culture: Some Reflections, pp. 73-82, *Indian Anthropologist,* Vol. 9 New Delhi.

19. Deen Vera Micheles, (1959), New Pattern of Democracy in India, p. 2, Cambridge, Harvard University Press.

16

Human Rights and Women: An Ignorance

NIRMALA KAUSHIK & MANJU

Introduction

Human rights are what each human being is entitled to allow her/his freedom to live a dignified and secured life of choice. We can understand the importance of human rights only when we rare confronted with violation of our own rights. Human rights include rights related to safety of the person, the right to be free from coercion by other individuals, groups or governments, the right to social benefits, rest and leisure, and the right to be a good basic education.

Women rights are human rights. In many countries, men and women are equal and that they enjoy the same right and freedom. Equality is important for effective enforcement of human rights. All the citizens should be treated as equals that all should get equal protection of law without any discrimination of caste and creed and all should get equal opportunity. Women throughout the world live in constant fear and conditions of deprivation very often for their simple reason that they are women. Numerous international and regional instruments have drawn attention to gender related dimensions of human rights issues, the most important being the UN Convention on the

Elimination of All Forms of Discrimination against women (CEDAW), adopted in 1979. In 1993, 45 years after the Universal Declaration of Human Rights was adopted, and 8 years after CEDAW entered into force, the UN world conference on human rights in Vienna confirmed that women's status as human beings entitled to rights should have never been in doubt. And yet this was a step forward in recognizing the rightful claims of one half of humanity, in identifying neglect of women's right as a human rights violation and in drawing attention to the relationship between gender and human rights violations.

In 1994, the International Conference on population and Development in Cairo (ICPD) articulated and affirmed the relationship between advancement and fulfillment of rights and gender equality. It also clarified the concepts of women's empowerment, gender equality and reproductive health and rights. The programme of Action of ICPD asserted that the empowerment and autonomy of women and the improvement of their political, social, economic and health status was a highly important end in itself as well as essential for the achievement of sustainable development.

Women Right

The independent India witnessed many forces of social change particularly towards women. Realizing the suffering and hardships of women, the Government of India passed many legislations to remove the injustice done to women. These legislations paved the way for the upliftment and progress of women.

Social Legislation for Women

1. The Hindu marriage Act of 1955 stipulate the marriageable ages as 18, but now amended to 21 for women.
2. The Hindu succession Act of 1956 ensures the right to inherit their parental property.
3. The Dowery Prohition Act of 1961 gives severe punishment with imprisonment for the dowery seekers.
4. The Hindu widow remarriage Act of 1956 legalised the widow remarriage.

5. The Hindu marriage Act of 1967 gave legal sanction to the self respect marriages.
6. The Hindu succession Act of 1989 provide right to have equal share in the inheritance property.
7. The Indecent Representation Act of 1999 prohibits the indecent representation of women in magazine, newspapers, posters, handbills etc.

In spite of all these rights women are facing many problems day by day like sexual harassments, Incest, rape and domestic violence etc.

Women and Violence

Violence against women takes a dismaying variety of forms, from domestic abuse and rape to child marriages and female circumcision. Violence affects the lives of many women worldwide, in all socioeconomic and educational classes. It cuts across cultural and religious barriers, impending the rights of women to participate fully in society. Violence against women is a universal problem that must be universally condemned. But the problem continues to grow (United Nations Secretary General, Boutros Boutros - Ghali, 1995). Violence against women constitutes a violation of basic human rights and is an obstacle to the achievement of the objectives of equality, development and peace (Beijing Conference, Government, 1995).

Sexual Harassment

Sexual harassment means that someone is bothering you by saying or doing unwanted or unwelcome things of a sexual or gender related nature like touching you inappropriately, making offensive jokes, making sexual requests and display sexually offensive pictures etc. It does not have to be sexual in nature. It can also mean that someone is bothering you simply because you are a man or women. Making stereotypes about one gender or the other can be a form of sexual harassment. It is a pattern of behaviour that happens frequently over a period of time.

Sexual Harassment in Employment and Housing

Someone says or does something to you of a sexual nature that you do not welcome. This includes behaviour that a person knows or ought to know you do not welcome.

When boss, landlord, or other authority figure uses their position of power to sexually harass you. By being in a vulnerable situation, it is difficult for you to speak out about the situation.

Sexual Solicitation

A person suggests that if you become sexually involved with him or her, he or she will give you a better grade or some other type of incentive.

Sexual Harassment and Reprisal

A person who has authority or power denies you something important, punishes or threatens you for refusing a sexual request, or for complaining about inappropriate sexual behaviour or comments.

Sexual Harassment and a Poisoned Environment

Sexual harassment can have a bad effect on, or poison, the places where you live, work or receive services. Evan if the harassment is not directed at you, it can still poison the environment for you or others.

Incest, Rape and Domestic Violence

Some females fall prey to violence before they are born, when expectant parents about their unborn daughters, hoping for sons instead. In other societies, girls are subjected to such traditional practices as circumcision, which leave them maimed and traumatized. Women are victim of incest, rape and domestic violence that often lead to trauma, physical handicap or death. Rape is still being used as a weapon of war, a strategy used to subjugate and terrify entire communities. Soldiers deliberately impregnate women of different ethnic groups and abandon them when it is too late to get an abortion. More women today were suffering directly from the effects of war and conflict than ever before in history (Secretary General Boutros- Ghali).

Coomaraswamy (1994) focused on three areas of concern where women are particularly vulnerable in family (domestic violence, traditional practices, infanticide) in the community (including rape, sexual assault, commercialized violence such as trafficking in women, labour exploitation, female migrant workers etc.) and by the state (including violence against women in detention as well as violence against women in situation of armed conflict and against refugee women).

Kinds of Violence Against Women

Domestic violence: Violence against women in the family occurs in developed and developing countries alike. In United States, a woman is beaten every 18 minutes. Indeed, domestic violence is the leading cause of injury among women of reproductive age in the United States. The highly publicized trial of O.J. Simpson, the retired United State football player acquitted of the murder of his former wife and a male friend of her, helped focus international media attention on the issue of domestic violence and spousal abuse. According to Special Rapporteur's report many Government now recognize the importance of protecting victim of domestic abuse and taking action to punish perpetrators. This report highlights the importance of adopting legislation that provides for prosecution of the offender. It also stresses the importance of specialized training for law enforcement authorities as well as medical and legal professionals, and of the establishment of community support services for victims, including access to information and shelters.

Traditional Practices

In many countries, women fall victim to traditional practices that violate their human rights. The persistence of the problems has much to do with the fact that most of these physically and psychologically harmful customs are deeply rooted in the tradition and culture of society.

Female Genital Mutation

Every year an estimated 2 million young girls undergo genital mutilation and suffer from its adverse health effects. In France, a Malian was convicted in a criminal court after his first baby died of a female circumcision related infection. The procedure had been performed on the infant at home. A Nigerian woman was granted refugee status since she felt that she might be persecuted in her home country because of her refusal to inflict genital mutilation on her baby daughter.

Son Preference

Son preference affects women in many countries. Its consequences can be anything from foetal or female infanticide to neglect of the girl child over her brother in terms of such essential needs as nutrition, basic health care and education. In China and India, some women choose to terminate their pregnancies when expecting daughters but carry their pregnancies to term when expecting sons. In India, genetic testing for sex selection has become a booming business, especially in the country's northern region. A study of amniocentesis procedures conducted in a large Bombay hospital found that 95.5 per cent of foetus identified as female were aborted compared with a far smaller percentage of male fetuses.

Dowery Related Violence and Early Marriage

In some countries, weddings are preceded by the payment of an agreed upon dowery by the bride's family. Failure to pay dowery can lead to violence. Early marriage, especially without the consent of the girl, is another form of human rights violation. Early marriage followed by multiple pregnancies can affect the health of women for life.

Violence in the Community

Rape: Rape can occur anywhere, even in the family, where it can take the form of marital rape or incest. It occurs in the community, where a woman can fall prey to any abuser. It also occurs in situations of armed conflict and in refugee camps. In the United States, national statistics indicate that a woman is raped every six minutes. In 1995, the case of a Brazillian jogger raped and murdered in New York City's Central Park drew international attention once again to the problem. The incident occurred only a few years after an earlier sensational jogger assault case in which the victim-an American assaulted in the same general area of the park barely survived after her assailants left her for dead.

Sexual Assault within Marriage

In many countries sexual assault by a husband on his wife is not considered to be a crime, a wife is expected to submit. It is thus very difficult in practice for a woman to prove that sexual assault has occurred unless she can demonstrate serious injury. Sexual assault cases send the wrong message to perpetrators and to the public at large, that female sexual victimization is unimportant.

Prostitution and Trafficking

Many women are forced into prostitution either by their parents, husbands or boyfriends – or as a result of the difficult economic and social conditions in which they find themselves. They are also lured into prostitution, sometimes by mail order bride agencies that promise to find them a husband or a job in a foreign country. Most women initially victimized by sexual traffickers have little inkling of what awaits them. Many women and girl children are trafficked across borders, often with the complicity of border guards. The extent of trafficking in women and girl children has reached alarming proportions, especially in Asian countries.

Pornography

Pornography represents a form of violence against women that glamorizes the degradation and maltreatment of women and asserts their subordinate function as mere receptacles for male lust.

Conclusion

It is concluded on the above discussion that in spite of many rights for women, women are facing so many psychological as well as physical problems. Women are not feeling secure at work place and home also. In society they are feeling many gender inequalities. Women are not utilizing their rights properly. After a strict discipline in India, many mishappnings are going on day by day. Government should use some other strategies to overcome the problems of women.

References

Desai, N. & Thakkar, U. (2001), *Women in Indian Society*, National Book Trust India.

Ghali, B. & Boutros (1995), *An Agenda for Peace*, United Nations Publication.

http://www.ohrc.on.ca/en/issues/sexual_harassment.

http://www.un.org/rights/dpi1772e.htm

Narira Adhikar, published by Orissa Sahitya Academy.

Samantaray, J. (2005), Human Rights and Women: An Introspection, *Orissa Review.*

Samantaray, J., *Narira Sthiti O' Pragati*, Image Publications, Bhubanneswar.

United Nations Department of Public Information (1996), Human Rights, *Women and Violence*, United Nations Department of Public Information

Vora, N.N. *A Look on India in 20th century*, (NBT).

Index

A

Acts of Atrocities, 2

Burning of Houses, 2

Massacre, 2

Rape, 2

Adivasi (s), 130

Human Rights, 98

Lands, 105

Tribal Rights, 97

Adivasi/Tribal Culture, 96

Administration, Civil, 65

Adopted Human Rights Act, 137

Adoption Agencies in Andhra Pradesh, 112

Adult Franchise, 10

Agrarian Labour Women, 229

Agricultural

Castes, 2

Operations, 2

Aids and Relief Measurements, 53

AIDS, 113

All India

Depressed Classes Federation, 6

Haryana Sangh, 6

Alleviation of Women's Poverty, 167

Alma Alta Declaration, 298

Ambedkar, Dr, Baba Saheb Bhimrao, 6, 98

American

Declaration of Independence, 54

Revolution, 145

Revolutionaries, 220

Amnesty International, 88

Ancient Indian Tribes, 97

Andaman and Nicobar, 185

Andhra Pradesh

And Orissa, 105

High Court, 190

Angul-Talcher Area, 184

Anju, Dalit Teenager Girl, 23

Anti-

Atrocities Law, 44

Discrimination Laws, 11

Rape Movement, 154

Slavery International, 88

Terrorists Acts, 214, 215

Armed Force (Special Power) Act, 1958, (AFSPA), 258

Armed Forces, 60

Arora, Gujjar, – Gond Khond, 131

Arya Samaj, 5

Asia, Africa, and Latin America, 55

Asian Countries, 52, 53, 228

Asia-Pacific Region Labor, 150

Assam, 60

Company London, 61

Labor Enquiry Committee Report, 63

Tea Company, 61

Tea Plantation, 61

University, 70, 74

Association of Schools of Social Work, 272

Atrocities Act, 30, 31

Awareness of Human Rights, 287

B

Babylonian Code of Hammurabi, 164

Backward Class, 59

Bahujan Samaj Party (BSP), 15

Bamanghaty Disturbances, 117

Bangladesh, 119, 126

Bhutan, Nepal, Myanmar, 256

Barak Valley of Assam, 68, 70, 76 see under Valley also

Basic

Principles—of Human Rights, 222

Rights and Freedoms, 85

Behavioural Change Communication, (BCC), 278

Beijing Platform of Action, 167

Benami Transfers, 105

Bengal

Provincial Committee, 65

Tea Association, 61

Bengali

Population, 68

Samaj, 67, 68

Bhagawat Gita, 51

Bharat

Jan Andolan, 91

Nirman, 46

Bhils In. Bhilanchal, 97, 98

Bhils, Gonds, Mundas, Santhals and Nahals, 94, 97

Bhuria Committee Recommendations, 118

Bible and Quran, 164

Bill of Rights, 54

Bokaro Thermal Power and Steel Plants, 185

Bonded

Child Labour in Carpet Industry, 109

Labour (erers), 115, 122, 137, 185

Labour Act, 115, 121

Labour from Rajasthan, 115, 122

Slavery, 56

Survey of India, 93

Brahmin Community, 19

Brahmo Samaj, 5

Missionary, 63

Brahmputra River, 63

British

Magna Carta, 54

Planters, 68

Policy, 5

BSF, 258

Buddhism, 96

Buddhist Philosophy, 51

Buotros Buotros Ghali, UN Secy Gen, 309, 311

C

Case Studies, 116

Tribal of Mayurbhanj District Orissa, 116

Tribals in Uttar Pradesh, 122

Tribals of

Jharkhand and Madhya Pradesh, 126

Meghalaya, 118-119

Tamil Nadu, 133

Uttarakhand, 120

Caste

And Communal Violence, 2

And Gender Based Discrimination, 9

Atrocities, 3, 4

Based Discrimination, 10

Disabilities, 4

Discrimination in Labour/ Consumer Markets, 34

Endogamy, 67

Groups, 67

Chanda, 67

Majhi, 67

Malakar, 67

Sukalbaidya, 67

Hindu Landlord, 17

Oppressed, 6

Relationship in Hindu Society, 2

Society, 2

Structure, 2, 3

System, 3, 5, 6, 67, 284

Violence, 2

Violence and Untouchability in India, 29

Categories of Labourers, 62

Cha Shramik Union, 71

Chaneli—Jair Budhi, 129

Charter of UN, 85

Chhatisgarh, 130

Child

Abuse, 111

Labor, 109, 115, 137, 156, 148, 150, 152, 153

Labourers, 58
Marriage, 200
Pornography, 109
Prostitution, 109
Sexual Abuse, 111
Children Engaged in Match, Glass, Silk, Beedi – Handloom Industry, 151-152
China, 234
Singapore, Malaysia, 52
Chotanagpur, 62
Tribal Belt, 184
Christian Community, 135
Civil
Administration, 65
And Political Rights, 144, 212, 213, 244
Marriage, 109
Rights Protection, 35
Political, Economic and Cultural Rights, 144
Political, Social, Economic and Cultural Rights, 52
Civilization,
Agriculture, 2
India, 2
Class Structure, 66, 68
Coalmines in Talcher (Orissa), 184
Colonial
Forestry, 98
Period, 66
Policy, 98
Revenue Administration Sardars –, 117
Commercial
Farmers/Industries, 179
Sex Workers, 114
Commission
For Social Development, 236
Scheduled Caste/Tribes, Report, 36
Committee on Plan Projects, 105
Community Development Program, 202
Concept of Empowerment, Defined, 247
Constitutional Provisions of Human Rights, 159
Contractor System, 98
Convention for Elimination of DAW, 103, 253, 263, 308
Counseling Centres, 107
Counter Terrorism Committee, 215
Cow Slaughter, 18
Crimes
Against Women, 107
Against Scheduled Castes/Tribes, 13
Against Women, 169
Criminal
Courts, 64
Justice Administration, 35

Politicians, 57

Tribes, 91

Tribes Act (CTA), 1871, 96

Tribes Act (CTA), 1911, 92

Tribes Act (CTA), 1952, 93

Cross Border Terrorism, 56

CRPF, 258

Cultural

Identity, 67

Imperialism, 52

Custodial Deaths, 56, 164

Customs and Traditions, 59

D

Dalit

Agricultural Labourers, 33

Children, 31

Communities, 35, 37

Converts, 33

Defined, 7

Groups, 11, 20

Homes, 32

Human Rights Violence, 34

Organization, 46

Priests, 33

Rights, 12

Sikhs, 32

Various Names, 7

Violence and Crime Against, 13

Workers, 33

Dalits, 17, 18, 21, 29-30, 59, 89

In India, 35

Socio-Economic and Political Discrimination by Caste Hindus, 16

Statutory and Legal Safeguards, 8

Damodar Valley Project, 185

Dargakone Tea Garden, 67, 70, 72

Declaration on Elimination of Violation against Women, 245

De-Criminalization, 113

Degradation of

Environment, 91

Human Rights, 54, 221

De-notified Tribes, 91

Denudation of Forests, 104

Devadasi System, 42

Developing Societies, 50-57

Development Projects, 176, 178

Directive Principles, 160-163

Disadvantaged Sections, 10

Discrimination

Against Women, 33, 168

In Labor Market, 33

And Inequality, 1

District

Auraiya, 23

Bhandara, 28, 29

Bhopal (MP), 198

Champaran, 123

Chhatarpur (MP), 22

Darrang, Kamrup, Nowgond, 61

Dibrugarh and Sibsagar, 60, 61

Dindigul (Tamil Nadu), 17

Gumla and Palameu (Bihar) 184

Jhajjhar (Haryana), 18

Nilgiri, 134

Rohtak, 19

Tiruchi, 17

Domestic Violence Bill, 108

Dowry, 108, 200, 312

Deaths, 56, 169, 251

Related Crimes, 251

Related Violence, 312

System, 1342

Draft Declaration of Old Age Rights, 235

E

Earthquake Reconstruction Program in Gujarat, 32

East India Company, 60, 61

Economic

And Social Council, 236

Development, 176

Empowerment, 165, 250

Growth, 196

Rights, 144

Social and Cultural Rights, 86

Social and Political Rights, 59

Economy, 56, 62, 125

Education

A Fundamental Right to Child, 110

And Awareness, 80

And Economic Development, 10

And Training Program, 236

Educational Committee, 206

Educationally Backward Sections, 201

Electoral Rolls, 100

Elimination of Discrimination, 10

Emigrants, 62

Employment Generation Scheme, 207

Empowerment of Women, 198, 203, 259

Encroachment, 105

Enforcement of Human Rights, 261

Environmental Economic Problems, 192

Ethical Principles of Social Work, 273

Ethnic Communities, 100

Europe Convention on Human Rights, 215

European

Missionaries, 119

Planters, 65

Tea Gardens, 65

Ex-Criminal Tribes, 91

Extremism, 229

F

Famines and Food Security, 62

Female

Education and Employment Status, 153

Foeticide, 169

Genital Mutilation, 312

Infanticide, 169

Literacy Rate, 76

Feudal State, 33

Foeticide, 111, 113

Food Insecurity, 178

Forced Displacement and Resettlement, 176-196

Human Rights Perspective, 176-196

Forced Labour, 56

Forest

Law, 123

Resources, 91

Forms of Atrocities among Bhoksas, 122

Freedom Movement, 6

French

Declaration of Rights of Man, 54

Revolution, 145, 212, 220

Fundamental

Human Rights, 212, 257

Rights, 89, 158-163, 178

Rights and Education, 56

Rights and Human Rights, 159

Rights to Property, 190

G

Gandhi, Mahatma (Gandhiji), 6, 201

Gang Rape, 47

Gangetic Belt of India, 57

Gaur Brahmin Shishan Sanstha, A Brahmin Organization, 19

Gender

Based Discrimination, 200

Discrimination, 102

Equality, 158-175

Constitutional Provisions in Indian Constitution, 158-175

Inequality, 102

General Assembly of United Nations, 50

Generation Rights, 145

First Generation, 145

Second Generation, 145

Third Generation, 145

Genocide, 88

German World War I Troops, 254

Ghotul System, 133

Girl Child, 102, 111, 251

Global Agency, 231-242

Globalization, 177

Glorious Revolution, 145

Goala, Koiri Bher, Pasi, 67

Gond

In Gondwana, 97, 98

Inhabited States, 130

MP—Orissa, 130

Kingdom, 130

Language, 130

Society, 132

Tribal Community, 132, 133

Gondwanaland, 130

Gorkha

Regiment, 66

Soldiers, 66

Gram

Panchayat, 197, 204, 206, 208

Mendori, 198, 205

Sabha, 206

Great Religious Revolutions, (GRR), 50

Buddhism, 50

Christianity, 50

Hinduism, 50

Islam, 50

Gurkha Rifles from Narayanganj (Bangladesh), 65

Gurugranth Sahib of Sikhism, 51

H

Habitual Offenders Act, 92

Hard Core Terrorists, 53

Haryana Vikar Party, 20

Head Hunting, 137

Health and Communication, 74

Heavy Electricals Ranchi, 185

Hindi Speaking Bill, 67

Hindu

Caste System, 5

Community, 18

Gods, 120

Law, 5

Population, 3

Social Order, 2, 6

Society, 5

Vedas, 164

Hinduism, 67, 68

Degradation of-, 68

HIV/AIDS, 276

Holocaust or Genocide, 50

Hong Kong, 53

Human Rights, 50-57, 74, 75, 85-99, 210-219

Act, 89, 137

Act, 1913, 146

And Development, 58-78

And Fundamental Freedoms, 267

And Role of UNO, 54

And Social Work Practices, 267-283

And UN, 268

And Women, 168, 307-314

Awareness, 80-84

Categories, 268-272
Commission, 181, 195, 225
Functions and Powers, 225-228
Committee of UN, 59, 146
Declaration, 142-157
Education, 166, 170-172
Education and Women, 171
Education Program, 57, 229
For Women, 259
In India, 88
Instruments, 58
Laws, 88
Movement, 55, 225
Phases, 144
Principles, 86
Salient Features, 288
Social, Economic and Political, 199
Violations, 15, 46, 58, 88, 92, 102, 107, 118, 243-265, 254, 255, 257, 304, 312
Against Women, 254
Against Dalits, 15
And Women Empowerment, 243-265
Forms, 16
Human Rights, 243-265
Workers, 157
Human Sacrifices, 129
Hunting and Food Gathering, 125

I

India's Tea Industry, 60
Indian
Army, 185
Council of Indigenous and Tribal People, 91
Entrepreneurs, 66
Forest Act, 91
Judiciary, 57, 229
Judiciary And Human Rights, 163
Patriarchal System, 102
Penal Code, 17, 30, 37, 44, 93, 227, 252
Society, 1, 7, 11, 30, 59, 201
Tribal Communities, Violation of Human Rights, 85-99
Tribals, 109
Tribes, 103
Indira Kushwa, Dalit Village Sarpanch, 22
Industrial
And Mining Complexes, 104
Development, 191
Industrialization, 98, 184, 192
Infanticide, 111
Information, Education and Communication (IEC), 278
INLD, 20
International
Bill of Human Rights, 51

Bill of Rights on Women, 103

Conference on Population and Development in Cairo, (ICPD), 308

Congress of Human Rights, 170

Convention for Civil and Political Rights, 51, 244

Convention on Civil, Cultural and Political Rights, 86

Convention on Economic, Social and Cultural Rights, 244, 298

Convention on Economic, Social and Political Rights, 86

Convention on Urbanization, 191

Customary Laws, 87

Federation of Human Rights, 88

Federation of Social Workers, (IFSW), 272

Human Rights, 167

Human Rights Covenants, 12

Humanitarian Law, 88

Labor Organization (ILO), 101, 150, 151

Convention on Elimination of the Worst Forms of Child Labour, 109, 110

Protection of Human Rights, 54

Terrorists Group, 215

Irrigation Projects, 104

J

Jagir Singh, Dalit Agricultural Laborer, 21

Jaintia, 256

Janpad Panchayat, 204

Of Phende, 198

Janta Party, 203

Japan, 53, 233

Japanese Troops Rapid—, 254

Jayant Patel Committee, 188

Jharkhand Movement, 91

Jharkhand—Orissa, 126

Jhoom Cultivation, 119

Juangs, 116

Judicial System, 55, 118, 225, 251

In India, 57, 229

K

Kandhamal (Orissa), 107

Terrorists, 107

Kanthas, 116

Karan Singh, 19, 20

Elected Dalit Sarpanch, 19

Mysterious Disappearance, 19

Karimganj, 65

Kartik Oraon, 127

Khairlangi Massare, 28, 39

Khanwar Tribe of Madhya Pradesh, 98

Khasi

And Jaintia Hills, 119

People, 119

Tribes, 119

Kidnapping and Abduction, 14

Kol Insurrenction, 117

Korean Women, 255

Kuran Sharif of Islam, 51

Kurukh Literary Society, 127

L

Labour Market, 239

Labourers

Recruiting Districts, 61, 62

Recruitment Areas, 61

Land

Acquisition Act, 91

Acquisition, 193

Alienation, 117, 138

Alienation Forms, 105

Alienation in Tribal Areas, 105

For Land Based Compensation Policies, 182

Grabbing, 137

Records Manipulation, 105

Reforms, 92

Rights, 115

Latin America, 150, 166

Law Enforcement, 15

Agency, 59

Leasing and Mortgaging of Lands, 105

Legal

Autonomy, 101

Safeguards, 34, 35

Legal/Regulatory Measures, 8

Legislative Measures, (LM), 11, 34, 35

Bonded Labor (Abolition) Act, 1976, 11

Employment of Manuel Scavengers and Construction of Dry Latrines Act, 1913, 11

Land Reforms Act, 11

Protection of Civil Rights Act (PCR), 1955, 11, 13, 14

SC/ST (Prevention of Atrocities) Act, 1989, 11, 13, 14

Linguistic Identity, 67

Literacy, 111

Rate, 76

Local Self Government, 10, 200, 201

M

Madhya Pradesh, 229

Orissa, Jharkhand, 57

Madras and Bombay Legislatures, 6

Magna Carta, 145, 220, 221, 244

Mahanadi Coalfield Ltd., 184

Maharashtra, 109

Manipur, 257

And Nagaland, 256

Women, 257

Maoist Terror Group, 107

Marginalization, 178

Marital Rape, 312

Mass

- Conversion of Mahars to Buddhism, 32
- Media, 59
- Maternity Benefits Act, 112
- Matrilineal and Matrilocal Society, 119
- Mega Projects and Industries, 56
- Meghalaya, 119, 256
- Mehta Committee, 202
- Mehta, Balwant Rai, 202
- Migration, 234
- Militant Mercenaries, 53
- Militants, 257
- Militants and Insurgents, 60
- Ministry of Rural Development, 199
- Minority
  - Commissions, 89
  - Community, 18
- Minto-Morley Reforms, 201
- Modernization, 2
  - And Urbanization, 137
- Mohini, A Kumhar Women, 21
- Monetary Economy, 186
- Moneylenders Feudal Lords, 104
- Mon-Khmer, 119
- MP (Madhya Pradesh)
  - Families, 186, 187
  - Panchayati Raj Avam Gram Swaraj Adhiniyam, 204
- Multinational Corporations, 177
- Muria Gonds, 133
- Muslim Rule in India, 5

N

- Nainital (Now Udhampurnagar), 120, 123
- Narmada
  - Control Authority (NCA), 186
  - Tribunal Award, 189
  - Water Dispute Tribunal, 187
- National
  - Children Rights Commission, 147
  - Commission for Dalit Human Rights, 39, 41
  - Commission for Minorities, 147
  - Commission for Safai Karamcharis (NCSK), 11, 43
  - Commission for Scheduled Caste, 43
  - Commission for Scheduled Castes and Scheduled Tribes, 10, 18, 147
  - Commission for SC/ST (NCSCST), 38, 39
  - Commission for Scheduled Tribes, 43
  - Commission for Women, 147, 155, 169, 259
  - Commission on Backward Areas Development (1980), 104
  - Development Planning, 89
  - Forest Policy, 98

Human Rights Commission (NHRC), 11, 29, 45, 46, 57, 89, 115, 122, 134, 164, 229, 259, 262

Human Rights Commission for Scheduled Castes, 43

Rehabilitation Policy, 195

Natural

Calamities, 62

Justice, 80

Naxalbari Movement, 91

Naxalism, 56, 229

Naxalite Movement, 98

Nazi Germany, 50, 221, 255

Nepal Population, 123

Nepotism, 57

Nerahat Firing Range, 184-185

Nilgiris Mountains, 136

Nomadic Tribes, 92, 93

Non-Governmental Organizations (NGOs, 32, 39, 47, 59, 60, 76, 88, 99, 192, 235, 246, 257, 262

North East India, 256

Assam—Sikkim, 256

North Eastern

Himalayas, 93

Region of India, 60, 61

Notorious

Industries, 152

Rape Cases, (NRC), 154

Bhumika-Assam Rape Case, 154

Gumta Behn Case, 154

Mathura Case, 154

Maya Tyagi Rape Case, 154

Piperia Rape Case, 154

O

Old Age Dependency Ratio, 233

Operation Rhino, 258

Oraon

And Gonds, 133

Gods and Goddesses, 129

Gotras, 127, 128

Language, 127

Society, 128, 129

Tribal Communities, 129

Tribes, 128, 129

Orissa

And Jharkhand, 229

Law Reforms Act, 117

Scheduled Areas Transfer of Immovable Property Regulation, 1956, 117

Other Backward Castes (OBCs), 2, 15, 45, 205

Other Backward Communities, 34

P

Panchayat,

Bagan, 70, 71

Caste, 70

Goan, 70, 72, 77

Guarantor of Human Rights, 302

System, 302

Panchayati Raj, 201

Institutions in India, (PRII), 197-209, 248

Human Rights, 197

Women And-, 197

System, 200, 205

System in India, 202

Panchayats, 202

Pandey, Radhakrishna, Silcher Congress Leader, 65

Pann-Caste-Christians, 107

Partition, 2

Patherkatta/Kanjars or Grihar, 125

Main Areas, UP—Mid Western Terai Region, 125

Paudi Bhunyas, 116

Peasantry Agrarian Labourers, 57

Pehrawar Sangarsh Samiti, 20

People's Walk, NGO, 17

Physical

And Sexual Abuse, 166

Security, 240

Planning, 278

Planning Commission, 90, 105, 198

Plantation

Labourers, 62

Workers, 62, 72

Planters, 62, 64

Policy of

Liberalization, Privatization and Globalization, 35

Reservation for SC/ST, 200

Political

Economy, 192

Rights, 59

Rights of Women, 199

Polygeny System, 109

Population,

Bengali, 68

Tribal, 89, 116

Pornography, 313

Post-World War II, 254

POTA (Prevention of Terrorism Act), 214

Poverty Stricken Countries, (PSC), 53

Bangladesh, 53

Bhutan, 53

Nepal, 53

Pakistan, 53

Philippines, 53

Sri Lanka, 53

Power Structure, 66, 70

Praja Mandal Movement, 90, 117

Prarthna Samaj, 5

Pre-British Judicial System, 5

Prenatal Diagnostic Techniques—Act, 1994, 113

Prevention of Atrocities (POA), 35, 37-40, 44, 45, 167

Primitive Tribal Groups, 134
Privacy Rights, 215
Privy Council, 5
Project Affected People (PAP), 187
Projects Sites, 185
  Bastar, 185
  Bhakra, 185
  Dahanu, 185
  Hirakund, 185
  Koraput, 185
  Malkangiri, 185
Promotion and Protection of Human Rights, 164
Prostitution, 113, 114
  And Trafficking, 313
Protection of
  Civil Rights Act, 9, 31
  Human Rights, 50
Public Health Centre, (PHC), 134

R

Rabidas, Dusad Dom, 67
Racial and Ethnic Groups, 54
Rajasthan—Bihar, 109
Ram Chandra Deo Singh Committee, 187
Ramakrishna Mission, 5
Rape
  Camps, 255
  In Police Custody, 153
Ravidas Samaj Mahasabha, 20
Recruitment of Labor, 63
Rehabilitation
  And Resettlement, 187
  Of Bonded Labour, 115
Relief and Rehabilitation, 182
Religious Violence among Tribes, 107
Reservations, 9
  In Education, 34
Right to
  Common Heritage of Man, 59
  Education, 189
    Marriage, 295
Rigvedic Period, 3
Rio de Janeiro Declaration on Environment and Development, 101
Ritual Pollution and Rights, 5
Role of Women, 198
Royal Commission on Decentralization, 201
Rural Society, 202
Russian
  Revolution, 145
  Troops, 255

S

SAHRDC, 39
Saints, 5
  Kabir, 5
  Nanak, 5
  Ravidas, 5

Sale of Girl Children in Andhra Pradesh, 112

Sankan, Dalit Agricultural Laborer, 17

Santhal

In Santhal Desh, 97

Parganas, 62

Rebellion, 90

Saoras, 116

Sardar Sarovar

And Problems, 186-191

Dam, 186, 187

Project, 188

Sarhul Festival, 129

Sati Pratha, 200

SC/ST/OBC, 147, 284 305

Scavengers, 16

Scheduled Caste, 2, 6, 9

Scheduled Caste Women, 40, 41, 43

Scheduled Caste/Tribes, 8, 10, 11, 13, 18, 36, 40, 134, 154, 190, 246

And Women, 203

Commission, 18

(Prevention of Atrocities) Act, 1989, 9, 17, 21, 35, 36, 46, 89, 107

Scheduled Tribes, 116, 121, 131

And Forest Dwellers Act (Recognition of Forest Rights), 2006, 134

Communities, (STC), 134

Hathuneyakan, 134

Irulas, 134

Kota, 134

Kurumbas, 134

Paniyan, 134

Toda, 134

Communities in Tamil Nadu, 133

Reservation, 259

Second World War, 50, 51

Security

Committee, 206

Council, 215

Physical, 240

Self-Determination, 59

Sen, Amartya, 165

Senior Citizens, 235

Sex

Determination, 102

Selective Abortions, 111, 112

Slavery, 255

Workers, 114

Sexual

Abuse, 169, 246

Assault, 313

Harassment, 56, 111, 137, 255, 309, 310

Violence in Tribes, 103

Shamlat Land, 20

Shifting Cultivation, 98, 120, 123

Short Stay Homes, 108

Shoshit Jan Andolan, 91
Silcher Medical College, 74
Singapore, 53
  And Malaysia, 52
Singrauli Region, 179
Slavery, 56
Social
  And Economic Justice, 51
  Awareness, 80
  Communities in India, 92
  Conference, 6
  Disabilities, 6
  Discrimi. :ation against Women, 252
  Environment, 80
  Environment for Dalits in Uttar Pradesh, 15
  Justice, 32, 35, 54, 56, 225, 272, 284
  Legislation for Women, (SLW), 308
    Dowry Prohibition Act, 308
    Hindu Marriage Act, 308
    Hindu Marriage Act, 309
    Hindu Succession Act, 308
    Hindu Widow Remarriage Act, 308
    Indecent Representation Act, 309
  Relationship, 8
  Security, 147
  Stratification, 1
  Structure, 2, 66, 198
  Traditions, 52
  Violence, 8
  Work Profession, 272
Societies Based on Slavery, Serfdom or Capitalism, 102
Socio-Economic Reforms, 163
Son Preference, 312
South Korea, 53
Special
  Courts, 44
  Economic Zone, 177, 195
  Hunting Ceremony, 129
State Backward Commission, 285
Status of
  Dalits, 30
  Human Rights, 60
Stratification System of Tea Garden Society, 67
Sub Saharan Africa, 150
Supreme Court of India, 56
Surekha Bhotmong, Dalit Women, 28
Swaraj Bhawan, 205

T

TADA (Terrorists and Disruptive Activities (Preventive Act), 1987, 214
Tamil Nadu, 109, 115
Tana Bhagat Movement, 90

Tea

- Companies, 61
- Garden Districts, (TGD), 60
  - Cachar, 60
  - Darrang, 60
  - Goalpara, 60
  - Kamrup, 60
  - Karbi Anglong, 60
  - Lakhimpur, 60
  - Nowgong, 60
- Garden in India, (TGI), 60
  - Arunachal Pradesh, 60
  - Assam, 60
  - Manipur, 60
  - Nagaland, 60
  - Tripura, 60
- Garden Labourers, 66
- Garden of Assam, 64, 66, 72, 74, 77
- Garden Setting of Assam, 58-78
- Garden Society, 66, 67, 69
- Garden Society of Assam, 60

Technology Electronics, 56

Tehri Dam Project, 178

TELCO Experience of Displacement, 191, 192

Terai Valley of Nepal, 123

Terrorism and Human Rights, 210-219

Terrorist and Disruptive Activities, 56

Terrorists Acts, 212

Tharus Buksa, Second Largest Tribe of Uttarakhand, 120

The Rape of Nanking, 254

Theosophical Society, 5

Toda, 134, 135

- Christian Settlements, 135
- Community, 135
- Kota, Paniyan of Tamil Nadu, 137

Traditional

- Civil, Political Rights, 55
- Healers, 42
- Indian Society, 200
- Musical Instruments, 127
- Techniques of Cultivation, 69

Trafficking, 113-115

- In Minors, 114

Transfer of Land, 121

Treaty of Versailles, 54, 220

Tribal

- Autonomy, 100
- Communities, 56, 62, 117, 126, 131, 137
- Development Program, 105, 134
- Geographical Regimes, 97
- Groups, 98, 100
- In India, 126
- Institutions, 98

Lands, 104, 105, 106
Population, 89, 116
Research Bureau, 116
Reservations, 107
Sub Plan, 118
System, 104

Tribes, 116, 138, 185
Asur, 185
Bhokasa, 138
Bhumijas, 116
Bhunyas, 116
Gond, 116, 129-133, 138
Hos, 116
Kandha, 107
Kanjar, 138
Khewar Berojia, 185
Kisan, 185
Kurukh, 126
Maria, 129
Munda, 129, 185
Oraon, 126, 129, 138, 185
Patterkatta, 126
Santhal, 116, 129
Tharu, 123, 138

U

UN, 50, 51, 54, 55, 58, 86, 99, 101, 170, 211, 215, 220, 221, 245, 275
Centre for Human Settlement, 289
Charter, 50, 86, 88, 156, 189, 211, 222, 223
Conference on Human Rights, 52
Convention on Elimination of all Forms of Discrimination on Women, (CEDAW), 174
Convention for Rights of Child, (CCR), 149, 298
Declaration, 191
Declaration on Rights of Indigenous People, 93
Development Programs, 198
General Assembly, 87, 103, 245, 268
Human Rights
Declaration, 220-230
Violation, 88
International
Convention on Civil and Political Rights, 215
Women's Year, 199
Laws, 88
Principles for Older Persons, 237, 238
Security Council, 88
World Conference, 308

UNICEF, 249

UNICEF, Framework of Women Empowerment, 249

Uniform Civil Code, 174

Universal
Declaration by UNO, 51
Declaration on Human Rights (UDHR), 50, 51, 55, 56, 86-88,

99, 146, 159, 164, 174, 221, 224, 225, 228, 236, 243, 244, 254, 268, 275, 280, 297

Treaty, 88

Declaration on Rights of Indigenous People, 101

Human Rights, 245

Rights, 145

Universality of Human Rights, 52

Universalization of Human Rights, 243

Untouchability, 2, 6, 9, 31-33, 43

Untouchability (Offence) Act, 1955, 9, 31

Untouchables, 3

Upanishads, 51

Urbanization, 234

US, 51

Germany, France, Italy and UK, 52, 55

Patriot Act, 215

Uttar Pradesh, 31, 32, 115

Uttarakhand, 115

Uttarakhand Scheduled Tribes Restriction on Transfer of Land and Restoration of Alienated Land Act, 121

V

Valley,

Barak, 60, 68, 70, 76

Brahmputra, 60, 119

Chitwan, 122

Dang, 122

Deukhuri, 123

Ganges, 96

Surkhel, 122

Varna System, 4

Varnas, 3

Vedas, 51

Verbal and Physical Abuse, 33

Vienna Declaration, 1993, 167, 210

Village Swaraj, 201, 202

Violation, 64

Against Dalits (VAD), 1-49

Against Human Rights, 143, 144, 147

Against Women, 164, 245

Kinds of-, 310

And Discrimination in India, 1

Caste, 44

Caste and Communal, 2

Crimes, 8

Communal, 2

Defined, 7

Domestic, 103, 107, 138, 165, 255

Of Human Rights, 53, 54, 59, 88, 120, 121, 137, 138, 168, 211, 221, 225, 229, 256

Of Land Rights, 104

On Dalits, 17

Organized, 1

Physical, 4, 34

Sexual and Psychological, 245, 246

Sexual, 8, 103, 104, 138

Social, 8

State, 8

W

Wage Labourers, 41

Domestic Work—Embroidery Work, 41

War

Crimes, 88

On Terrorism, 217

Warren Hastings, Gov. General, 60

Welsh Missionary, 119

Western

Ghats, 93

Societies, 53

Widow Marriage, 200

Witchcraft and Women, 42

Women

And Violence, 309

Atrocities, 126

Trafficking, 137

Trafficking (Prostitution) Act, 113, 114

Women's

Development Decade, 199

Empowerment, 173, 248, 249, 250

Human Rights, 244, 255

Movement, 115

Participation—, 166

Rights, 168, 171, 199, 307, 308

Workmen's Breach of Contract Act, 62

World

Assembly on Ageing, 236

Commission on Dams (WCD), 181

Conference on Human Rights, 168, 211, 245

Conferences, Beijing, 168

Cairo, 168

Vienna, 168

World Health Organization (WHO), 110

Brasilla Declaration on Aging and Health, 232

World Organization against Torture, 88

World War I, 54

World War II, 51, 54, 87, 220

World's Population, 232

Y

Year for Development of Women, 199

Year of Women Empowerment, 201

Z

Zilla Parishad, 204

Zygmunht Baumen, German Social Scientist, 50